Great
Rober

The Civil War in Spain:
    "For an introduction to the Spanish Civil War, its causes, and its results, there is no better book."
    —*Chicago Tribune*

The Life and Death of Nazi Germany:
    "Robert Goldston's book is extraordinarily welcome. It splendidly performs the task a work of history should perform. . . . I offer the highest possible praise." —Peter Gay,
        The New York Times Book Review

The Russian Revolution:
    "Brilliant. . . . It is probably the best short summary on the Russian Revolution yet to be produced."
        —*The New York Times*

The Rise of Red China:
    "Robert Goldston has a marvelous knack for making the complex simple and for capturing the dramatic essence of great world events. He has done it with *The Russian Revolution* and now in *The Rise of Red China.*"
        —Harrison Salisbury

The Great Depression:
    "This is a good, authentic, and well-organized overview of the '30s."
        —*School Library Journal*

COMMUNISM: A NARRATIVE HISTORY

by Robert Goldston

A FAWCETT PREMIER BOOK

Fawcett Publications, Inc., Greenwich, Conn.

COMMUNISM: A NARRATIVE HISTORY

A FAWCETT PREMIER ORIGINAL

for LOUISE AND FRANK NOVITCH

CONTENTS

PART THREE
THE GIFT OF TONGUES

PART FOUR
REALITY IN SEARCH OF SOME IDEAS

COMMUNISM:
A NARRATIVE
HISTORY

Prologue

THE AGE OF OPTIMISM

> Happiness, in Europe, is a new idea. But today we
> know that the unhappy are the really important
> powers of the earth; they have the right to speak
> as the real masters of the governments that neglect
> them.
>
> —*François Noël Babeuf*

All during July 1789, Paris was swept by frightening rumors. It was said that King Louis XVI, on the advice of certain of his reactionary ministers, would crush the newly formed National Constituent Assembly then meeting at Versailles. It was said that the hard-won reforms and liberties proposed by the Assembly would be suppressed at the point of bayonets. It was said that the king had gathered royalist regiments together to assault Paris itself and "discipline" its revolutionary people. By July 14, tensions in the ancient French capital had reached the explosive point. On that day, armed with paving stones, knives, clubs, and what few weapons they could find, and led by a few soldiers who had escaped from prison, the mobs of Paris boiled out of their slums and assaulted the Bastille, an old royal fortress-prison which, to the poor inhabitants of the Faubourg St. Antoine seemed the very symbol and substance of royal tyranny and feudal oppression. The Bastille fell quickly, yielding up its handful of political prisoners and the blood of its small band of guards. This all-but-unplanned outburst of violence succeeded; within a few days the royal regiments had been recalled, the more reactionary of the king's advisors were in headlong flight to the frontiers and Louis himself came to

Paris to protest his equalitarian sympathies to its citizens. Ever after, Bastille Day would be celebrated as the festival of French liberties.

One of those present at the storming of the Bastille on that riotous July 14 was a twenty-nine-year-old clerk named François Noël Babeuf from the little town of Roye. Babeuf was employed in the office of the registrar of seignorial rights at Roye—the place where the duties, taxes, and contracts that bound the local peasantry in obligation to their aristocratic masters were recorded. Hurrying back to Roye, Babeuf burned these seignorial archives and then, as both government official and journalist, threw himself with desperate energy into the cause and the work of the Revolution.

The son of a Protestant in Catholic France, Babeuf had grown up in the utmost poverty. He learned to read and write from papers he picked up in the streets; his father taught him Latin and mathematics. And from his father too, he imbibed an admiration for the heroes of the ancient Roman republic; on his deathbed the old man presented him with a copy of Plutarch's *Lives* and advised him to emulate Caius Gracchus, an ancient Roman champion of the people's rights. Thereafter the youngster called himself Gracchus Babeuf, the name under which he was to enter history as one of the founders of socialist thought.

But young Babeuf's republican zeal and socialist sympathies were not inspired solely or even primarily by either paternal example or the excitement of events in revolutionary France; they were a natural result of the study of thought that had been accumulating and seeking an outlet for more than a century—just as that body of thought itself was a natural product of the emergence of the modern world from the shackles and restraints of feudalism.

Along with the diminution of plagues and barbarian invasions, the revival of trade and the consolidation of nation-states in Europe during the fifteenth, sixteenth, and seventeenth centuries, partly inspiring these events, partly inspired by them, had come the Renaissance (rebirth) of independent, nonreligious study and speculation. Influenced by the rediscovery of the works of the antique world of Greece and Rome and by the thought and writings of numerous scholars which had continued during the misnamed "Dark Ages" and through medieval times, Renaissance philosophers were groping toward a new view of man and man's place in the universe. No longer satisfied with the medieval Catholic-feudal hierarchy of God, angels, pope, king, lord, artisan, and serf, thoughtful men, attempting to grasp the concept of "natural law" in the physical sciences, sought to discover natural law in human social relationships. They were seeking to formulate concepts of human behavior which might explain human history as something more than heroic myth and might explain and justify the relations of men in this world as something other than the reflection of an unfathomable divine will.

The awakening of the medieval mind to social problems is perhaps most excitingly seen in the work of Giovanni Vico, a humble Italian scholar born in Naples toward the close of the seventeenth century. Vico had read the work of the English philosopher Francis Bacon, who proposed to apply the principles of experimentation and inductive reasoning to the study of natural science; Vico had also read the work of Grotius, who suggested that both philosophy and theology ought to be studied in terms of human rather than divine will. Vico thought it possible to apply these principles to the study of human history and society. Accordingly, in 1725 he published a scholarly treatise entitled: *Principles of a New Science Dealing with the Nature of Nations, Through Which Are Shown Also New Principles of the Natural Law of Peoples.*

In his *New Science* Vico expressed some conclusions which were, for his time, truly revolutionary. "In that dark night," he wrote, "which shrouds from our eyes the most remote antiquity, a light appears which cannot lead us astray; I speak of this incontestable truth: the social world is certainly the work of men; and it follows that one can and should find its principles in the modifications of the human intelligence itself." At a time when history was still generally considered to be either the unfolding of God's immutable plan on earth or the record of the impact of "great men" individually on events, Vico's was a revolutionary concept indeed. In another place he advises us that history and societies may only be understood in terms of their primitive origins and environments, and finally: "Governments must be conformable to the nature of the governed; governments are even a result of that nature." But although Vico was prepared to sweep the gods, monsters, myths, and heroes from the stage of human history, his thinking did not encompass one of the key concepts which were to inspire his successors. Living and working under the shadow of the

Inquisition (which by 1700 had all-but-completely stamped out Renaissance learning in Italy), Vico did not arrive at the conception of history as progress. He still conceived of man as perfectible only in Heaven; he did not imagine his perfectibility or that of his social institutions here on earth.

Yet the concept of human progress was to be found not only in Francis Bacon, but in both the thought and nature of Vico's times. If, as scientific philosophers from Bacon to Sir Isaac Newton were to establish, the natural world obeyed natural laws, and if these laws could be known to men, then the physical world could be manipulated by men. If this were true, then man could change his own environment according to the dictates of his own intelligence—and by so making that environment more hospitable to human life, man could relieve many, perhaps most, of the tensions, needs, and hungers which had assailed him since prehistoric times. This in turn ought to have a direct effect upon human nature itself. Thus by the application of human reason, humanity ought to be able to perfect itself in this world irrespective of what might or might not happen in the next.

Obviously the key element in this concept would be education; the transmission of that knowledge which would enable man to conquer his environment. During the eighteenth century this task enlisted the energies and talents of some remarkable men; Denis Diderot, D'Alembert, Condorcet, and Jean-Jacques Rousseau in France all contributed to a massive, new, and revolutionary *Encyclopedia (Encyclopédie)* which was to address itself to the compilation and diffusion of all of man's assessable knowledge. Lest there be any doubt about the overall aims of the French Encyclopedists or the depth of their optimism about the possibilities of the human condition, Diderot himself (the *Encyclopedia*'s general editor) wrote: "In fact, the purpose of an encyclopedia is to assemble the knowledge scattered over the surface of the earth; to explain its general system to the men with whom we live, and to transmit it to the men who will come after us; in order that the labors of centuries past may not be useless for the centuries to come; that our descendants, *by becoming better instructed, may as a consequence be more virtuous and happier. . . .*" [Italic's added.]

The optimism of the Encyclopedists was supported not only by rationalistic theory, but also by the nature of the age. Based on the principles of the new physical sciences, various inventions were making their appearance, inventions which seemed to promise the opening of an era in which, for the first time in human history, man might be relieved of his overriding concern to simply wrest food and shelter from his environment. Mechanical power would, within a now foreseeable future, liberate man for higher pursuits, including the refinement of his own intellect and character. The eighteenth century, too, was witnessing the fruition of the centuries of exploration and pioneering which had preceded it. The New World, if still but thinly settled in the interior, had proven man's ability to dominate and transform his environment. Europeans had seized two huge "new" continents for exploitation; they controlled the seas of the world; European penetration and eventual domination of the Far East and Africa were already clearly visible on the horizon. Reversing the balance of preceding ages when Asia (or the threat of Asia) had dominated Europe, Europe was now about to dominate the world.

Furthermore, the triumph of human reason seemed vindicated at home by the emerging Industrial Revolution (especially in England) and the fight for economic and political power of a new "middle class" whose strength was derived from trade, commerce and manufacture, and the manipulation of a money economy rather than from inherited properties in land and serfs or the whim of God or king. The success of the new middle classes, theologically justified by the Protestant Reformation, was to be attributed to their brains, energy, and daring as individuals, not to divine intervention or age-old usage.

One of the direct consequences of European penetration of North America was the emergence of the concept of the natural nobility of man in a state of nature. To such European thinkers as Rousseau (who had never seen either the North American wilderness or its Indian inhabitants), the idea of "natural man" seemed a logical corollary to the idea of human progress. If man was capable of improving himself, it was only society which obstructed his efforts; where no society existed, man would be found to possess uncorrupted virtues, as did, theoretically, the North American Indians and, to a somewhat lesser extent, the North American white pioneers. "Nature," wrote Rousseau in his best-selling novel *Émile,* "made man happy and good, but society depraves him and makes him miserable." In this concept of man's natural nobility when unfettered by social forms may be found the seeds of both anarchism, which proposes the abolition of the state, and Marxist political theory, which predicts its "withering away."

The practical application of these enlightened ideas in the real political world had been proposed in England by John Locke at the end of the seventeenth century. Natural man, to Locke, possessed "natural rights" and among these were the rights to "life, liberty, and property." It was to protect these rights, Locke claimed, that men had instituted governments. When governments deprive men of these rights, the people are entitled to overthrow the governments. Locke's ideas were seized upon by the English middle classes as a justification of their struggle against royal absolutism and of their triumph in the "Glorious Revolution" of 1688. Rousseau, in his most important book, *Social Contract,* iterated Locke's ideas, holding that government had originated as a contract between society and the king. The people had given the king his authority in return for his services; therefore it is the people's right to depose an unjust or absolute monarch; they (the people) are the true sovereigns.

Going into greater detail than either Locke or Rousseau about the possibilities of instituting reasonable governments among men was Charles de Montesquieu, an enlightened French nobleman who had spent many years traveling and been much impressed by the relative liberties enjoyed by Englishmen. In his treatise on governments, *The Spirit of Laws,* Montesquieu held that the abuses of government power could best be avoided by the separation of government functions. The executive, legislative, and judicial branches of government should hold equal powers—as each of these would maintain a jealous watch on the others, none would dare to violate the rights of citizens.

The ideas of all these philosophers of the Enlightenment seemed so self-evident to them and to their followers that opposition to them could only be explained by greed, lust, and madness. Yet opposition was powerful. The Catholic hierarchy, from Pope to village priest, found the divorce of man from God abominable; the ruling classes, from king to pettiest aristocrat, found their privileges and authority intolerably threatened. They responded with persecution, censorship, and the police power of the state. At one time Diderot himself was imprisoned; his great *Encyclopedia* was heavily censored, and its publication held up for many years.

The men who perhaps did most to popularize and give currency to the ideas of the Enlightenment (while contributing but little original thought to it) were the clever French satirist François Marie Voltaire and the English radical Tom Paine. Both were possessed of great talent and scathing pens; both turned the fierce light of an unquenchable anger upon the follies and cruelties of ruling classes driven to extremes of lunatic repression by their own sense of inadequacy and impending doom. Voltaire ridiculed king and aristocracy in tales and pamphlets which were entirely too entertaining to be successfully suppressed. He addressed himself in particular to a savage attack upon the Catholic clergy in France. Imprisoned and exiled, he continued to mock the "establishment" so successfully that a few years after his death (in 1778) he was to be hailed as the man who had laughed the "old regime" out of existence, the genius of that French Revolution which he had but dimly apprehended.

Tom Paine, coming to the North American colonies on the eve of the American Revolution, brought with him the courage and talent to express the ideas of Enlightenment philosophers in phrases that all could understand. His pamphlet *Common Sense,* appealing to natural law and the natural rights of man, was probably the most effective piece of propaganda ever written. It convinced the overwhelming majority of Americans of the necessity and inevitability of their separation from the English crown. Revolutionary leaders such as Sam Adams and Thomas Jefferson acknowledged that without Paine's forceful pen, independence would have been long delayed.

The American Revolution seemed indeed, to thoughtful men on both sides of the Atlantic, to be the culmination and fulfillment of the ideas and dreams of the Enlightenment. American leaders were committed to Enlightenment assumptions such as the social contract, the natural nobility of man, and even the particulars of Montesquieu's system of government. John Locke's phrase about "life, liberty, and property" was written into the Declaration of Independence (Jefferson, with a surer understanding of the human spirit, substituted "happiness" for "property"). Above all, the American Revolution, and later, the construction and adoption of the United States Constitution, offered the spectacle of a nation *consciously* organizing itself through the application of human reason to the social and political environment. Through the actions of American revolutionaries a whole new set of ideas had entered upon the stage of real history—not merely to inspire men, but as practical guides through the law of their unfolding lives. To European observers it was the triumph and vindication of human reason itself. In this respect, as the first act of man's practical attempt to organize his social world by the lights of his intellect, the American Revolution was to serve as model and inspiration for more than a century of future revolutions.

The first tremors of the Age of Revolution following upon the American success were quickly felt in France. There, beginning in 1789, the vast masses of the French people, led by those middle-class elements which could no longer tolerate the idiocies and repressions of the old regime, with one mighty shrug cast from their backs the entire archaic royal-feudal system and heritage. But if the French Revolution (so important in world history that it is commonly referred to simply as "the revolution") was partly inspired by the American, it was bound to develop differently, as it coped with entirely different problems. The American Revolution did not address itself to the destruction of caste or class; in the pioneering wilderness of the New World there was no feudal heritage of class to destroy. The American Revolution was not inspired by widespread poverty and despair or the desire to transfer property to the masses; with an entire virgin continent ripe for exploitation before them, the Americans knew relatively little poverty and less despair (with, of course, the exception of black slaves whose "natural rights" remained unrecognized in the United States Constitution). And as for property, there remained the possibilities of limitless expansion to the West. The American Revolution, for all its generalized ideals, had been basically a nationalist revolution—the Americans had decided to develop and exploit their environment for their own benefit, not for the benefit of distant England. Today the American Revolution might be called a "war of national liberation."

The French Revolution, with its slogan "Liberty, Equality, Fraternity" (a slogan in which the emphasis, somewhat different from "Life, Liberty, and the Pursuit of Happiness" reflects the differences between the two revolutions), had to cope, first of all, with the existence of large groups of people —the royal party, the aristocrats, the Catholic hierarchy, most of the military—who were irrreconcilably opposed to its aims and ideals. The power of these groups, compared with that of the American Tories, was vast indeed. Secondly, France was not separated by an immense body of water from those foreign European powers whose ruling classes, recognizing the threat implicit in the French Revolution to their own continued existence, were prepared to intervene to crush it. Thirdly, French revolutionary leaders did not have the advantage which colonial revolutionary leaders enjoyed of a long, practical experience with political power in local legislatures and the very old traditions of the practice of the English Common Law; nor were the masses they led anywhere near as literate or politically mature as most American colonists. Finally, and perhaps of greatest importance, property in the form of land—the means of production, wages, food, the necessities of life—was one of the central issues of the French uprising. The middle classes sought an end to feudal restrictions on trade and their opportunity to exploit their environment; the professional classes sought an end to censorship, both royal and religious, and the opening of careers to men of talent irrespective of their backgrounds; intellectuals sought the freedom to think and express their thoughts and an end to royal and religious superstition and power; the peasantry (the great majority of the nation) sought to wrest ownership of the land from church and nobility; the city workers, especially in Paris, sought bread and shelter and a reasonable standard of living.

From these impulses behind the French Revolution all else was to follow; the Reign of Terror (about 20,000 people lost their heads to the guillotine within a few years and thousands more were imprisoned or exiled), by which the revolution tried to dispose of its domestic enemies; the burning of the chateaux and the murder of landlords throughout France, by which the peasantry expropriated the land; the raising and arming of mighty new revolutionary armies, by which the revolution sought to defend itself against foreign enemies; the abolition of all remnants of feudal laws and its signs and symbols, even down to the changing of the names of months and the attempt to substitute 1789 as "Year One" in a new calendar that should no longer depend on the birth of Christ; the expropriation of church property and suppression of Catholic worship, by which the revolution sought not only to dispose of a powerful opposition element, but also to dispose of God Himself—substituting Reason as the new god.

It seemed then, that through both the American and French revolutions, although both might follow their separate courses, the basic ideals of the Enlightenment, for which so many men had striven for so long, were now to be triumphantly established as the universal law of mankind. Free, and guided by science and reason, men were now to create a society in which all would be happy, all virtuous. All the world was new and "to be alive" at that time, as the English poet William Wordsworth observed, "was very heaven." The essential optimism of the age about man and his possibilities seemed fully vindicated.

And yet, somehow, the Golden Age was not only not ushered in at the beginning of the nineteenth century—it seemed as remote as ever. Something had gone wrong with the French Revolution—somewhere within the welter of its events and the careful reasoning of its ideals, contradictions lurked. And since these contradictions are best illuminated through the fate of the clerk of the seignorial archives in the little town of Roye, it is time to return to Gracchus Babeuf.

After burning the seignorial archives at Roye, Babeuf instituted a one-man revolutionary campaign in his province of Somme. He went to the innkeepers and informed them that the Constituent Assembly had abolished the old wine tax which he urged them not to pay; he began selling the landlords' expropriated estates to the peasants who had, in any event, already seized them; he started a campaign to divide up village commons land among the poorest peasants. In all this he was doing no more than what the Revolutionary government in Paris had decreed. But Somme was not Paris, and the local landlords and police kept trying to jail him on trumped-up charges. In 1793 he was given a post in Paris in the Bureau of Subsistence of the Commune (the city government), and there he uncovered proof that government officials were deliberately fostering a famine in Paris in order to make money in food speculation. Once again he was pursued by the authorities on false charges.

In July 1794 (in Revolutionary France the new month "Thermidor"), the Jacobins, members of a revolutionary club who had risen to supreme government power, were guillotined as the Revolution, like so many since, began to devour its own children. With their passing, something close to civil war seized France. Royalists, republicans, the surviving Jacobins, and opportunists of all descriptions struggled for power throughout the country. At last, in 1795, after the revolutionary National Convention had been forcefully suppressed by a young artillery officer named Napoleon Bonaparte, a new constitution was adopted by which the country was to be ruled by a five-member Directory. The earlier constitution of 1791 was repealed; under the new one only those who held a significant amount of property were allowed to vote. So reactionary was the new constitution that exiled royalists declared it would satisfy them very well if only there could be one Director instead of five.

In a small newspaper which he was now publishing, *The Tribune of the People,* Babeuf denounced the new constitution of 1795, the Directorate, and the conniving of financiers and politicians which had produced a terrible famine in Paris. The newspaper was promptly suppressed and Babeuf sent to jail; while he was in prison his seven-year-old daughter died of starvation, a victim of that very famine which had first alerted him to government corruption.

As soon as Babeuf emerged from prison he founded a political club which was to be called the Society of Equals. In a manifesto (declaration) of the Society it was stated that "there must be no more individual property in land; the land belongs to no one. . . . We declare that we can no longer endure, with the enormous majority of men, labor, and sweat in the service and for the benefit of a small minority." The Society, suppressed by the indefatigable Bonaparte, went underground and prepared a new constitution. Under it all the goods and means of production (mines, mills, factories, distribution centers) in France were to be declared national communal property. Thus the right to work would be guaranteed by the state. Furthermore, equal education would be guaranteed to all; the state itself was to supervise the care and training of young children; people were to eat at communal tables; and all the necessities of life were to be supplied by the government. Attracting scattered remnants of the now illegal Jacobin club, the Society of Equals plotted an insurrection against the Directory.

The inefficiency and corruption of the Directory had by now reduced France to misery. The government's money was all but worthless and in Paris alone there were an estimated 500,000 people living on the edge of starvation. Babeuf's Society of Equals moved ahead with its plans for insurrection; but on the eve of their projected uprising, in the beginning of May 1796, they were betrayed by a police spy. Babeuf and other leaders of the Society were arrested and charged with conspiracy against the government. At his trial Babeuf conducted his own defense, and his speeches to the court constitute not only a tremendously eloquent and moving document, but also offer a closely reasoned analysis of what

had gone wrong with the Revolution, what would be needed
for the establishment of a truly just society, and the first
coherent statement of socialist aims and outlook.

The cause of revolutions, Babeuf declared, was the bend-
ing beyond what the people could bear of the human springs
of society. The people had a right to rebel against this pressure
because society's aim ought to be the greatest good for the
greatest number. Nature has ruled that all men must work—
he who escapes this duty commits a crime against humanity.
He is also a criminal who would earn his bread through the
sweat of other men's brows; the consumption of goods by
any man in excess of his needs is nothing other than theft.
Furthermore, in trying him, Babeuf pointed out, the court
was really trying the great philosophers of the Enlightenment
whose ideas had inspired him. The revered Rousseau had
written of "men so odious as to dare to have more than
enough while other men are dying of hunger." And Gabriel
de Mably long ago had declared: "If you follow the chain
of our vices you will find that the first link is fastened to
the inequality of wealth." Diderot had said that every citizen
should take from the community what he needed and give
to the community what he could and that anyone who attempted to restore the abominable principle of private property should be looked upon as a dangerous lunatic!

It was here, in his defense, that Babeuf touched upon the
basic contradiction which had emerged from the Revolution.
What had happened was that the middle classes, in order to
win power, had aroused the great masses of the nation to
exile and expropriate the royalists, clergy, and aristocrats.
But they had not been against the principle of property itself—quite the contrary. Once their aims had been satisfied,
they were quite content to put an end to the Revolution
and to further "dangerous" revolutionary ideals. In abetting
the peasants' seizure of the land, they had transformed a
revolutionary peasantry into a lower middle class of small
landowners who, once having achieved their basic aim (land
ownership), would now fight to the death any attempt to
redistribute or nationalize the land. And the peasants were
the overwhelming majority in France. Those who had won
nothing from the Revolution were the city workers who had
formed the spearhead of the revolutionary struggle. But
these were now exhausted by their years of struggle, repelled
by the bloodshed of the Terror, and as disorganized and
leaderless as they had been when they stormed the Bastille.

The French Revolution had cast down a monarchical-feudal order and established a middle-class capitalistic one, based on the sanctity of private property. But only by taking an ax to the principle of property itself could the needs of city workers and the very poor of the nation be resolved. Thus, Babeuf pointed out, the Revolution was by no means finished. Since the fall of the Bastille, all the terrible pageantry of the Terror, foreign invasions and wars, the madly shifting spectrum of political groups and parties in power—all of this had but reflected a struggle between those who, having won something from the Revolution, were now desperately determined to hang onto it, and those who felt that the Revolution had not gone far enough to either fulfill Enlightenment ideas or to raise the masses of people out of misery. But for now, Babeuf well realized, the Revolution had come to an end. Addressing his family, seated in the gallery of the courtroom, he said:

> But, oh, my children . . . I have but one bitter regret to express to you: that, although I have wanted so much to leave you a heritage of liberty which is the source of every good, I foresee in the future only slavery, and that I am leaving you a prey to every ill.
>
> I have nothing at all to give you! I would not even leave you my civic virtues, my profound hatred of tyranny, my ardent devotion to the cause of Liberty and Equality, my passionate love of the People. I would be making you too disastrous a gift! What would you do with it under the monarchic oppression which is certainly going to descend on you? I am leaving you slaves, and it is this thought alone which will torture my soul in its final moments. I should equip you for this situation with advice as to how to bear your chains more patiently, but I do not feel I am capable of it.

On May 27, 1797, Babeuf and his associates were sent to the guillotine. But before his execution, with an optimism infinitely more sober and patient than that which had marked the Age of Enlightenment, Babeuf wrote to a friend: "I believe that in some future day men will give thought again to the means of procuring for the human race the happiness we have proposed for it."

Part One

SOME IDEAS IN SEARCH OF REALITY

Chapter One

THE SEARCH FOR UTOPIA

> All my life may be summed up in one idea: to guarantee to all men the free development of their faculties. Forty-eight hours after our second publication, the party of the workers will be organized: the future belongs to us!
>
> —*Comte de Saint-Simon*

That future day, predicted by Babeuf, on which men would once again give thought to the welfare of their fellows, came only a few years after his death. But although many of Babeuf's successors were of his generation and had, like him, lived through the French Revolution, although they shared the same background of rationalistic Enlightenment ideas, their outlooks were influenced more by the Industrial than by either the American or French revolutions. And too, they had experienced somber events which Babeuf had only foreseen: the solidification of a middle-class, property-based society in France; the monarchical tyranny of Napoleon Bonaparte; a decade and more of international wars that devastated much of Europe; and, finally, with the defeat of Napoleon, the refastening of the Bourbon monarchy on France and the "freezing" of a rigidly reactionary social status quo on as much of Europe as the tsar of Russia, the king of Prussia, and the emperor of Austria-Hungary could control.

The new breed of socialist thinkers who wrote after 1800, while still clinging to the Enlightenment faith in man's perfectibility on earth, were faced with the inescapable evidence that despite revolutions man was certainly not perfecting

27

himself in European society. Furthermore, they realized that
the remaking of that society was entirely too complex a
matter to be solved by a simple act of enlightened will. In
fact they were beginning to question whether man could
truly be said to possess "free will"—that is, whether what
he thought to be freely-arrived-at decisions were not, in fact,
heavily preconditioned by his political, social, and economic
circumstances.

Nor could post-French Revolution socialists share the
Enlightenment's optimism about the advent of mechanical
power and industrialization. The Industrial Revolution, which
was to free men from toil for higher pursuits, was simply
not working out that way. On the contrary, in England,
where the Industrial Revolution was most advanced, increasing numbers of people were being sucked into a working
class which lived in the most abject misery and degradation.
On the Continent, and especially in France (where the factory system of gathering large groups of people into one
place to work for wages actually preceded mechanization),
the newly emerging working classes seemed, in some ways,
worse off than feudal serfs had been. Under feudalism, for
all its harshness, the lowest orders of society had at least
the security of a defined place in the social order; relationships between social classes had been defined in terms of
duties, rights, and obligations. But in the new industrial
society it seemed that no one was obligated to anything but
personal gain, that the relationships between men had been
reduced to the impersonality and vulgarity of wages, dividends, profits—money. The industrial machinery which was
to liberate the human spirit was, apparently, devouring increasing numbers of human beings.

The socialist thinkers of the beginning of the nineteenth
century were later to be characterized by Karl Marx as
"utopian" to distinguish them from himself and his followers
who had, he supposed, developed a "scientific" socialism. The
phrase "utopian socialism" is borrowed from the title of a
book by Sir Thomas More, *Utopia* (1516), in which the
English philosopher described a virtuous, intelligent, near-
perfect but totally imaginary society. The word "utopian"
was used by Marx and his followers in the pejorative and
derisive sense, meaning "unrealistic." But in the confused
welter of thought that engulfed Europe after the collapse of
revolutionary ideals, some early socialist thinkers were able
to discern the emerging problems of an industrial society

with remarkable clarity; and some of their proposed solutions, if short-lived, were nothing if not "real."

One of the earliest, and in some ways the most remarkable of these utopian socialists was Claude Henri de Rouvroy, Comte de Saint-Simon. A nobleman descended from one of the most illustrious of French aristocratic families, Saint-Simon had dropped his title at an early age but not his belief in the importance of the family Saint-Simon. He went to America and fought on the side of the colonists during the American Revolution; but, repelled by the excesses of the French Revolution, he took no part in that. As the scion of a noble family he was imprisoned by the revolutionists during the time of the Terror and spent months in a dungeon, wondering whether he would be guillotined the next day. It was during this period that he imagined that his great ancestor Charlemagne appeared to him to declare that he, Saint-Simon, was to be as great a philosopher as Charlemagne had been a warrior.

Released from prison and inspired by Charlemagne's advice, Saint-Simon undertook to educate himself in every area of human knowledge. In turn he systematically studied physics, mathematics, medicine, languages, philosophy, and history. He undertook extensive travels in Germany and England to broaden his viewpoint; he sought out for conversation and stimulation as many of the learned men of his day as he could reach. And although his program of self-education left vast gaps in his knowledge, although to the specialized professional thinkers of his day and to the even more narrowly specialized experts of our own day his career was to seem hopelessly amateurish, Saint-Simon was able to see aspects of the new industrial social fabric which escaped others. He was perhaps fitted to do so by the very contradictions of his character and background. A noble of the old regime, he had fought for revolutionary ideals in America; inspired by Enlightenment ideals, he nevertheless had viewed the French Revolution as primarily a "destructive process"; committed to scientific inquiry, he nonetheless believed in the reality of the ghost of Charlemagne. His character, in fact, faithfully reflected the chaos of the collapse of the old order and the birth pangs of the new.

Addressing himself to one of the central contradictions of eighteenth-century philosophy, Saint-Simon, in an impressive series of books and pamphlets published beginning in 1802, pointed out that Enlightenment thinkers had erred in assuming that human beings were capable of acts of free will. On the one hand, these thinkers had insisted that nature, the physical world, was ruled by immutable natural laws; by assuming that man himself could escape these laws, they had divorced man from nature. But the effect of natural law on man was expressed through human social laws, and these laws influenced and preconditioned much of what man imagined to be his free will. Therefore the liberals in the traditions of the American and French revolutions, with their insistence on absolute individual liberty, were simply mouthing a meaningless slogan.

The revolutions in which the world was immersed—political, industrial, and scientific—had unleashed vast new sources of power, knowledge, and production. If society was not to sink into absolute chaos, these great new powers would have to be organized and directed rationally. In fact, the power of production, the economic factor in society, was and had always been basic to the nature of society. Political and social evolution in history was really the story of economic evolution, and society's true business was the rationalizing and balancing of conflicting economic interests in such a way as to promote the greatest good for the greatest number. This perception of the economic springs of the social world, this insistence upon the importance of economics in human evolution was perhaps Saint-Simon's greatest contribution to socialist thought.

How then was the social world to be organized to achieve these ends? To the ex-nobleman, it seemed self-evident that all men were *not* created equal. Obviously some men were more courageous or more talented or wiser than others. Therefore society was not to be based on the ideal of equality but rather on the ideal of inequality modified by Christian love. Mankind could be divided into three overall groups: the wise men, the men who owned property, and the men who were neither wise nor propertied. In Saint-Simon's hierarchy the wise men, including scientists and artists, were to inspire society with their goals, devise new inventions for the betterment of the human condition, and form a sort of supreme spearhead of human spiritual leadership. The wise men engaged in these noble pursuits were to be supported by general taxation, which would cheerfully be contributed by the other classes in their own obvious self-interest. Occupying a less exalted position, but in actual governing command of the state, were to be the men of property. These men, because they possessed enough personal income to work without salary for the state, and because they were better educated and more intelligent, would direct the affairs of society unselfishly for the betterment of all its members. The lowest order of Saint-Simon's hierarchy, the men without property, would naturally see that it was in their own interest to support this order; after all, when the unpropertied had attempted to run the state for themselves, as during the French Revolution, not only had they produced terror and famine, but they had lost control of affairs to the abominable military upstart, Napoleon. Despite the apparent inequalities of this scheme, Saint-Simon insisted that the purpose of it was to improve the physical, moral, and intellectual lot of the poorest class.

It will be noticed immediately that Saint-Simon's proposed society looks both to the past and to the future. Its order might be described as feudal if for the scientist-artist class one substituted the Catholic clergy; for the propertied class, royalty and aristocracy; and for the unpropertied class, artisans and serfs. It might be described as present-day bureaucratic communism if one were to substitute for the three classes the Communist party, the governing bureaucracy, and all the other members of Soviet society.

But although Saint-Simon's hierarchy seems both undemocratic and rigid, it by no means exhausts his thought as expressed in a continuing series of works. From a scientific viewpoint, he could see no possible profit to be derived from a struggle between employers and workers; were not their ultimate interests the same? They should cooperate, and to ensure that cooperation the ownership of the means of production (mines, mills, factories, etc.) was not to be private, but social and communal under the direction of scientific state-appointed managers. The state, he held, was under an obligation to provide work for all, and everyone was obligated to work for society according to his individual powers. He vigorously denounced the exploitation of workers under the private-ownership system of the means of production, and his proposed solution, if dictatorially paternal, was intended to be benevolent.

How did Saint-Simon propose to introduce his new social order? What social engines did he expect would establish it? Simply an appeal to reason—to the reason of governments and propertied classes. Enlightened self-interest would motivate them—and something more: a rebirth and redefinition of Christian virtues. In his last book, *The New Christianity,* anticipating later deist thinkers, Saint-Simon attempts to construct, out of both Catholic and Protestant thought, a new religion. The admonition "Love thy neighbor," he points out, now means "organize society in such a way as to improve the lot of all men, especially the very poor." The last words Saint-Simon ever committed to paper were addressed to the rulers of the Holy Alliance, the tsar of Russia, the king of Prussia and the emperor of Austria-Hungary, who between them had been stifling European progress since the fall of Napoleon:

> Princes! [Saint-Simon declares] Hear the voice of God, which speaks to you through my mouth: Become good Christians again; throw off the belief that the hired armies, the nobility, the heretical clergy, the corrupt judges, constitute your principal supporters; unite in the name of Christianity and learn to accomplish the duties which Christianity imposes on the powerful; remember that Christianity commands them to devote their energies to bettering as rapidly as possible the lot of the very poor!

Saint-Simon's confidence in appealing to reason and love may be traced to a lingering of Enlightenment optimism. But this optimism was difficult for him to sustain in the face of the complete indifference with which his writings were received, as was shown by his attempted suicide in 1823. By the time of his death in 1825 (he died in absolute poverty, having spent his entire fortune trying to propagate his ideas), Saint-Simon's hopes, like Babeuf's before him, were no longer centered on the present, but on the future.

The disciples of Saint-Simon were later to devote themselves almost exclusively to the religious aspect of his thought; one of them, Auguste Comte, based his widely popular "positivist" religion on Saint-Simon's attempt to reconcile God and science. The economic and social side of Saint-Simon's philosophy was to be developed not so much by his disciples as by certain of his younger contemporaries working along parallel lines. These men, not content simply to appeal to the generosity or self-interest of the age, proposed that their various schemes be clothed in reality, that socialist communities might be founded within contemporary society which by the example of their success would bring about change. If Saint-Simon may be said to have been a propagandist of the word, these men were propagandists of the deed.

François Charles Marie Fourier was a shop clerk and traveling salesman who had experienced the insufficiency of the promise of the French Revolution: he had watched the people of Lyons sink into degradation as the textile mills had come to dominate the city's trade, and he had experienced famine in Marseilles. Nevertheless, like Saint-Simon he had clung to the old Rousseauist idea that man is naturally good and only society corrupts him. In several books published after 1808, Fourier advanced the view that not only was man naturally good, but his various "passions," if properly understood and manipulated, could be woven into a productive and harmonious social fabric. Whereas the Revolutionary tradition had sought to repress what it considered some of man's evil instincts, Fourier held that there were, rightly viewed, no evil instincts in man, only a misapplication of natural functions. Furthermore, he believed he had discovered the form through which man's passions might profitably be organized.

Recognizing that society must be organized in accordance with its primary function, production, Fourier advocated the establishment of small communities which he called phalansteries (the word is derived from the Macedonian military unit, the phalanx) which would be based on a rational division and application of labor. Fourier's phalansteries were to consist of 1,500 or 1,600 persons—a number not too unwieldy to administer but sufficiently large to ensure a wide variety of tastes and abilities. All the members of this community were to live together in a single large building (designed by Fourier); there was to be universal suffrage, equal education for all, and complete equality between men and women. But Fourier did not advocate equality of income or the abolition of property rights. Each member of the phalanstery was to be rewarded according to his labors and the community itself was to be based on private capital. Five-twelfths of the phalanstery's total production was to be awarded to labor; four-twelfths to capital and three-twelfths to special talent. But his intricate system of dividends to be paid on investments so favored the small investor that a Fourierist phalanstery would actually resemble, financially, a cooperative stock-sharing corporation.

Since men were possessed of so many and such various passions, there was some kind of work that everybody enjoyed performing. It was only a question of finding the right man for the job. Disagreeable or heavy work would be more highly paid and the performance of such tasks rotated within the community. No one would be made to work at a job he disliked; furthermore, people would shift jobs regularly so as to maintain their interest—no one would labor at the same task for more than two or three consecutive hours. Efficiency would be promoted by men's natural desire for praise from their fellows. An example of Fourier's matching of a human passion to a necessary job was his suggestion that since children seem to love to play in dirt, it would be well to make them the phalanstery's garbage collectors.

Fourier announced to the world that he would remain at home every day at noon prepared to discuss his plans with philanthropic capitalists ready to finance them. Although he kept this appointment punctually for ten years, no public-spirited patron ever appeared. He died in 1837 without a single phalanstery ever having been founded.

Yet Fourier had met and influenced some important people, especially two American journalists, Albert Brisbane, a writer, and Horace Greeley, the editor of the New York *Tribune.* Bringing Fourier's ideas back from Paris, these two propagandized them so successfully in the United States that during the 1840's no less than forty different groups set forth to establish phalansteries. They would buy several thousand acres of land, erect large central dwelling and dining halls according to Fourier's design, establish farms and mills and light industries and attempt to live according to the Fourierist doctrines. The large spaces, political freedom, and ample rewards to be won from exploiting the natural wealth of a new continent seemed to promise ideal conditions under which to experiment with this new social form. Yet few of the Fourierist phalansteries lasted more than a decade. All sorts of troubles afflicted them, but perhaps the most central was simply the fact that people, rich or poor, raised within the framework of an exploitive and competitive society, could not "remake" themselves at once into model socially oriented citizens of a cooperative community. Although one or two of the phalansteries lasted until well after the Civil War, most came to grief amid a welter of lawsuits by the 1850's.

A much more practical and successful advocate of the establishment of "demonstration" social communities to show the way to a new world was Fourier's English contemporary,

Robert Owen. Born in 1771, Owen had left home at the age of ten to work in the cotton mills of Manchester; his experience of the miseries of the Industrial Revolution in England was nothing if not personal. So successful was Owen at the cotton trade (he was largely self-educated, like Saint-Simon and Fourier) that by the time he was twenty he had risen to be manager of an entire cotton-spinning factory at New Lanark in Scotland. From this position he could clearly see that not only was capitalist industrialism destroying the impoverished workers, it was also degrading the capitalists themselves. "I was completely tired," he wrote, "of partners who were merely trained to buy cheap and sell dear. This occupation deteriorates and often destroys the finest and best faculties of our nature. . . . Under this system, there can be no true civilization; for by it all are trained civilly to oppose and often to destroy one another by their created opposition of interests. It is a low, vulgar, ignorant, and inferior mode of conducting the affairs of society. . . ."

When Robert Owen first came to manage the New Lanark mills (in 1791) he found the workers there demoralized by wretched conditions. Many of them were ex-farmers forced from their small holdings by the commercialization of agriculture; others were elderly men and women cast off from former employment for whom in the Great Britain of 1791 no social provision whatsoever was made; still others were young children between the ages of five and ten shipped in by local orphanages. All were thoroughly degraded, drunken, given to thievery; the refuse and wreckage of a heartlessly competitive society. Purchasing a controlling interest in the mills, Owen set about redeeming this most unpromising human material. He paid his workers higher wages and had them work shorter hours; during hard times he continued to pay high wages despite losses. He ploughed profits back into the community of New Lanark in the form of schools, cheap and decent workers' housing, adult education, and a health and savings fund for the workers. Within two decades Robert Owen could point not only to the greater efficiency, profits, and workmanship of his mills, he could point to a working-class population seemingly transformed from utter demoralization to sturdy independence. All who came to witness his self-wrought "miracle" had to agree that his workers were healthy, educated, cheerful, honest, and devoted to Robert Owen. What Owen believed he had done was demonstrate practically, realistically, and successfully the central concept of the Enlightenment; that by changing men's social and economic environment one could change human nature itself. In his journal, *The New Moral World,* he wrote: "Any general character, from the best to the worst . . . may be given to any community . . . by the application of proper means."

Unlike Fourier, Owen believed that contemporary nations might be persuaded to undertake the reforms on a universal scale which he had indicated in his writings and at New Lanark. He invited prominent English and foreign politicians, economists, and prelates to witness for themselves the success of his experiment. He accepted invitations to address learned conferences and devoted much time to lobbying in the English Parliament for such measures as his cherished law against child labor (a law ultimately defeated by the machinations not only of greedy cotton spinners but of such liberal politicians as Robert Peel). At first the politicians listened to Owen. He was a practical and successful businessman, after all, and he seemed to have discovered a way of coping with the dangerously growing discontent of the working classes. But the ruling classes soon discovered that Owen's "solution" was more than merely ameliorative—if generally applied, it promised to undermine the entire existing social order. In 1817, while attending an international conference at Aix-la-Chapelle, Owen was told bluntly by a highly placed diplomat that the governments of the world were as well aware of both the problems and their potential solutions as was Owen. But if the working classes became educated and independent, how were the ruling classes to continue to control them?

Until that moment, despite earlier disappointments, Owen had believed that he had only to instruct and persuade the powerful of the world; now he realized that he was faced not only with ignorance or apathy, but with conscious opposition from men who simply did not care what became of their fellows so long as their own personal profits and privileges remained undisturbed. If his success at New Lanark was not sufficient incentive and example for the world, he would construct others. Accordingly, he traveled to the New World and in 1825 established an Owenite community, modeled on New Lanark, at New Harmony, Indiana. He established other such communities at Orbiston, Scotland, and Ralahine, Ireland, between 1826 and 1835. But all, after a few brief years, were doomed to failure. For the truth, to which Owen's modesty always blinded him, was that the success at New Lanark had been due, not so much to ideal principles or to the innate nobility of man in a proper environment, as to Robert Owen's personal intervention and supervision. A consummate businessman, he was able to make idealism profitable; a generous and extremely intelligent man, he was able, through the force of his personality, to inspire close associates; a man inflamed with a real faith in his fellows and dedicated selflessly to their betterment, he had the strength and self-confidence to play the part of a benevolent but absolute "father" to his followers. When, as in the later communities, he was not himself in constant residence, these communities fell into the hands of less able men and soon came to grief.

From about 1830 to 1834, more because of his vast popularity with the English working class than because of any real interest on his part, Owen found himself at the head of the nascent English trade-union movement. He was the nominal leader of the Owenite Cooperative Movement and the Grand National Consolidated Trades Union. But the long, grinding struggle of labor to gain its rights bit by bit was not really congenial to Owen, who, to the end of his life, remained convinced that man's perfectibility on earth could be won at a single stroke. Within a few years his trade union movement went to pieces. He died in poverty in 1858 (his idealism had triumphed over his business sense in the long run), still persuaded that "the happiness of self [can] only be attained by conduct that must promote the happiness of the community."

The seeds of exemplary utopianism, implicit in Saint-Simon, explicitly defined by Fourier, and bodied forth by Owen, gave rise to many other attempts to construct model paradises on earth. There were the Icarians, led by Étienne Cabet, who established several utopian communities in the United States, and there were the followers of the American utopian socialist, John Humphrey Noyes, who established a remarkably successful and long-lived community at Oneida, New York. But these ventures were not solely dedicated to equalizing man's economic environment; they included semireligious doctrines and such experiments in social dynamics as "complex marriage." All eventually failed—the principal Icarian settlement at Nauvoo, Illinois, and the Oneida community, lapsing into normal private ownership and the acceptance of normal American mores. The permanent

significance of the utopian socialist movement in practice
was that it led to the establishment and growth of producers'
cooperative societies, which remain today a vital and significant part of the economic structure of the Western world.

And utopian socialism had a very important negative effect
on the world of socialist theory. It was, after all, based on
the concept of man's inherent goodness and nobility and his
resultant perfectibility given the correct social conditions here
on earth. It presupposed the success of an appeal to generosity
of spirit and human reason. But the "man" conceived of
by the utopian socialists was an abstraction born in the
minds of optimistic Enlightenment philosophers. If, for example, man was essentially noble and remained noble in a state
of nature, how was it then that this noble natural man had
devised all those means of social oppression which had de-
based him? And, in any event, where in all of human history
could any trace be found of naturally "good" men living in
a naturally "good" society? The utopian socialists were
forced to point to contemporary "natural societies" such as
those of the North American Indians with which they were
totally unfamiliar, or to a purely imaginary prehistoric
"society" for which they had only their personal intuitions
as evidence. During the early years of the nineteenth century
the sciences of physical and social anthropology were just
coming into existence as was the science of archaeology. Had
the utopian socialists lived to examine the bodies of knowledge
brought forth by these new sciences, it is hard to believe they
could have retained their essential optimism about human
nature. Indeed, the picture of the evolution of life on earth
that was shortly to be painted by Charles Darwin seemed,
in its earlier, less sophisticated phase, to establish ruthless
struggle and conflict as the core of Natural Law.

And irrespective of whether or not "natural (utopian)
man" was to be viewed optimistically or pessimistically, he
remained an abstraction. He could be found only in fiction
or in the imagination, not in history. Yet man, real man
with all his failings and contradictions, is the basic building
block of any society. Even to begin to understand the nature
of man in society due weight must be given to *all* available
evidences of human behavior, no matter how detestable.
And at least until such time as man's self-knowledge matures,
it would seem that those societies which preserve the greatest
freedom and widest possible scope for the eccentricities of
human behavior are the most rational. A society based on

any "abstract man" must be as ephemeral as were the utopian communities of the early nineteenth century, or as repressively rigid as are the totalitarian states of our own day. In either case, such societies are doomed to failure.

Yet the utopian socialists, with their insistence upon the importance of science and production as the motive forces in human society, with their demonstration of the possibilities, if not the practicalities of cooperation rather than competition, above all with their view of man himself consciously at the controls of social development, did represent progress in the human understanding of social environment. And by omitting myths, heroes, and divine intervention their abstraction of man, however faulty, represented an advance toward reality.

Chapter Two

THE SEARCH FOR HISTORICAL MAN

Philosophy makes no secret of the fact that her creed is the creed of Prometheus: "In a word, I detest all the gods." This is her device against all deities of heaven or earth who do not recognize as the highest divinity the human self-consciousness itself.

—*Karl Marx*

The abstract, or ideal, man of the utopian socialists had been maturing in the imaginations of English and French thinkers for centuries. Early socialist theory had naturally developed in England, where the Industrial Revolution was much more advanced than elsewhere, and in France, which had been since 1700 the seedbed of revolutionary political ideas in Europe. The word *socialism* itself had first appeared in print as a description of the principles of Fourier and Robert Owen in the *Cooperative Magazine* in London in 1826. But the next phase of socialism, its transformation from "utopian" to "scientific" principles, was to be largely dominated by German thought. In fact, the emergence of socialism in its contemporary form may be said to be the result of the fusion of English and French political ideas with German philosophy; the catalyst of that fusion, Karl Marx, was to give his name to the entire body of socialist thought which today dominates nearly half the world.

Karl Marx was born in 1818 in the German city of Trier on the Moselle River near the Franco-German border. Although basically German, Trier had often in its history been occupied by the French, most recently during the era of

Napoleonic conquests which drew to a close only a few years before Karl Marx's birth. Not only was Trier more cosmopolitan than most German towns, it had had a heavier dose than most of those ideas of the French Revolution which, as Napoleon boasted, his troops "carried in their knapsacks."

Karl Marx's ancestors for many generations back had been highly respected rabbis in the Jewish community of Trier—the rabbinate being the sole possible outlet for Jews of intellect imprisoned by the medieval ghetto laws of. pre-nineteenth-century Germany. One of the results of the Napoleonic domination of Trier had been the relaxation of some of these ancient anti-Jewish restrictions. Hirschel Marx, Karl's father, had taken advantage of this new freedom to study law and make himself a modestly successful political career in Trier. And when the French were finally expelled from the city by Prussian troops, who once again imposed anti-Jewish laws on the population, Hirschel Marx, who had studied Kant, Rousseau, and Voltaire and considered himself a "freethinker," had his entire family baptized Christians. He eventually rose to be a judge and head of the Trier Bar Association.

Karl Marx himself was to disregard and discard his Jewish and rabbinical heritage; he saw both the "Jewish problem" as defined by anti-Semites, and the miseries experienced by Jews still struggling to escape medieval bondage, as subsidiary symptoms of the disease of capitalist exploitation. Yet there was to be in Marx's writing and career more than a hint of the tremendous moral force of the Old Testament prophets; the subtlety and earnestness of his thought made him appear to be the great secular rabbi of the nineteenth century; against opponents he thundered with the wrath of Jehovah. . . . It may be that the rebellious impulse in Marx sprang not only from his absorption of Enlightenment ideas, but also from his family heritage of struggle against oppressive laws and anti-Semitic taboos.

Marx attended the Friedrich-Wilhelm School in Trier, where his brilliance was fully recognized by his teachers. Later, in 1835, he went to the University of Bonn. There, somewhat uncharacteristically, he plunged into a student life of drunkenness and brawling and did very little serious studying. He joined a poets' club which was under the surveillance of the political police, went heavily into debt, and generally scandalized the university authorities. At their suggestion (and with the hearty approval of his long-suffering father),

Karl was transferred to the University of Berlin in the fall of 1836. There, to please his parents, he made a show of studying law but actually immersed himself in the study of philosophy.

When Marx reached Berlin, German philosophy was still dominated by the teachings and thought of Georg Hegel. Hegel held that society, "the state," was the realization and fulfillment of absolute reason. It followed that the individual must subordinate himself to the state, which was ultimately the working out here on earth, through reason, of some divine "Idea." Already, in 1836 some younger German philosophers were rebelling against Hegel's "Absolute Idea." They were called "Left Hegelians," and most, such as Bruno Bauer, Moses Hess, and Ludwig Feuerbach addressed themselves to the demolition of what they considered to be a carryover of Christian idealism in Hegel. Marx joined them with certain reservations which we shall discuss later. But unlike certain of his contemporaries, Karl Marx found in Hegel a principle of historical change that could be useful in the real world.

Hegel saw history as the organic progress of man on earth, guided by the Absolute Idea. The world was, therefore, in constant process of change—but this process always took place in a cycle of three phases. The first of these phases was called by Hegel the *thesis*—a process of unification and affirmation. The second he called the *antithesis*—a process of splitting away from the *thesis* and combating it. The third phase, which Hegel called the *synthesis*, was a process by which elements of the *thesis* and the *antithesis* were unified and reconciled on a higher plane. A very much simplified example might be an argument between yourself and a friend. Your friend makes a general statement which may be described as the *thesis*. You counter this with a negating argument which may be described as the *antithesis*. But as your discussion progresses, both you and your friend realize that a third viewpoint, incorporating some elements of both sides of the question is really closer to the truth. This third viewpoint would be the *synthesis*. Hegel called this entire process "dialectic" (derived from the Greek word *dialego,* meaning to discuss or debate), since it was inspired by Plato's dialectic technique of arriving at truth by reconciling two opposing statements. But unlike Plato, Hegel saw the dialectic as operating not only in the realms of discussion and logic, but also in the real world and in human history.

As an example of the dialectic working in history, Hegel proposed the ancient Roman republic. This republic, by unifying people, territory, and certain political ideals was to be regarded as a *thesis*. But over the years, under the influence of increasing prosperity, the republic's citizens became greedy and cynical and its political ideals decayed until, by the time of Julius Caesar, the state itself had been fragmented by civil war. This decay and anarchy were to be regarded as an *antithesis*. But Julius Caesar and, later, Augustus, were able to reunite the elements of Roman society through force of arms and impose upon it a new, autocratic form of government. This new government created a much larger unification, the Roman Empire; and this for Hegel was a *synthesis*. Later we will examine the uses to which Marx was to put Hegel's dialectic. Basically, he was to project it into the present and the future as well as the past, something Hegel had not contemplated.

Karl Marx graduated from the University of Berlin in 1841, with the reputation of being the most brilliant student of his generation. Early in 1842 he commenced writing articles for a liberal newspaper published in Cologne, the *Rheinische Zeitung*. His articles, criticizing censorship and exposing the increasing miseries of the Rhenish wine-producing peasants, were incisive and savagely satirical. So popular did they become that by October 1842 Marx had been appointed editor-in-chief of the newspaper. But under his direction the *Rheinische Zeitung* lasted only five months before it was suppressed by the authorities for criticizing the Russian tsarist government.

In June 1843, Marx married his childhood sweetheart, Jenny von Westphalen, a girl four years older than himself and remarkable for her beauty and intelligence. She had been raised in a liberal, cosmopolitan home not unlike Marx's own; their families had been neighbors in Trier for many years. Disgusted by the suppression of his newspaper and by increasing evidences of political reaction in Germany, Marx took Jenny to live in Paris in the fall of 1843. There he set about reading Saint-Simon, Fourier, and other French socialists, and there, in August 1844, he established a life-long and vital friendship with a young German writer named Friedrich Engels.

Friedrich Engels was born in the industrial German milltown of Barmen in 1820. His father was highly successful in the textile business, owning mills not only in Barmen but also in Manchester, England. Young Engels' background was instructively different from Marx's. Whereas the elder Marx had held himself to be a free-thinker, the elder Engels was a Calvinist religious fanatic of the most puritanical kind. While Marx's family had encouraged his interests in poetry and reading and music, Engels' father strongly disapproved of such "frivolities." And yet, from this background, young Engels emerged a much more spirited, gay, and light-hearted optimist than Marx. He enjoyed good wine and good music; he was an accomplished athlete who delighted in riding, fencing, and swimming; although he was a serious student and thinker, there runs through his writing a basic sympathy for and vital interest in all things human that is largely absent from the heavier works of Marx.

In the fall of 1841, Friedrich Engels went to the University of Berlin (arriving just after Marx's graduation) where he quickly came under the influence of Hegelian theory and of the new Left Hegelians. One of these, Moses Hess, who had traveled in England and France, was a convert to some of the theories of Saint-Simon; he soon converted Engels to socialism. But in November of 1842, Engels' university career came to an end when his father sent him to Manchester, England, to learn the operations of the family's English mills.

Possessed of a quick and acute intelligence, Engels mastered the rudiments of the textile trade. But during the twenty-two months he spent in Manchester he learned something much more important: the practical, immediate effects of industrialization upon the population of an industrial city. The years from 1842 to 1844 were years of economic depression for English textile mills. Engels visited the slums of Manchester and saw working people crammed like rats into miserable little hovels; he saw them eating garbage, poisoning themselves with ptomaine-tainted bits of rotten meat, doping themselves with cheap gin and their children with laudanum, living amid piles of their own excrement, dying young and fast from typhus, malnutrition, and cholera. He saw young women supporting their unemployed fathers by working in the mills by day and prostituting themselves at night; he saw children of five and six fed into the mills where their growth was stunted and their minds were paralyzed.

And Engels also saw that industrial commerce had depraved the rich—the mill owners and operators—by atomizing society so that it had become little more than a collection of individuals driven by fear and greed. Once, traveling into

Manchester in the company of a prosperous mill operator, Engels had discoursed on the terrible misery of the working people and the terrible physical blight that industrialization had brought to the city itself. "And yet," the mill operator remarked as they parted, "there is a great deal of money made here. Good morning, sir."

Above all, Engels began to perceive in England that politics was really a function of class interests. He watched the liberal English politicians ally themselves with their supposed enemies, the conservatives, to fight against such legislation as the Child Labor Act, the Factory Act, and the Poor Relief Law—all measures that threatened their mutual economic interests. When Engels met Marx in Paris in 1844, he was able to bring to their intellectual discussions a large and thorough practical knowledge of many of the realities of that industrial-capitalist system that both men were eager to see destroyed.

This meeting of Marx and Engels was one of the most important intellectual events of the nineteenth century. Each man complemented the other in various ways. Engels' thoroughgoing knowledge of the working class and industrial problems became grist for the vast scholarship and mighty mills of Marx's mind. Engels' writings, if not nearly so "profound" as those of Marx, exhibited a vitality and exuberance which did much to counterbalance the inhuman brilliance and "heaviness" of his partner's work. While Marx was given to crusty intolerance of those who disagreed with him and to morbid suspicions about the motives of friends as well as foes, Engels maintained a better sense of proportion. Yet it was always Marx who dominated their relationship, in a sense almost replacing the father Engels hated. Years later Engels was to write: "Marx was a genius, the rest of us were talented at best."

If Marxism may be said to be the result of the encounter of German philosophy with French and English political ideas, it will also be seen that the first task Marx and Engels had to perform was to engage the ideal speculations of German philosophy in the real world of men. French and English philosophy, although incorporating many an "ideal" or abstract element, had generally been practical, even pragmatic. In the social, political, and economic spheres it either justified existing conditions or predicted new real conditions. But German philosophy, with its conceptions of "Absolute Will," "World Spirit," "Ideal Will," and "Divine Reason," among many others, remained almost totally abstract; it was neither rooted in nor very much concerned with the real world. Marx and Engels were later to see this difference as caused by the fact that Germany—still primarily a collection of small principalities, largely unindustrialized—had seldom offered scope for men of intellect to advance their ideas in the real world in an area which since the time of Martin Luther had been the battlefield of conflicting religious beliefs and since the time of the Holy Roman Empire the battlefield of rival European political ambitions. German philosophers had, as it were, been forced by native social, political, and economic conditions to retire into "pure" rather than "practical" philosophy. Heinrich Heine, the great German poet (and a friend of Marx and Engels) had observed: "The land belongs to the Russians and French, the sea belongs to the British; but we possess in the cloudland of dreams the uncontested domination."

It was through the analysis and rejection of the works of the Left Hegelians that Karl Marx was able to bring German philosophy out of the clouds and down to earth. In 1841 the most important of Hegel's younger disciples, Ludwig Feuerbach, had published a book called *The Essence of Christianity*. In it Feuerbach pointed out that Hegel's "Absolute Idea," which was supposed to be working itself out in the real world through human reason as exemplified by man's social organization, was simply an assumption on Hegel's part—an assumption which he would never be able to prove. It was, in fact, nothing less than the old Christian conception of the Word of God. But this itself was an unprovable assumption. In order to understand Christianity, Feuerbach declared, it would be better to discard all assumptions resting upon the divine and to assume that Christianity, like all other religions and systems of thought, was a product of the thought and imagination of man himself—to be understood only by an examination of man's real social world. Feuerbach not only analyzed the supernatural right out of Christianity, he was also able to show that the valuable moral and ethical aspects of Christian thought could be deduced from the necessities of men in the real world and therefore required no divine sanction. But Feuerbach, when he referred to "man," was still assuming the existence of an abstract "Man," who was possessed of an abstract "Reason." He even went so far as to propose a substitute religion, incorporating Christian ethical and moral ideals for his abstract man, which would be acceptable because they were sanctified by reason.

In 1845 Karl Marx analyzed Feuerbach's book and wrote down a set of notes which were to be published years later as his *Thesis on Feuerbach*. In it Marx pointed out that Feuerbach, like almost all philosophers before him, had been baffled by the question of human reason. The real world exists, but does it exist only because it is perceived by human intelligence, or is it possessed of a reality of its own, a reality which may even give rise to human reason itself? Marx dismissed this question as irrelevant. Reason, he held, could only be known as it exerted itself upon the real world. Our very self-consciousness, our knowing that we know, rises from the interaction of the human intelligence and the material world. Man seeks to act on the real world, as he must, to survive; when he observes that his actions have had some real impact on that world, then and then only does he know that his reason not only exists, but that its conceptions were correct.

Turning to the thought of such utopian socialists as Fourier and Owen, Marx pointed out that these men had assumed that different economic and social conditions would produce a different type of human character. Perhaps. But Owen himself had been a product of those very social conditions which he denounced. How then could he account for his own intelligence, generosity, and idealism? From what sources could an enlightened educator educate? Almost all philosophers had evaded this question, Marx said, by devising some sort of Abstract Man, generally within the framework of some abstract religious ideal. But in actuality both man and man's reason were integral parts of his social world; both human character and human intelligence could only be understood as parts of specific social conditions at any given time. Therefore the "ideal" problems of philosophy could only be apprehended as elements of real social conditions; and they could only be resolved through man's continuing attempts to transform the real social world. The last lines of Marx's *Thesis on Feuerbach* express his attitude: "The philosophers hitherto have only interpreted the world in various ways: the thing is, however, to change it."

To Marx and Engels the trouble with all these Abstract Men was their apparent inability to have any impact on the real world. But the real world does change, as history proves. And men change it. What are the dynamics of this process? Where can one find the social engines which carry society forward? To answer this question Marx brought Hegel's dialectic to bear: the *thesis, antithesis,* and *synthesis.* But Hegel had imagined this as an ideal process carried forward by an Absolute Idea. Not so, declared Marx; it is a real process of the real world; it is nothing less than the continuing succession of struggles between an exploited and an exploiting class. These classes arise throughout history as the means of human production change. When, for example, during the Middle Ages the means of production were primarily small-scale agriculture and domestic artisanship, feudal society, with its hierarchy of classes, developed as a faithful reflection of this system of production. But when barter was replaced by a money economy, when larger-scale agriculture became possible, when commerce became international and as the factory system replaced domestic artisanship, a new society, the middle-class capitalist system with its own hierarchy of social classes, came into being. Thus one might say that feudalism was a historical *thesis;* but as the means of production changed a new class, that of the emerging bourgeois merchants, capitalists, and factory owners, came into being to challenge the feudal order—and this new class may be said to be a historical *antithesis.* From the struggle between these two has emerged a new *synthesis* which is nothing other than modern capitalist society.

This was all very well as an analysis of the past, but what of the future? Was capitalist society the end of social history, or did it contain within itself an *antithesis* which would one day destroy it? Marx perceived that the developing *antithesis* to the capitalist order was the growing working class in capitalist society. In 1843, writing an article called "A Critique of the Hegelian Philosophy of Law," Marx proposed the working class, or proletariat, as the *antithesis* of capitalist society: "A class in *radical chains,* one of the classes of bourgeois society which does not belong to bourgeois society, an order which brings the breakup of all orders, a sphere which has a universal character by virtue of its universal suffering and lays claim to no *particular right* because no *particular wrong* but complete wrong is being perpetrated against it, which can no longer invoke a *historical* title, but only a *human* title. . . . The *proletariat* represents the dissolution of society as a special order."

That Marx's proletariat did not become yet another abstraction but remained a conception of real people working under real conditions was in no small measure the result of Engels' influence. Engels, in 1844, wrote *The Condition of the Working Class in England in 1844,* a work which filled in the word "proletariat" with facts and figures. Here the older English political economists such as Ricardo and Adam Smith were exposed as apologists for the harsh exploitation of the English workers; here the capitalist phenomenon of recurring "boom" and "bust" periods were shown to be inevitable cycles due to the blind greed of competing commercial interests; here the food, habitation, wages, and untold miseries of the English working class were described in minute detail.

Karl Marx was later to claim that this conception of the working class as the inherent *antithesis* of capitalist society was his only original contribution to the theory of socialism. While this claim may be too modest, it may be convenient here to point out that Marx and Engels, like most great originators of social theories or systems, were actually harvesters and organizers of the thought of very many men. To cite only a few examples: from the writings of Saint-Simon they had learned that modern politics was really the science of organizing the productive forces of the state; from Fourier they had imbibed distrust and even hatred of the middle-class owners of the means of production; from Robert Owen, the idea that the factory system itself must be the seedbed of social revolution; from the French historians Augustin Thierry and François Guizot, the idea of history as a record of class struggle; from Théodore Dézamy, the importance of the proletariat as the liberating class in capitalist society. All these thinkers and many many more, both famous and obscure, had influenced Marx and Engels. In their books jointly written from the time of their meeting in 1844 until the revolutionary year of 1848, books such as *The Holy Family, The German Ideology,* and *The Poverty of Philosophy,* the reader may trace the development of their thought as it has been influenced both by earlier and contemporary writers and as it seeks a coherent form and voice of its own. In turn, the writings of Marx and Engels began to reach men influential in the many, scattered reformist, working-class, or socialist movements which had managed to maintain a faltering, underground existence during the decades of post-Napoleonic repression in Europe.

This repression, which had first affected Marx when it closed down his *Rheinische Zeitung,* pursued him to Paris. He was expelled from the French capital in 1845 at the insistence of the Prussian government, which was worried about the activities of German radical expatriates in exile. Marx took Jenny to Brussels and continued his work; Engels, shifting back and forth between the family mills at Barmen and Manchester, joined him there whenever he could. While they continued to study and write, the storm clouds of revolution were once again gathering over Europe.

Since the days when the king of Prussia, the tsar of Russia and the emperor of Austria-Hungary had decided to make Europe safe for absolute monarchy, much had changed. The Industrial Revolution was now in full swing over the continent. The middle class, which had thought itself freed by the French Revolution, grew increasingly restive under the re-imposed monarchies in Franch and Spain. Behind them could be discerned the continuing and growing discontent of ever-more-miserable working classes. Pressures for reform had led to a brief revolution in France in 1830 which had replaced the traditionalist monarchy of the Bourbon kings (reimposed after Napoleon's downfall) with the constitutional monarchy of the "citizen king," Louis Philippe. This "July Revolution" in France had touched off similar risings in Belgium, Poland, Italy, and some of the small German principalities. East of the Rhine these uprisings were soon quenched by Prussian, Russian, or Austrian troops; and in France itself it soon became apparent that Louis Philippe was no more than a mask behind which the very wealthiest capitalists manipulated both the French economy and the nation in the interests of their own purses. Europe from 1820 to 1848 resembled a large vat of boiling water: once or twice the lid had been blown off to allow some steam to escape; each time the ruling classes had pressed the lid back down until, by 1848, an explosion was almost certain.

Nor had the traditions of the French Revolution been forgotten; secret societies devoted to the principles of François Babeuf had reappeared in the working-class quarters of Paris. In the late 1830's they merged with groups of exiled German radicals to form the League of the Just. Gradually through the years this semisecret organization gained strength as it attracted to it all those, from Utopian Socialists to radical nationalists, who could not abide the repressive pressures of the reactionary European system. Marx and Engels came into close touch with the leaders of the League of the Just in Brussels. These in turn were much impressed by the forceful thought and brilliant writings of the two young Germans. In 1847, now coming increasingly under the domination of

Marx and Engels, the League of the Just changed its name to the Communist League and authorized Marx and Engels to prepare a manifesto which would set forth the aims and policies of the new organization.

What the Communist League received from the ready hands of Marx and Engels was a compression of all their thoughts and conclusions up until that moment, expressed in language so trenchant and fiery that *The Communist Manifesto* must be reckoned one of the most brilliant and explosive political documents of all time. In little more than fifty pages Marx and Engels were able to present their theory of history, analyze current European society, project a program of action and issue a ringing battle cry to arouse intellectuals and workers everywhere. *The Communist Manifesto* effectively destroys almost all previous conceptions of Abstract Man and brings to light a new idea—Historical Man; that is, man seen as a social being working out his destiny through his own devised history. Without precisely realizing it, perhaps, it was toward this new conception of man that Marx and Engels had been struggling for years. From that time forward, not only Abstract Man, but also Abstract Ideals were to be measured against this new image. And in the light of social, historical man, much idealism seems either futile or mendacious. Thus in *The Communist Manifesto* Marx speaks of the ideal concept of justice: "Justice for whom? Under capitalism it is the proletariat who get caught most often and punished most severely, and who also, since they must starve when they are jobless, are driven to commit the most crimes." As for liberty, "Liberty for whom?—You will never be able to liberate the worker without restricting the liberty of the owner." As for such conceptions as God and truth, Marx pointed out that the world would never know what these words meant until it produced philosophers who were no longer involved in exploitive societies.

As for the transition from feudalism to capitalism marked by such events as the French Revolution, Marx commented, "Wherever the bourgeoisie has risen to power, it has destroyed all feudal, patriarchal, and idyllic relationships. It has ruthlessly torn asunder the motley feudal ties that bound men to their 'natural superiors'; it has left no other bond between man and man but crude self-interest and callous 'cash payment.' It has drowned pious zeal, chivalrous enthusiasm, and popular sentimentalism with the chill waters of selfish calculation. It has degraded personal dignity to the level of exchange value. . . ."

The program of action outlined in the *Manifesto* was clear and direct in its advocacy of "the forcible overthrow of the whole extant social order." It proposed:

1. Expropriation of landed property, and the use of land rents to defray state expenditures; 2. A vigorously graded income tax; 3. Abolition of the right of inheritance; 4. Confiscation of the property of all émigrés and rebels; 5. Centralization of credit in the hands of the state, by means of a national bank with state capital and an exclusive charter; 6. Centralization of the means of transport in the hands of the state; 7. Increase of national factories and means of production, cultivation of uncultivated land, and improvement of cultivated land in accordance with a general plan; 8. Universal and equal obligation to work; organization of industrial armies, especially for agriculture; 9. Agriculture and urban industry to work hand in hand, in such a way as, by degrees, to obliterate the distinction between town and country; 10. Public and free education of all children. Abolition of factory work for children in its present form. Education and material production to be combined.

And, at the end, the famous words with which Marx and Engels on behalf of the Communist League declared war to the death against capitalist society, the words which have since their day rung again and again around the world, the words with which Historical Man hurls defiance to previous abstract conceptions of himself: "Let the ruling classes tremble at the prospect of a communist revolution. Proletarians have nothing to lose but their chains. They have a world to win. PROLETARIANS OF ALL LANDS UNITE!"

Chapter Three

THE STAGE OF HISTORY

> What astonished me most in Marx was his passionate
> partisanship in political questions, which did not
> jibe with the calm objective method he recommended
> to his disciples. . . .
>
> —*Maxím Kovalévsky*

It must not be thought that Marx and Engels developed
their ideas only through reading or by pondering industrial
statistics in the cloistered atmosphere of library and study;
they also hammered out their views in response to immediate
practical needs, personal conflicts, and important historical
events in which they were deeply involved. To understand
both the vitality and the limitations of their theories it is
necessary to trace their development through the stormy
social history of mid-nineteenth-century Europe.

During the last weeks of February 1848 that explosion
toward which European social pressures had been building
since 1830 and to which *The Communist Manifesto* had been
hopefully addressed, took place on the streets and in the
working-class districts of Paris. Once again, as in 1830 and
1789, the spark was ignited by the dissatisfied middle classes
while the fuel was supplied by working-class miseries. The
citizen-king, Louis Philippe, behind whom the very richest
of the French capitalists had thought to shelter, had proven
inadequate even as a mask. Deteriorating economic conditions
in France made the bourgeoisie apprehensive of another
terrible working-class revolt. A graft-ridden system of taxa-
tion-through-bribes bore most heavily on the less wealthy
middle-class small manufacturers and shopkeepers. A muddled

foreign policy squandered millions of francs on the conquest of Algeria while threatening to involve France in a hopeless war against England and other continental powers. These factors destroyed Louis Philippe's usefulness even to his most avid supporters. The worried mill and mine and railway owners, the troubled manufacturers, the dissatisfied intellectuals, all pressed for constitutional reform. Since censorship was strict and public meetings forbidden, they did this through a series of "private" banquet parties at which fiery speeches denouncing the monarchy were made. When Louis Philippe banned one of these banquets in Paris on February 22, 1848, large and riotous crowds assembled to demonstrate against the government. More ominously, barricades and red flags began to appear in Parisian working-class districts. When the king learned that even his army would not support him, he abdicated (on February 24, 1848) and fled into exile. Immediately afterward the middle-class lawyers and journalists who had actively led the popular demonstrations in the streets proclaimed the Second French Republic.

The Austrian statesman Metternich once remarked, "When France sneezes, all Europe catches a cold." The events of 1848 proved him correct. This same Metternich, chief architect and guardian of the reactionary political system imposed on Europe after Napoleon's downfall, was now forced to flee in disguise when Vienna erupted into bloody rioting. The Austrian Emperor, Ferdinand I, was forced to promise his people a constitution and to permit autonomy within his empire for the Hungarians and Czechs.

Success in Austria quickly inspired uprisings in Prussia and in the small German principalities. Street fighting broke out in Berlin and the Prussian king, Frederick Wilhelm IV, was forced to appoint liberal ministers, promise a constitution, and agree to work for German unification. And with both Austria and Prussia, the two dominating states of Germany, caught up in revolution, German liberals from the small principalities decided that the hour of German unification under a liberal democratic form of government had arrived. They held elections for a national assembly, which met in Frankfurt to work out a democratic constitution for a unified Germany.

Upon hearing of the success of the French uprising, Karl Marx sent an address from Brussels to the French provisional government; he also contributed almost all of his money to buy arms for the Belgian workers. When the Belgian police learned of this, Marx was expelled from the country; he went immediately to revolutionary Paris where he set up a new headquarters for the Communist League. In April 1848, when Marx and Engels heard of the rising in Germany, they hurried to Cologne. There they quickly won control of the German branch of the Communist League and Marx began publishing a newspaper, the *Neue Rheinische Zeitung*. He used its popular columns (the newspaper quickly became famous throughout Germany) to goad the deputies assembled at Frankfurt to broader democratic reforms and, above all, to haste. His satire was never more biting, his exposition never more brilliant than during the months of the *Neue Rheinische Zeitung*.

But from his journalistic pulpit of 1848 Marx did *not* preach a proletarian revolution. His theory of historical change, the organic development of society through the processes of the dialectic presupposed that capitalist society would supplant feudalism *before* any question of a proletarian revolution could be raised. To imagine a communist seizure of power direct from the hands of a feudal society would be to short-circuit the dialectic, to attempt to establish a new political and social order before the necessary change in society's productive base had been accomplished. Any such attempt, Marx felt, was doomed to failure. Furthermore, to encourage the workers to fight for socialism before capitalism had established itself was to lure them into a futile and bloody trap. Not only did Marx carefully restrict his propaganda to liberal, democratic demands, he also, having come into control of the German Communist League, abolished that organization! He did not want to see the liberal energies of the German working class diverted from immediate democratic goals to hopelessly premature and, under the circumstances, "utopian" ones.

And the Frankfurt assembly, dominated by lawyers, journalists, and university professors who had almost no political experience, devoted itself to idealistic talk and planning while the Prussian and Austrian monarchies desperately hurried to reestablish their authority at home as a base from which to stamp out rebellion in the small German states. The deputies at Frankfurt were high-minded and generous men, but it must be remembered that they emerged from a German society which, at the middle of the nineteenth century, had still not fully shaken itself free of feudal shackles, had still not established a German nation-state, had never known an

authoritative parliament, had no rooted traditions of common-
law liberty, and had not even any real traditions of revolution
as had the French and English.

While the deputies debated in Frankfurt, the Austrian emperor, whose higher army officers remained loyal to him, was
able to stamp out the rebellion of the Czechs. Then, with
the help of Russian troops sent by the tsar, he drowned the
Hungarian uprising in blood. At the same time, Frederick
Wilhelm of Prussia was able to establish a truce in a dis-
tracting war he'd been waging against Denmark and to turn
his loyal troops loose against the citizens of Berlin; martial
law was soon imposed in Prussia. When the Frankfurt assembly at last concluded their deliberations with a constitution and offered Frederick Wilhelm the crown of all Germany
as a constitutional monarch, the Prussian king felt secure
enough to reject it, declaring that he would never accept "a
crown from the gutter." The Frankfurt assembly resumed its
debates, but by this time, the beginning of 1849, Austrian
and Prussian troops were on the march into the small German
states. Wherever they appeared, liberal sentiment was quickly
smothered.

During all these discouraging events Marx and Engels
played active and courageous parts. When Marx's *Neue
Rheinische Zeitung* stung the Cologne authorities too much
and some of the middle-class liberals of the small German
states began to waver at the prospect of advancing Prussian
troops, Marx found himself pestered by police agents, lawsuits, and threats. Once, two army officers went to his house
to bully him, but Marx bluffed them out at the point of an
unloaded revolver. But finally in June 1849 the Cologne
authorities closed down the *Neue Rheinische Zeitung* and
Karl Marx and Jenny went once again into exile in Paris.

Engels meanwhile found himself charged with high treason
for urging the Frankfurt assembly to commence armed resistance against the Prussians. He fled to Brussels, was expelled by the Belgian police to France, made his way back
into southern Germany, and there enlisted in the forces preparing to fight oncoming Prussian troops. He took part in
four engagements, realized soon enough that the liberal
democratic elements in Germany were not, after all, seriously
prepared to fight against the Austrians and Prussians, and
retreated with his unit into Switzerland. By this time the
Frankfurt assembly had been dispersed by Prussian troops,
many thousands of German liberals were fleeing to America,

and the last embers of the 1848 revolutions were being stamped out from the Rhine to the Russian border.

Marx, in Paris, soon found that the "revolutionary" French Second Republic had run into the same problem which had destroyed the First Republic. The middle classes, having achieved their aims, had turned upon their working-class allies to prevent any further social changes which might endanger the principle of private property. The bourgeois leaders of the uprising of 1848 had sought to assuage working-class grievances by the promise of establishing national work-shops—factories owned by the government—to assure full and steady employment. Had these actually come into being they would, of course, have been in direct competition with private businesses. French workers soon learned that the na-tional workshops were to be little more than outdoor leaf-raking enterprises designed basically to siphon off some of the idle poor from Paris to the provinces. When, in the spring of 1848, even these travesties of "national workshops" were abolished by the provisional government, the red flag and barricades once again appeared in the working-class districts of Paris. The rising, which took place in June 1848, unlike the revolution of the previous February, was a real intrusion of class warfare into history. Led not by bourgeois malcon-tents but by themselves, the French workers were not striving so much for abstract political ideals as for basic economic and social necessities. The reaction of the democratic pro-visional government was fierce. Thousands of workers were killed by government troops in Paris; many more thousands dispersed into the countryside. Censorship and police restraint of radical thought returned with a vengeance.

Affrighted once again, as they had been after 1789, by the dangers to their private land-holdings implicit in a working-class revolution, the vast mass of French small farmers elected highly conservative deputies to the new government in the early spring of 1849. The Emperor Napoleon's nephew, the shrewd and unscrupulous Louis Bonaparte, was elected presi-dent of the Second Republic, thereby assuring its doom. In December 1852, with the temporary support of almost all segments of French society except the working classes, Louis Bonaparte had himself elected emperor—Napoleon III. The establishment of the Second French Empire marked the dismal end of the revolutionary struggles which had begun with such high hopes barely four years before. But by this time, harassed by the French police, Marx and Engels had long since fled to England.

Excluded now from direct participation in the European historical drama by the failure of the revolutions of 1848, Marx and Engels turned once again to the writing and philosophy of history. Engels found himself obliged to go back to the family mills in Manchester in order to earn enough money, not only for himself, but for the now penniless Marx, who lived in abject poverty in London. They analyzed the failures of 1848 in two brilliant books, *The Class Struggles in France* and *The Eighteenth Brumaire of Louis Bonaparte,* which stripped away all the immediate political maneuverings and the clouds of parliamentary rhetoric to lay bare the bones of what had been a struggle for economic power in French society. And Marx himself, going every day from ten in the morning to seven in the evening to the British Museum Reading Room, devoted his immense energies to the writing of a *Critique of Political Economy* (published in 1859) which was to be nothing less than an advance sketch of his classic work *Capital (Das Kapital).*

Marx's life in exile in London was incredibly harsh. He would not work at anything but his writing. "I must follow my goal through thick and thin," he declared, "and I shall not allow bourgeois society to turn me into a money-making machine." Like so many middle-class revolutionists, Marx was somewhat neurotic about money. He seemed constitutionally incapable of earning or saving it, yet his self-imposed isolation from bourgeois society was also essential to his work. Only by remaining outside it could he be certain of the selflessness of his motives in attacking it. A normal man, entangled in the web of social and economic relationships within which most men live, could hardly have summoned the fierce dedication, bitter contempt, and towering anger with which he anatomized his world. But what this uncompromising dedication meant in human terms is revealed in a letter to a friend written by Jenny Marx after the Marxes had been evicted from their squalid London dwelling in 1850 for failure to pay the rent:

> I shall describe to you a day in this life just as it is, and you will see that perhaps few other refugees have gone through anything like it. Since wet nurses are here much too expensive for us, I decided, in spite of continual and terrible pains in my breasts and back to nurse the child myself. But the poor little

angel drank in from me so much secret sorrow and grief with the milk that he was constantly unwell. . . . He has not slept a single night since he came into the world—two or three hours at most. . . . As I was sitting like this one day our landlady suddenly appeared. We have paid her over the course of the winter over two hundred and fifty *thalers,* and we made an arrangement with her that in future we were not to pay her but the landlord, who had put in an execution. Now she denied this agreement and demanded five pounds which we still owed her; and as we were unable to produce this sum at once, two bailiffs entered the house, took possession of all my little belongings: beds, linens, clothes, everything, even my poor baby's cradle, and the best of the toys that belonged to the little girls, who were standing by in bitter tears. . . .

The next day we had to leave the house. It was cold and rainy and dreary. My husband tried to find a place for us to live, but no one was willing to have us when we mentioned the four children. At last a friend came to our rescue, we paid, and I quickly sold all my beds in order to settle with the chemist, the baker, the butcher, and the milkman, who had been alarmed by the scandal of the bailiffs' arrival and who had come wildly to present their bills. . . . The only thing that really crushes me and makes my heart bleed is that [Marx] is obliged to endure so much pettiness, that there should be so few to come to his aid, and that he who has so willingly and gladly come to the aid of so many, should find himself so helpless here.

The grinding poverty of these years was somewhat relieved in 1851 when Charles A. Dana and Horace Greeley, publisher and editor respectively of the New York *Tribune* (and imbued, it will be recalled, with Utopian Socialist ideas) invited Marx to submit a regular column to their paper. This work Marx largely turned over to Engels, who had a better command of English. But even this scanty income declined when the *Tribune* was forced to retrench by the American economic depression of 1853–55. Then in April 1855 Marx's only son died at the age of eight, a victim of the poverty and slums in which the family lived. It was a blow from which Marx never truly recovered. Writing to Engels in Manchester, Karl Marx said, "The house seems deserted and empty since the death of the child who was its living soul. I have had all sorts of bad luck, but now I know for the first time what a genuine misfortune is. . . . I feel myself broken down."

In describing Marx's private life, we are not really leaving the stage of social history. Marx himself was experiencing no more than the common miseries of European working classes everywhere during the mid-nineteenth century. The fact that these miseries were, in his own case, largely self-invited did not make them less real. Furthermore, the patience with which he endured them and the grim persistence with which he pursued his work despite them, have left an aura of sanctity around his name for those who continue to cleave to his theories. The martyrdom of Marx (and of other revolutionary idealists) has supplied present-day communism not only with a roster of "saints," but also a legacy of grim moral righteousness which is a very real force in the contemporary world.

While Marx advanced from his *Critique of Political Economy* to the writing of the first volume of *Capital*, which was to be the detailed exposition and explanation of the entire body of his theories, the shattered working-class movements in Europe were gathering strength again after the disasters of 1848–1852. In Germany the working-class movement had fallen largely under the domination of a young adventurer who professed Marxist ideas, named Ferdinand Lassalle (1825–64). Enjoying a stormy relationship with Marx and Engels (who viewed his deviations from Marxist orthodoxy with extreme suspicion), Lassalle personally combined a romantic outlook with revolutionary fervor. This was objectively reflected by the fact that his programs supposed a fusing of working-class aims with middle-class liberal aims. A brilliant orator, Lassalle quickly built up a large following in Germany. He urged that the German working-class "must become itself a monster employer . . . in the massed and concentrated form of the factory, with its enormous advantages in productivity." Control of industry was to be given the workers by the state itself, and this aim was to be achieved by socialist workers' organizations capturing control of the state through universal suffrage and the forms of democratic politics. Thus Lassalle made himself the prototype of the socialist leader who, whatever his rhetoric, eschews violent revolution as a means of achieving socialism, substituting for it legal democratic processes. In 1863 Lassalle put himself at the head of the Universal German Workingmen's Association, the first organized nationwide German socialist party.

Working-class and liberal agitation in Germany, and especially in Prussia, had brought about a constitutional crisis under the regime of the Prussian king, Wilhelm I. Eager to exclude Austria from the old competition as to which of their nations would dominate the small German principalities, Wilhelm I attempted to strengthen his army. But the Prussian parliament refused to vote the necessary taxes. When he was on the point of abdication, however, Wilhelm found a chief minister who declared himself capable of ruling without the support of parliament. This was Otto von Bismarck, a tough Prussian landowner who had come to realize that the only sure means of preserving the power and privileges of the Prussian ruling class within Prussia itself was to stamp out liberalism throughout Germany. This was to be accomplished by straightforward political and military conquest of all Germany by Prussia. But since the interests of the Prussian landowning aristocracy, the *Junkers,* of whom Bismarck was representative, were essentially the preservation of their feudal society, Bismarck was prepared to treat both workers and middle-class capitalists with an impartially iron hand. His aim was above all to ensure the hegemony of the Prussian king and aristocracy; hence the hegemony of Prussia; hence the unification through war if necessary of all of Germany. To achieve these aims, Bismarck was willing to purchase the neutrality of the German working-class by granting them many of their long-sought reforms. That these reforms would come at the expense of German capitalists was not of immediate concern to the Prussian feudal landowners; besides, the German capitalists were themselves to be won over by the expansion of commerce and trade which would accompany German unification. Bismarck's was, in certain respects, a form of state socialism.

When Bismarck came to power in 1862 he recognized the inherent potential for disruption among German workers loyal to Lassalle. Therefore, he was willing, at first, to bargain with Lassalle, to grant very minor reforms and promise others while he hurriedly prepared the Prussian state and army for its task of conquest. By 1864 Bismarck felt secure enough to sever his relations with Lassalle. In August of that year Lassalle was killed in a duel with a Rumanian adventurer. His Universal German Workingmen's Association survived him, however, until later it was fused with the Marxian Social Democratic Party.

The career of Lassalle was instructively ambivalent. He enjoyed precisely those bourgeois comforts—money, luxurious surroundings, love affairs, the feeling of personal power

—which Marx, in his isolation from society, scorned. It was, in fact, Lassalle's personal romanticism that brought about his untimely death. How was it possible, Marx and Engels asked each other, for a working-class leader to engage in such a light-minded venture as fighting a duel? And this personal ambivalence carried over into practical politics and socialist theory. Marx and Engels held that the proletariat would come to power by shattering the bourgeois state; Lassalle believed that proletarian power would be achieved by taking over the bourgeois state. Marx and Engels felt that the leaders of the working class would inevitably come from the middle classes—the proletarians having neither the education nor the leisure to devote themselves to the theory and practice of revolution—but that those middle-class leaders should, as much as possible, immerse and discipline themselves within the life style (if misery may be called a "style") of the working-class. Lassalle found association with workers personally repellent. He saw himself not so much as the self-disciplined disciple of the workers, as their benign, chivalrous champion and patron. These discrepancies between an essentially romantic view of revolution and the harder, more "scientific" view of Marx and Engels were eventually to be formalized in the split between Social Democrats and Communists which was to bedevil working-class movements down to the present day.

It was in the year of Lassalle's death, 1864, that certain groups of continental exiles in London combined with English labor leaders to found an International Workingmen's Organization, the so-called First International. It was an unstable and hybrid association. It included the supporters of the nationalist Giuseppe Mazzini who were interested only in the liberation and unification of Italy and not at all in the class war; and trade unionists whose revolutionary horizons were limited to such objectives as higher wages, winning strikes, and the eight-hour day. Marx, invited to join the organization, was soon able to win control of it from both moderates and nationalists. He prepared its statutes and, through his agents (he rarely attended meetings personally), dominated its proceedings. Soon branches had been established in most of the great European cities and in the United States. Membership rose eventually to about 5,000,000.

While Marx found it possible to work among such disparate forces (he showed himself, considering his fierce temper, remarkably tactful in handling International affairs), the inherent contradictions among First International socialists could not long be suppressed. Basically they revolved around the same question that had arisen between Marxists and Lassalleans: how socialist power was practically to be won.

An important element in the First International were the followers of the French socialist thinker Pierre Joseph Proudhon. In a book published in 1840, Proudhon had demanded, *What Is Property?* This question he answered by showing that "property is theft!" Marx, analyzing Proudhon's work, demonstrated that the saying "Property is theft!" implied that there existed such a thing as real rights in property, to be enjoyed or held privately. This theory he dismissed as "utopian." Proudhon laid heavy stress on cooperative societies, labor banks—any kind of working-class voluntary association which would provide an immediate alternative to the state itself. He envisaged a stateless society for the future, and thereby Proudhon ranks more importantly as an anarchist than as a socialist. A struggle between Proudhonists and Marxists within the First International was won by Marx in 1867; the Proudhonists were driven out, an early example of a Marxist "party purge."

Nevertheless, the Proudhonist vision of a stateless society could not be dispelled from socialist thought as easily as its supporters were from the First International. Anarchism, the theory that the state and all its symbols must be destroyed and that men will then live without the need of state or government at all, associating only voluntarily in small groups to manage necessary production, found its most eloquent champion in the person of Mikhail Bakunin. It was at the First International's annual congress of 1869 that Bakunin's magnetic personality and legendary reputation captivated enough delegates to hand Marx his first defeat within the organization.

Bakunin, born in Russia in 1814, studied the ideas of Georg Hegel in Berlin, as Marx had done. But for Bakunin, the Hegelian abstractions such as the Absolute Idea were sufficient in themselves. He did not subject Hegel's philosophy to the kind of searching criticism it received at the hands of Marx. Describing himself as a "pure revolutionist," that is to say, a revolutionist whose aims did not extend beyond revolution itself, Bakunin had no use at all for the patient strategy of Marx. He held it the revolutionist's business simply to destroy the entire extant social order. "The desire to destroy," he wrote, "is also a creative desire." He hoped to see "the whole of Europe, with Saint Petersburg, Paris, and London, transformed into an enormous rubbish heap." What would emerge from that heap was of less interest to him than its destruction. Bakunin entered vigorously, joyfully upon his career of "pure revolution." He enlisted himself in every revolutionary crusade he could find, from Polish nationalism to the grievances of Swiss watchmakers. He was captured by the authorities of several nations at various times and spent many years of his life in German, Austrian, and Russian prisons. Joining the First International in 1868, Bakunin was able to use his personal connections with Italian and Spanish revolutionaries to establish International branches in those countries.

At the congress of the First International in 1869, Bakunin demanded that the delegates vote into their program the abolition of the right of inheritance. Marx, who did not attend the congress personally, pointed out through his representatives that the right of inheritance was merely one of many evils of the capitalist system. What was necessary was to attack the entire concept of private property, not merely one of its symptoms. But Bakunin's oratory on the spot, combined with his legendary reputation as a revolutionary hero and martyr, so captivated the congress that although his own resolution   was defeated, so was Marx's—and by an even greater majority.

The fullest statement of Bakunin's views is to be found in a curious document he prepared in collaboration with a young Russian student exile named Sergei Nechaev. It was entitled *The Catechism of a Revolutionist*. This horrifying manifesto called upon the revolutionist to stamp out in himself all personal sentiments, especially such debilitating ones as mercy, love, pride, honor, or friendship. The revolutionist was not a man; he was a tool of the revolution, and he was to regard others either as equally expendable tools of the revolution or as outright enemies. Toward either he was to be absolutely ruthless, killing enemies and sacrificing fellow revolutionists as the cause demanded. His means were to include not only murder, arson, and dynamite; they were also to include the encouragement of both natural disasters, such as floods and famines, and artificial ones, such as police brutality, for all these would increase the fury of the people as their misery increased. That fury would one day break out in a tidal wave of killing and destruction. The revolutionist welcomed that day. He had trained himself to bear torture and face death; he was prepared to deal death impartially to all who opposed him. The revolution itself, the very upheaval—this was the only standard of morality and against its claims all else must be measured. Finally, when the present order has been drowned in blood and gutted by fire, the revolutionist will not offer a new social system; the survivors of the revolutionary holocaust, the manual workers, will have no need of one. They will inhabit a stateless and nongoverned world.

It will be seen that Bakunin's anarchism depended upon human will, pure and simple. There were no inevitable historical forces or progressions that men must patiently foster or await. Men had only to *decide* to destroy the old order. They could be encouraged toward this decision by demonstrations that would embolden them. A successful assassination, the successful burning of some public structure, the fiery explosion of a bomb—such acts of will would encourage other acts of will, until the will to destroy rose to sublime proportions.

It would be hard to imagine a viewpoint more exactly opposed to Marx's own. When at the trial of certain Russian anarchists in Saint Petersburg it was revealed that these followers of Bakunin had been passing themselves off as representatives of the International and claimed theoretical descent from Marx and Engels, Marx was horrified. So were other International leaders. It was seen now that Bakunin, behind his undoubted heroism and oratorical abilities, was actually politically quite irresponsible. Yet his control of delegates to the International posed a real threat of his capturing that organization. At the International's congress of 1872, Marx, rather than see Bakunin triumphant, forced through a measure transferring the International's headquarters to New York. There, as he well knew they would, distance and American conditions soon brought the First International to an inglorious end. Bakunin's followers maintained a rival International for a few years more, but soon after the death of their leader, in 1876, this too disappeared, except for its Spanish branch. If Lassallean democratic socialism may be said to be a conservative deviation from Marxist theory, Bakunin's anarchism was a radical deviation, so radical that its ties to socialist thought were tenuous at best and soon snapped.

The theoretical struggles between Marx and Bakunin were played out against the background of a new and startlingly significant revolutionary uprising in France, the Paris Com-

mune of 1871. Louis Bonaparte, self-proclaimed Emperor
Napoleon III, had struggled to be all things to all Frenchmen.
To the masses he granted a constitution which provided for
universal manhood suffrage; to the bourgeoisie he granted
liberal trade reforms and grants; to please devout Catholics
he allowed the church to control public education; to all
Frenchmen he offered the glories of foreign conquest. Nor
did he fail to remind them that his presence was perhaps the
unique factor which prevented bloody civil war. Of course,
attempting to please everyone, Napoleon III pleased no one,
and his foreign adventures promised just that domestic in-
stability so feared by France's conservative small farmers and
middle class. During his reign French troops fought in
Algeria, Indo-China, Mexico, Italy, Sardinia, and Russia—at
a heavy cost in blood and domestic taxes. In 1870 Napoleon
III was drawn into war against Prussia and the smaller German states by Bismarck; from the Prussian chancellor's viewpoint this was to be the final step in his campaign to unify
Germany under the Prussian king.

French troops, poorly led, were quickly overwhelmed by
German armies; Napoleon III himself was captured, and
victorious German divisions overran France. News of these
disasters led to an uprising in Paris and the proclamation of
a new republic. Led mainly by liberal journalists and politicians, this new republican government attempted to carry
on the war against the Germans. But Paris, after a terrible
siege, was forced to surrender because of famine, and the
French republican government had to accept a truce on
German terms. Before they made peace, however, the republican leaders attempted to consult the French people.
Elections were held to a new national assembly. Republican
leaders favored continued resistance to the Germans; French
monarchists favored immediate peace. The war-weary French
people elected a large majority of monarchist deputies to the
national assembly. Peace was duly made and the monarchists
moved their capital to Versailles in preparation for the res-
toration of a king. This was too much for the radicals and
working class of Paris to bear. Proclaiming themselves an
independent commune, the people of Paris raised the red
flag of revolution.

The Paris Commune established on March 28, 1871, was
to last only two months. But during that time an absolutely
new spectacle was offered to the world: the working class
itself actually achieved and exercised political power. The

Commune abolished both the police force and the army, their roles being undertaken by the people themselves; it opened the public schools to all children; it expropriated the Catholic clergy; it made all public offices elective. But the Commune hesitated to attack the roots of the bourgeois state. It did not confiscate the more than 3,000,000,000 gold francs in the coffers of the National Bank in Paris, attempted no general redistribution of property, and, in fear of civil war, refrained from marching on the republican government at Versailles. But that monarchist-dominated government had no hesitation at all in attacking Paris. On May 21 republican troops broke into Paris and during that week butchered an estimated twenty to forty thousand workers. Another fifty to sixty thousand were rounded up and imprisoned or exiled; the Paris Commune was drowned in blood that would be neither forgotten nor forgiven by the French working class.

Marx, watching these events from London, issued a manifesto in support of the Commune: *The Civil War in France*. In it he lavished praise on the Communards while chiding them for not having gone far enough. He pointed out that the proletariat could not achieve power by simply taking over the apparatus of the bourgeois state as the Communards had tried to do. What the working class had to do was to break the old state completely into pieces and construct in its place an entirely new proletarian state of its own. But if the Commune had been too conservative, if its end had been tragedy, nevertheless Marx recognized its significance for the strategy of socialism as a whole. "The struggle of the working class against the capitalist class and its state," Marx wrote, "has entered upon a new phase with the struggle in Paris. Whatever the immediate results may be, a new point of departure of world-historic importance has been gained."

And just as socialism had been forcing itself onto the stage of history, so Karl Marx's life represented, in a sense, the ebb and flow of practical and theoretic tides of work. We have seen him master German philosophy during the late 1830's and early 1840's. Then he attempted to cope with real revolutionary forces during the uprisings of 1848. When these were defeated he turned again to his studies, concentrating on political economy. During the 1860's, as a new wave of revolutionary activity prepared to break over Europe, he emerged once again into the practical world with the First International. Upon the defeat of the Paris Commune of 1871 and the conflict with Bakunin, Marx retired yet again to continue his massive work *Capital* (the first volume of which, published in 1867, had won him but scant recognition). Before his death in 1883 he was to appear once again as a protagonist on the historical stage.

The occasion for his last intervention in practical politics was the fusion of the new German Social Democratic Party (led by Wilhelm Liebknecht and August Bebel, two of Marx's most devoted disciples) with the remnants of the followers of Lassalle—an especially bitter and ironic pill for Marx to swallow. The question was the same one that had bedeviled socialist thinkers for decades: how was the proletariat to achieve power? It will be recalled that Lassalle had indicated that the working class should do so by capturing the bourgeois state through democratic proceedings. The Paris Commune had captured their fragment of the bourgeois state through revolutionary proceedings. But Marx had always spoken against the entire concept of taking over the bourgeois state through any kind of proceedings. To him it was necessary and inevitable that this state be smashed entirely. Only then could a "dictatorship of the proletariat" be established to bring to birth the new world.

Meeting in Gotha, Germany, in 1875, the German Social Democrats worked out a program of sufficient compromise to insure unification with the Lassalleans. When this program was forwarded to Marx for comment, he attacked it in blistering language. His *Critique of the Gotha Program* was so forceful that Marx's German disciples actually suppressed it for fear that its insistence upon the revolutionary dictatorship of the proletariat would undermine their political negotiations. These negotiations, though immediately successful, brought to birth a political party with, as Marx foresaw, contradictory objectives. The leaders and language of the party were Marxist; but its program was one of evolutionary reform. The German Social Democratic Party became, in effect, just another parliamentary political party whose aims were to be achieved through democratic, constitutional means. This was to have immense consequences for the future history of socialism. Throughout Europe, in the last quarter of the nineteenth century, Social Democratic parties modeled after the German were to be established and win vast followings. But only in those countries such as Russia, where no democratic political activities of any kind whatsoever were permitted, were these Social Democratic parties to remain revolutionary. In fact, the very word "socialism" was soon to necessarily imply democratic evolution, while the word "communism," though supposedly describing the same Marxist theoretical heritage, was to imply forceful revolution.

Thus Marx's last major intervention into the world of practical politics, like all his previous interventions, was to result in defeat. But it is time now to retire, like Marx himself, from the stormy nineteenth-century historical stage, in order to examine and evaluate the philosophy built by Marx and Engels as a means, not only of understanding history, but of acting upon it.

Chapter Four

CLASSICAL MARXISM

> *History* does nothing. It 'possesses *no* colossal riches';
> it 'fights *no* fights.' It is rather *man*—real, living
> man—who acts, possesses and fights in everything. It
> is by no means 'History' which uses man as a means
> to carry out *its* ends, as if *it* were a being apart;
> rather History is *nothing* but the activity of man in
> pursuit of his ends.
>
> —*Karl Marx*

Marx and Engels described their philosophy as dialectical materialism. We have seen how Marx adapted the Hegelian concept of dialectics as a means of analyzing history and identifying the social engines which bring about historical change. But what is meant by the word materialism in Marxist philosophy? Hegel's dialectic had been the function of an abstract, even divine "Ideal." For Hegel the real world was but a reflection of this Ideal. But Marx wrote: "With me, on the contrary, the ideal is nothing other than the material after it has been transposed and translated inside the human head." In other words, rather than the real world being a reflection of some Ideal, ideals and ideas themselves were reflections of the real world within the mind of man. Ideas and ideals were nothing other than human intellectual responses to the human material situation in the real world.

This view, of course, banishes *all* "ideals," whether Platonic, Hegelian, or Christian, to the limbo of human speculation. Religions of *all* kinds are the product of human imagination, not of any "divine" revelation or intervention. Such conceptions as "Ideal," "God," "Heaven," "Hell," "Soul"—all of these are born in the brain of man as he strives to cope with his real, material world. The fact that such concepts, through their influence among men, may in turn bring about changes in the material world, makes them no less mythical.

Some people, especially among latter-day Marxists, assume that this Marxist materialism is equatable with "economic determinism." That is, since man's situation in the real world is primarily that of an animal seeking to survive, all human thought and activities are economically motivated. Man, a helpless victim of his economic needs or his greed, may camouflage his thoughts or actions as he will; they are still economically determined. But economic determinism is so vast an oversimplification of Marxist thought as to be simply wrong. Neither Marx nor Engels ever assumed that all human thought or activity could be explained as being economically motivated; far from having any kind of "deterministic" view of human nature, they held as their ideal the concept of Renaissance Man, the human individual interested in *all* aspects of life and free to engage in as many varied activities as possible. If one had to guess who Marx and Engels would have considered the ideal man, it would probably be Leonardo da Vinci. Yet Marx and Engels themselves were partly responsible for the misinterpretations to which their theories lent themselves. After Marx's death, Engels wrote: "Marx and I are partly responsible for the fact that at times our disciples have laid more weight upon the economic factor than belongs to it. We were compelled to emphasize its central character in opposition to our opponents who denied it, and there wasn't always time, place and occasion to do justice to the other factors in the reciprocal interactions of the historical process."

If the Marxist materialistic description of man in society and man in history is not equatable with economic determinism, just what *does* it mean? It means not that *man,* in his infinite variety, but rather the *structure of society* in its various historical phases is determined by its organization of the means of production available to it. This organization of the means of production—the way society produces goods, feeds itself, disposes of labor or labor-saving machinery—may be viewed as the basis of the social structure. Such other human activities as art, science, government, education, law, the various professions, etc., spring from the economic organization of any particular society, and, in turn, influence that economic organization. Society, for Marx and Engels, may be pictured as one of those tropical trees whose branches are really roots. The original root and trunk of the tree is the organization of the means of production; from that trunk branches spring into the air which are the many varied activities of men. But these branches eventually return to the earth to become roots themselves which add to the sustenance of the tree and even change its form.

The products of man, then, his art, his learning, his science are not necessarily *determined* by economics; they are simply rooted within an economically determined society. To take the most extreme examples: the artist, the "pure" scientist, the philosopher—these men and their thought are not economically motivated, but they cannot, after all, escape the social totality into which they have been born. This social totality will influence their work, and their work will influence the social totality, so that even those men who may be said to be really economically motivated (to take another extreme example, the greediest of merchants) will have their views of society and their place in it modified by the work and thought of the "freest" thinkers.

We have here stated the meaning of *materialism*, in the phrase *dialectical materialism*, in its most positive form. But Marx and Engels, as Engels pointed out, did not always so state it. The truth is that neither of them ever came to grips with some of the knottier questions raised by their philosophy. For instance, what is the value to a succeeding society of the art and science of a preceding society? The means of production of the Roman world were organized around the institution of slavery; the means of production of the modern world are organized around the institution of mechanization. Does this mean that the greatest of modern poets is a better poet than Virgil, since his society's economic organization is certainly an "advance" over that of the Romans? Is the thought of a modern speculative scientist such as Einstein to be valued more highly than that of, say, Sir Isaac Newton, because of the discrepancies between the social totalities from which they emerged? Is there, finally, any absolute value to the thought and art of man independent of his social circumstances, or are such values always relative to their societies? Does, in fact, the emergence of new means of organizing social production always represent an "advance" over previous means? Just what does the word "progress" really mean? Progress from whose viewpoint? These questions are not satisfactorily answered by Marx and Engels; they are barely even posed.

Perhaps the immediate cause for this failure of Marxist philosophy is the fact that it was primarily meant not only as a description of social change, but also as a means of effecting that change. Therefore it had to *assume* that progress took place and that such progress—especially the next phase of it—was a liberating process, a "good" thing. Furthermore, by adapting Hegel's dialectic, Marx had thought to find the engine of social change in the rigid patterns of "class struggle," and his thought itself was to become enslaved to that engine. But what is the Hegelian dialectic, with its *thesis, antithesis,* and *synthesis,* but a mystical concept? In Marx's adaptation of the dialectic, History replaces God. It is History which "demands" change, History which "rewards" or "punishes" societies and their classes. History, for Marx, despite the quotation with which this chapter opens, has as much reality as Jehovah had for the ancient Jewish prophets. And the "will" of History, expressed through Its dialectical progress, is inevitable. Just as feudal society was inevitably swept away by the emergence of the middle class, so capitalist society must inevitably be swept away by the triumph of the proletariat. But if all this is inevitable, why struggle for it? Why not simply sit back and let History take Its course to the eventual triumph of socialism? Marx himself might have answered that this would be ignoble, perhaps impossible for any man equipped with the insight to understand historical change. Man, to Marx, was ultimately a social animal living in and through history; only through fulfilling his historical role could he fulfill himself personally. This involved not a supine acceptance of that role, but demanded active participation in it. This view is certainly an advance upon that of the various pre-Marxist idealists in that it presumes greater complexity in human nature. But does it presume *enough* complexity?

Before attempting to answer that question, which is at the very root of what is wrong with Marxism, it might be profitable to examine some of the Marxist practical mechanics, the more particular applications of Marxist philosophy to the historical world. The entire force of this application depends upon the role of the proletariat as the *antithesis* of capitalist society. It was from the clash of the proletariat with that society that the *synthesis* of the socialist world was to emerge. Was this eventual clash inevitable? Was the proletariat the

real *antithesis* of the capitalist order? Marx and Engels lived
during some of the worst decades of European industrialization. The portraits they drew of the lives of English and
European workers and their families were extremely accurate.
The mountains of statistics they unearthed to support these
portraits are extremely convincing; more than that, we have
voluminous independent evidence on the miserable nature
of working-class life in the mid-nineteenth century. There
was no question that the proletariat was indeed, at that time,
the likeliest and obvious *antithesis* to the capitalist world.
But would it always remain so?

Marx and Engels assumed that it would and that its
condition would become progressively more miserable and
alienated as time went on. Capitalism, they pointed out, was
based on competition; this was the very kernel of the system.
And competitions are eventually won. One industrialist's victory meant the defeat of another. Furthermore, it was certainly obvious that with the sophistication of industrial
processes, through the use of ever more efficient machines,
ever larger concentrations of labor power in factories, ever
wider nets of distribution, would work toward the elimination
of smaller productive units as they were gobbled up by larger
ones. And the greater the industrial units, the more capital
they would require, this capital itself then being concentrated
in larger and larger quantities in fewer and fewer hands.
Smaller businessmen of all kinds would eventually be forced
into the ranks of the proletariat; and precisely as the proletariat came to include more and more people, so its conditions of life and labor would deteriorate even further.
Eventually, capitalism would lead to a society composed of
a handful of extremely rich businessmen-industrialists at the
top and a vast mass of poverty stricken proletarians at the
bottom; the middle classes would vanish. At a certain point
the entire system would collapse under the weight of its own
misery.

But wouldn't governments intervene before this happened,
if only to preserve themselves from revolution? Governments,
to Marx and Engels, were only the organized powers of the
ruling classes, controlling society for their own benefit. Certainly they had pointed this out brilliantly in their studies
of the France of Louis Philippe and the France of Napoleon
III. And their entire analyses of the birth of capitalism from
the feudal world rested upon their appreciation of the importance of class struggle as the social engine that moved

society. How could governments, which were nothing more than the expressed and legally codified will of the ruling classes, work against the interests of those very classes? But, it might be objected, what if the ruling classes, in their own enlightened self-interest, so ameliorated the lot of the proletariat through government action as to progressively postpone revolution indefinitely? Subjectively, this was extremely unlikely. Ruling-class life, based on the exploitation of other human beings and motivated by competition and greed, brutalized and degraded the ruling class itself. Ruling-class self-interest would become less, not more, enlightened as time went on. Had this not been demonstrably the case with feudal ruling classes? It was bound to be the case with capitalist ruling classes, too. And objectively, no matter what their personal predispositions, the ruling classes were caught in the same historical dilemma as the proletariat. They could no more escape their role as oppressors within capitalist society than the proletariat could escape its position as the oppressed. Economics guaranteed the accuracy of this analysis.

The most important aspect of this economic "guarantee" of inevitable revolution was the Marxist theory of surplus value, sometimes called the Labor Theory of Value. Expounded at some length in *Capital,* this theory held that the worker had sold his capacity to work to the capitalist. The capitalist, purchasing this capacity to work, paid the worker as little as possible—just the minimum amount to keep him alive and productive. But this minimum amount really represents only a part of the worker's labor value. That is, the capitalist is paying the worker the worth of, say, six hours' labor, but forcing him to work eight, ten, or twelve hours. The products made by the worker during this extra time are sold for their value on the market. This value of stolen work hours is called by Marx, "surplus value" and represents the manufacturer's profit, profit he has robbed from his workers. It will be seen that this theory of surplus value assumes that the value of any given product is the labor which has gone into its manufacture—thus the phrase Labor Theory of Value.

What does it really mean to say that the value of a product is the amount of labor which has gone into it? What about such products as paintings, poems, books, antiques? And whose labor counts as labor? What about the labor of the manufacturer himself, of the distributor, of the merchant? The payment received by these nonproletarians was termed "profits." Did that mean that the wages of nonproletarians were somehow undeserved? Evidently, although in later volumes of *Capital* some attempt was made to rationalize this conception, for Marx only the labor of workers and farmers produced real value; all else was a parasitic draining of the real value of work. Marxist economics then guaranteed that, as industry became ever more efficient, more and more of the real worth of its products would accrue as profits to the undeserving capitalists, less and less would go as wages to the deserving proletarians—until the inevitable explosion took place.

If Marx satisfied himself in the inevitability of the revolution, what would be its actual mechanics? How were the proletarians to actually wrest power from capitalist society? It will be recalled that in his controversies with Lassalle and Bakunin Marx insisted that the proletariat could not capture the institutions of the bourgeois state; these institutions had to be totally destroyed and replaced by new ones. The new society had to be conceived within the womb of the old but born without an umbilical cord. This was to be accomplished by the Dictatorship of the Proletariat, another one of Marx's conceptions which has lent itself to vast misinterpretation in our own day. Briefly, it may be described as the emergency rule of the masses during the time necessary to consolidate new social institutions. The long night of capitalist oppression ends in a bloody dawn on the barricades; but the irresistible might of the proletariat (which, it will be remembered, now includes all but a handful of very rich members of society) triumphs quickly. To prevent absolute chaos and any attempt to reimpose the old order, the proletariat appoints representatives to preside in its name over the birth pangs of the new society. These representatives exercise an absolute dictatorship. They have the right to do so because they speak in the name of the overwhelming majority of the people. They may be required to act harshly, to exile, imprison, or even kill the enemies of the new society. But in this they are justified, too, because such people are enemies of mankind itself. But this dictatorship lasts only until the new society, safe from its enemies, has established its new institutions and reorganized the capitalist means of production and distribution. Thereafter, with bread, justice, and education assured them, the proletariat (which will no longer *be* the proletariat but rather simply all of society) will be able to enlarge its dignity and self-consciousness in such a way as to transform mankind. The new man, cooperative rather than competitive, social rather than alienated, fearless rather than greedy, will no longer require the coercive powers of the state. This marks the true dawn of communism. On that day society "proudly inscribes upon its banners: 'From each according to his abilities, to each according to his needs.' "

Let us now reexamine Marx's assumptions and conclusions in the light of what we know today. Of all the Marxist predictions, his concept of the future development of capitalism and the inevitability of class warfare is perhaps the most obviously false. One has only to compare the *imagined* future predicted by Marx and Engels with the real present. Marx's future workers live in indescribable filth amid crowded hovels, eating at near-starvation levels, their children growing up deformed and dwarfed through malnutrition, their minds benumbed by lack of education and despair. Their class consciousness, fed by dedicated liberators and intellectuals, grows until hatred for the oppressing ruling classes and their capitalist society burns like a lurid flame in proletarian eyes. These ruling classes themselves, as their fear and guilt mount, become ever more inhuman, ever more arrogant, ever more greedy and blind to their fate. Wages continue to fall, profits continue to rise; working conditions in the mines and mills and factories and on the farms become ever more terrible. The working day lengthens, the anonymity of the worker at his machine and the essential meaninglessness of his mechanized motions produce increasing misery. The governments, ever more tightly controlled by ever fewer capitalists, react with ever mounting hysterical brutality to any attempt on the part of the workers to improve their lot. Votes, petitions, trade unions—all the democratic apparatus of reform—produce nothing but increasing frustration for the proletariat, culminating in the ultimate Armageddon of a proletarian revolution. This was to be the Marxist future, and our present world.

But today it can be seen that in precisely those countries where industrialization has been most advanced, the proletariat has won the highest standards of living and the highest degree of political power. These gains have been won through struggle, yes—sometimes bloody struggle—but essentially within the confines of democratic reform, not revolution. It is certainly true that industry in its increasing complexity has tended towards monopoly; it is true that the richest capitalists have become fewer and fewer. But *control* of industry in capitalist society has become a prerogative of

broader and broader masses of people. Wages have risen,
profits proportionately declined; the economic, social, and
political power of trade unions has surpassed by far the
social influence of the very rich. What has happened is that
the immense productivity brought about by heavy industrialization has spread increasingly large shares of this world's
wealth into *everyone's* hands, including those of the proletariat. Indeed, in the most industrially advanced nations it
has not been the middle classes that have disappeared; it has
been the proletariat itself which has all but disappeared,
swallowed up into the middle class which has swollen enor-
mously. Beyond that, the increasing reorganization and integration of industry have led to less, not more exploitation of
human labor. With the advent of computerization, the day
is now foreseeable when human labor itself may occupy a
very minor role in production. Marx's future has simply not
come to pass. Such Marxist doctrines as the Theory of Surplus
Value, class warfare and the Dictatorship of the Proletariat
are simply irrelevant in capitalist societies today.

But Marxist doctrine is *not* completely irrelevant in much
of today's world. The painstaking analysis Marx and Engels
employed to describe the emergence of capitalism from feudal
society had a great amount of validity; and where feudal or
semifeudal societies have survived into the modern era, the
same processes described by Marx may be seen taking place,
modified by time and local conditions. Class warfare, proletarian revolution, the dictatorship of the proletariat (or rather,
the dictatorship of the party of the proletariat) have been
the lot of Russia and China. This Marxist historical progression threatens to be the lot, too, of South America, Africa,
and large sections of Asia. But in *every case without exception*
it has taken place in, or threatens to take place in, the *least*
industrially developed areas, the *least* capitalized areas, in
those areas where democratic forms have traditionally been
nonexistent or meaningless. The Marxist program of class
warfare, in all its ramifications, has, where it has occurred,
led to *the establishment of capitalist societies* (state capitalism
being but another form of capitalism) *upon the ruins of
former feudal or semifeudal societies.*

In other words, Marxism is a theory of capitalism. It *is*
inevitable that people everywhere will eventually demand an
integration and reorganization of the means of production
and distribution now available, which will ensure them better,
freer lives. And if private capital, for one reason or another,

is unable or unwilling to undertake this task, then the people will demand that the state undertake it and will capture the state if necessary to ensure that end. What has grown from the Marxist revolutions of the twentieth century has not been socialism, but state *capitalism* (which will be analyzed in a later chapter)—always emerging in nations where capitalism itself was never firmly rooted. Marx and Engels held that socialism was possible only *after* capitalism had fully developed itself and thereby fully exposed its "inner contradictions." But it is precisely in those countries where private capitalism has been most deeply entrenched and most fully developed that the prospect of Marxist class warfare and socialist revolution has proven most irrelevant.

We have seen how Marx and Engels, by basing their view of historical development upon the Hegelian dialectic, were actually introducing an element of mysticism into their philosophy; but this was not the only mystical element present. Underlying the entire Marxist conception of the rise and fulfillment of the proletariat is the assumption that the proletariat, the workers, are innately "good," while the other classes of capitalist society are innately "bad." The capitalists controlling society are inhuman monsters; but the proletarians, when they gain control, will prove themselves angels. The capitalist governments are little more than exploitation machines blundering from economic crisis to economic crisis and war to war. The government of the proletariat will be completely democratic and able to avoid both economic crisis and war. The proletarians of the future are almost ideal human beings because they have fulfilled their historical role and brought history (as the record of class warfare) to an end. With the advent of communism, true history, human history begins.

Marx and Engels had heaped scorn upon the Ideal Man of the utopian socialists. In his stead they had introduced Historical Man—a creature much more recognizable as a normal human being, a creature whose existence is proven by a study of history itself. But Historical Man remained an ideal conception. It was true that he was an advance upon the Ideal Man of absolutely free will imagined by Enlightenment thinkers, but he was still a long way from *real*. And if Marx's system of history was based on an element of the mystical ideal he inherited from Hegel, his justification for his life work was based on an essentially mystical view of the nature of Historical Man. But it is only by making such overwhelming, broad assumptions about the nature of the universe and the nature of man that any philosopher dares to construct a complete system. And Marxism is as complete a system as its inventors could make it. And here we come to what is perhaps the most basic objection to Marxism, its attempt to build an all-inclusive philosophical-historical-economic system upon an idealized and very *partial* understanding of man himself. For man is infinitely complex, infinitely varied. He eludes all ideal descriptions, will not fit into any preconceived pattern or system. Sociology, anthropology, history, psychiatry—all the sciences of man are still in the stone age of their development; and millennia from now it is unlikely that they will have arrived at any definitive description of human behavior under any and all circumstances. For man is capable of learning and capable of using self-knowledge to change himself as well as his external surroundings; therefore he will probably always elude those who seek to define him. Marx and Engels, who at times insisted upon this fact, nevertheless fell into the trap of extrapolating historical human behavior during a certain period into the future. Man himself has changed that future.

Yet one of the reasons that man in the present world has escaped some of the "inevitable" disasters predicted by Marxism has been the work of Marx himself. For in his voluminous writings, his brilliant interpretations, and painstaking analyses of nineteenth-century capitalism, Marx taught men much that they needed to know about themselves and their society. Like the Old Testament prophets he so closely resembled, he was able to awaken men's consciences to the injustices and inequities of their social and economic world. Furthermore, he demonstrated that man could and must organize his social environment for his own betterment. And Marx's utopian vision of the future and of man in that future, even if visionary, is nonetheless inspiring.

Karl Marx passed most of his life in desperate poverty. He lived to see not only his son, but also his wife and one of his daughters die, all victims of his dedication to his work. He lived to see only the first volume of *Capital* published (the rest, left in manuscript form, were brought-out by Engels and Kautsky after his death) and he never received much public recognition for that immense work. Marx himself referred to *Capital* as "the task to which I have sacrificed my health, my happiness in life, and my family." Yet he remained defiant. "I laugh at the so-called 'practical' men and their wisdom," he wrote, "If one had the hide of an ox, one could naturally turn one's back on the sufferings of humanity and look after one's own skin; but, as it is, I should have considered myself very unpractical if I had died without completing my book, at least in manuscript form." On March 14, 1883, Engels came to call on his old friend. He found the household in tears; Marx had suffered a hemorrhage. Engels found Marx dead in his study, slumped over the desk to which he had dragged himself from his sickbed.

Engels outlived his collaborator by twelve years; and with Marx's passing, something of the younger man's natural gaiety seems to have reasserted itself. Nevertheless, Engels remained modestly devoted to Marx's memory and spent most of his remaining years preparing the manuscripts of *Capital* for publication. Much to Engels' surprise, the first translation of *Capital* into a language other than English, was Russian. Neither he nor Marx had ever been able to conceive of Russia in terms of anything but an oriental despotism which would have to go through decades, perhaps a century, of capitalist development before socialist theory could have any relevance to it. Yet Marx and Engels had fashioned a theory of man in history and in industrial society which was not only an explanation of the nineteenth-century world, but also a weapon in that world. Now, as the century came to its close, other men were already sharpening that weapon, preparing to use it to change the course of history itself.

Part Two

THE WORD MADE FLESH

Chapter Five

RUSSIA IN SEARCH OF REVOLUTION

> Vladimir Ilyich and I recalled a simile that L.
> Tolstoy used somewhere. Once, when walking, he
> spotted in the distance the figure of a man squatting
> on his haunches and moving his hands about in an
> absurd way. A *madman!* he thought. But on drawing
> nearer, he saw that it was a man sharpening his knife
> on the paving-stones.
>
> —*Krupskaya Ulyanov* (Lenin's wife)

Russia, to Marx and Engels, had always represented both a threat and an enigma. A threat because, as the bastion of reaction and autocracy all through the nineteenth century, Russia had been instrumental in suppressing many a popular revolution, many a national-independence uprising. Russian armies had not only finally defeated the tyranny of Napoleon I, but when Cossack squadrons entered Paris in league with Austrian and Prussian troops, they provided many of the bayonets which supported the return of the hated Bourbon dynasty to France. The Russian tsar, in association with the emperor of Austria and the king of Prussia, was an essential pillar of the Holy Alliance, that structure of repression guided by Metternich which weighed so heavily upon all liberal and progressive movements in post-Napoleonic Europe. More than once during the century Russian troops stamped out Polish national uprisings. It was the Russian Army which preserved the Hapsburg regime in Austria during the storms of 1848; it was the omnipresent threat of Russian armies that gave pause to Prussian insurgents in 1848 and was, from time to time, conjured by Bismarck to cow liberals and moderates during his campaign to unify Germany under the Prussian yoke. And, of course, the tsarist tyranny within Russia itself had grown ever more notorious over the centuries.

It was no wonder, then, that Marx was surprised to learn that *Capital* had been translated into Russian in 1868, only one year after its publication. It gave him occasion to reflect, and he immediately set himself the task of learning the Russian language. His aim was to make Russia the central subject of the second volume of *Capital,* as England had been of the first. Later, his conflict with the Russian anarchist Bakunin for control of the First International spurred him to further investigation of Russian conditions; but he seems never to have really decided what he thought about Russia.

The core of the problem, the reason Russia remained an enigma as well as a threat, was the fact that Russia had not yet undergone the essential capitalist development which, according to Marxist theory, was prerequisite to any socialist revolution. Yet, as even the most casual observer could see, Russia during the nineteenth century, afflicted by uprisings, assassinations, and conspiracies, was fast becoming ripe for revolution. Did that revolution, when it came, have to be a bourgeois-capitalist overthrow of the essentially feudal Russian society, or was there not perhaps some shortcut by which the revolution could proceed at once to the establishment of a socialist state? Impatient Russian Marxists spent much time and effort seeking some evidence that Russia could prove an exception to the rigid Marxist historical pattern of feudalism-capitalism-socialism. They hopefully advanced the fact that Russian peasant villages had traditionally been communally organized; could not these village communes serve as the building blocks of a socialist rather than a capitalist system in what was, after all, overwhelmingly a peasant nation?

In 1881 a letter from the young Russian Marxist, Vera Zasulich, raised these questions. Marx, in reply, weighed the fact that the physical configuration of the Russian land did lend itself to mechanized, communal agriculture, that despite the lack of development of the means of production within Russia, the industrial strength of Western Europe might yet be made available. But in the long run, a Russian revolution that aspired to socialist rather than capitalist ends would have to *follow* successful socialist revolutions throughout the rest of capitalist Europe. The only concession Marx and Engels were prepared to make to "special" Russian conditions was the opinion that a large-scale uprising against the tsar might set off the coming socialist revolution in the *West*—presumably by removing the threat of tsarist intervention.

To understand both the uncertainty of the founders of Marxism about Russia, and, more importantly, the later adaptations of Marxist theory made by Russian revolutionists which today form the Communist dogma, it would be well to review certain developments within Russia itself over the centuries.

The repeated themes of Russian history have been unification, defense, expansion, and tyranny—and these problems may be traced to the physical geography of the country. The incredibly vast expanse of the Russian land (today, three times as large as the United States), plus the presence within it of no fewer than 170 different nationalities speaking over 200 different tongues, made its unification immeasurably more difficult than the unification of very much smaller and more homogenous Western European nations. The fact that this huge land mass, the bridge between Europe and Asia, presents but few natural barriers to invaders from either east or west, has made Russia the scene of repeated inundations of foreign hordes from the time of the ancient Persians under Darius (515 B.C.) to the time of Hitler—a geographical circumstance which has made Russians almost morbidly sensitive about their defenses. This same lack of natural geographical barriers to invasion has in turn invited that continuous Russian expansion which today has filled one sixth of the land area of the world. These three factors combined—the necessity for unification and defense, and the lure of expansion—go far toward explaining the centralized tyranny under which Russians have lived since earliest times. They also help to explain the tardiness of Russian national development in relation to the countries of Western Europe.

The Slavic peoples of Russia entered late upon the stage of world history. Not until six centuries after the fall of Rome—a thousand years after the birth of Christ—did a coherent civilization appear in Russia, and much of it was foreign-inspired. Following the old river trade routes from the north, Scandinavian merchants, raiders, and migrants pushed their way south towards the Black Sea. There they encountered the trade and cultural penetration of Greeks, Arabs, and other Mediterranean peoples pushing north along the river Dnieper. The fusion of this foreign penetration along natural trade routes with the local Slavic population produced the Federation of Kiev, a loosely organized region embracing much of the Ukraine and dominated by the great commercial city of Kiev on the banks of the Dnieper.

Kievan culture was largely derived from the Byzantine Empire, the successor to the Roman Empire in the Near East. From the imperial capital of Byzantium (later Constantinople), Kievan traders brought back the arts, handicrafts, learning, and Greek Orthodox Christianity which were to mold Russian culture; even the Russian alphabet was based on the Greek. But with the fall of Byzantium to the Crusaders in the early thirteenth century, and with rising pressures of internal dissension, the Kievan civilization decayed. No longer able to defend themselves against the raids of barbaric nomad tribes from the East, the peasants, traders, and merchants of Kiev began to migrate to the relative safety of the great northern forests. There they came under the domination of the princes of Muscovy, semibarbaric hereditary rulers of the area around Moscow, which was then little more than a collection of wooden huts.

In 1237 complete and overwhelming disaster fell upon the Russian land; vast Mongol armies under the brilliant leadership of Batu Khan (a descendant of Genghis) invaded and conquered the Eurasian plain, sweeping everything before them to the gates of Vienna. Slaughtering the entire populations of various areas along their way, deporting whole races, the Mongols fastened a grip on Russia which was to last for centuries. The entire central and southern portions of the country fell to the Tatars. Kiev was burned to the ground, Moscow and other cities enslaved. Skilled craftsmen were carried off to the Mongol capital of Sarai in central Asia, trade came to a standstill, and crushing taxes were imposed on the starving peasants. While the Dark Ages gave way to a Renaissance in Western Europe, Russia struggled to emerge from the Mongol domination.

The Khans saw no need to station troops in Russia; the terror of their name was sufficient to ensure obedience. Instead they appointed certain Russian princes to collect taxes and slaves for them. Among these, the princes of Muscovy eventually won the right to be sole tax collectors for the Great Khan. Every year they sent caravans of Russian slaves, gold, timber, and furs to the south, to the fabled lands of the Golden Horde, which stretched from the Ukraine to Turkestan.

Using the threat of the Mongol terror, the princes of Muscovy were able to first dominate and then wipe out the petty principalities of northern Russia. Where the prince of Muscovy's power extended, peasants, traders, merchants, and the lesser nobility *(boyars)* were reduced to absolute dependence upon his whim and his protection; the Russian Orthodox Church was reduced to a servile branch of government. The princes of Muscovy were careful not to arouse the anger of the Great Khan in the East as they slowly widened their domains and gathered strength. By 1480 the power of the Golden Horde had fallen so low, while that of the princes of Muscovy had risen so high, that the princes felt free to defy the Khan, refuse to pay further taxes, and so end three centuries of foreign domination.

This slow conquest of northern Russia by the princes of Muscovy, their continual subversion of the Mongol power, was accomplished at a terrible price. The nobility had been impoverished and reduced to complete dependence on the princes; the Orthodox Church existed only on their sufference; the peasants, living almost always on the edge of starvation, found their ancient primitive liberties destroyed. By the beginning of the sixteenth century there was no power in all the broad land of Russia save that of the prince of Muscovy. His tyranny was absolute, with no group, no institution to gainsay his word. From this time until the late nineteenth century the history of Russia becomes very much a personal history of the country's rulers. Behind the throne one is aware of vast, silent multitudes suffering, sometimes conspiring; around the throne fawning courtiers sparkle momentarily and are then snuffed out. From time to time a general, a statesman, a poet makes his appearance. But Russia is the personal property of its ruler, the people his absolute slaves. Government policy, law, religion, commerce, trade, life, and death all reflect the often-crazed personal whims of the inheritors of the princes of Muscovy.

In 1533 Ivan IV became prince of Muscovy. Fourteen years later he assumed the title of Tsar (Caesar) of All the Russias. He is better known to history as Ivan the Terrible. He faced three problems which were to plague all his successors and which still have not been finally settled. First, there was the constant need to organize, to centralize, in order to control the vast and sprawling Russian domains. This was to be accomplished by making everyone—noble, priest, tradesman, and peasant—a servant of the state under rigid bureaucratic control. Second, there was the old danger of invasion either from the technologically more advanced West or by the semibarbaric nomadic tribes of central and eastern Asia. This problem was to be solved only by constant warfare and the maintenance of huge standing armies. Third was the problem of the technological and cultural backwardness of the nation. This was to be solved by the large-scale importation of engineers, craftsmen, and advisors from the West.

Like most of his successors, Ivan found it much easier to smash the decaying power of the Mongol khanates and expand into the limitless Asiatic plateaus than to defend himself (largely against Poland and Sweden) in the west. His reign was marked by constant warfare, desperate oppression, and savage cruelty. In this it was not remarkable. There has hardly been a tsar in Russian history who would not as well have deserved to be named "the Terrible."

Under Ivan, the Russian conquest of the Mongols was completed, and all the vast land of western Siberia annexed. But the exhaustion from this effort, and the struggle for power which occurred when Ivan's son died without leaving an heir to the throne, led to the Time of Troubles, a time of peasant uprisings and civil war that lasted until a *boyar* (noble) named Mikhail Romanov assumed the throne in 1613. His descendants were to rule for more than three hundred years in an unbroken line.

The Romanovs brought no new policy to the throne as they struggled with Russia's same age-old problems. They continued to increase the autocracy of the tsar, degrading all classes more and more. In 1649 Alexei Romanov produced a new legal code which divided and froze the Russian people into rigid classes. Peasants were bound to the land, townspeople to their town or city. The Church and the nobility were declared to be closed classes, and both were strictly regulated by the tsar. Thus at a time when feudalism was fast crumbling in the West, something very much like it was formally codified and frozen into existence in Russia.

But if the tsars were absolute rulers at home, they remained apprehensive of foreign, especially western, enemies. Recognizing that only by adopting western technology could they hope to preserve their empire, the Romanovs now strove to modernize their nation. Peter I, remembered as Peter the Great, who ruled from 1682 to 1725, made a mighty effort to "westernize" his people. He issued regulations and laws which even went so far as to abolish beards and attempted to change the old native costumes of his people. Importing engineers from France. Scotland, and England, and architects from Italy, Peter built a large and modern city on the shoes of the Baltic Sea. His "window on the West" was named Saint Petersburg in honor of his patron saint and cost the lives of untold thousands of workers toiling along the swamps of the river Neva.

By the time of Peter's death in 1725, Russia had become a world power; and if its peasants remained sunk in illiterate slavery, its nobility made haste to copy Western tastes and culture. French became the fashionable language at court (which Peter had moved from Moscow to Saint Petersburg), and the Russian people were more than ever separated from their newly educated masters.

After a brief repetition of the Time of Troubles, during which tsars came and went (often murdered by members of their own families), peasant rebellions flared and died, and the nobility won back a small measure of independence, Catherine II (the Great) seized the throne from her insane husband in 1762. Although she liked to consider herself an enlightened ruler (she was a friend of Voltaire's), in actuality she did nothing to relieve the misery of her people. A succession of her lovers, promoted to the rank of general, succeeded in conquering the Ukraine and the Crimea from both the Turks and local tribesmen. Her foreign policy in the West led to the dismemberment and enslavement of Poland among Russia, Prussia, and Austria. This mistake of destroying the buffer kingdom between Russia and Prussia was to cost Catherine's descendants dearly.

During these centuries of Romanov rule, while Russia remained a prison for its people, Russian influence in the rest of the world was steadily growing. It reached a peak under Catherine's grandson, Alexander I. It was during Alexander's reign that Napoleon launched his *Grande Armée* into the icy fastness of the Russian wilderness. The deadly winter, the guerrilla warfare of the peasants, a scorched-earth policy which culminated in the accidental burning of Moscow, and the valor of the huge Russian armies led by the brilliant General Mikhail Kutuzov, utterly destroyed the French forces —and with them Napoleon's dream of a world empire.

The hardy serfs, with their fierce Cossack cavalry, swept across Europe to join the British, Swedes, and Prussians in bringing Napoleon's empire to an end. Russian divisions marched down the Champs Élysées in Paris, while Russian diplomats now found themselves exercising great influence in Western capitals.

But at this peak of imperial glory the Romanov power had reached its zenith. By exposing his army officers to Western ideas and ways of life, Alexander was undermining his own position. When he died suddenly in 1825, a group of these officers attempted to overthrow the autocracy in favor of a more democratic, constitutional monarchy. Known as the Decembrists because of the month in which they struck, they were quickly and efficiently crushed by the new tsar, Nicholas I. Their palace revolution had little hope of success in any event; for although they enjoyed the backing of certain elements among the lesser nobility, the army officers and a few landowners, they were almost as far removed from the enslaved masses of the Russian peasants as was the tsar. The Decembrists did succeed, however, in throwing a scare into Nicholas. His response to the uprising was to inflict thirty years of the most savage repression upon all classes of his people.

In the realm of foreign affairs, aside from lending his armies to the crushing of European uprisings in the West, as we have seen, Nicholas's policies were mostly aimed at gaining control of Constantinople and the straits between the Black Sea and the Mediterranean. This meant war with Turkey and led eventually to the humiliating defeat inflicted upon Russia by France and England during the Crimean War (1854–1856). It was this disaster which prompted Nicholas's successor to the throne, Alexander II, to institute a few long-overdue reforms.

Alexander II may have had some slight personal regret for the hideous conditions under which his people toiled, but his primary concern was with the technological and social backwardness that had led to defeat in the Crimea. He traced these conditions to the continued existence of serfdom. For this reason, in 1861, Alexander abolished serfdom throughout Russia. But instead of giving the land to the peasants who had for centuries worked it, much of it was sold to the rich while the rest was declared state property. This half-measure of liberation only succeeded in driving many peasants off the land completely, into vagabondage, while those who remained found themselves sunk in a morass of debt that effectively continued their former slavery. Reforms in the universities, the press, the judicial system, the army, and local government followed emancipation of the serfs. But these reforms, again, were not so much designed to help the people as to make the government more efficient. And they whetted the people's appetite for more liberty, thereby increasing the frustration of the small minority of educated Russians. Alexander faced, in the declining years of his life, a widespread and increasingly bold opposition. Revolutionary plots against the government made the tsar a hunted man in his own empire. On March 13, 1881, one of these plots caught up with Alexander II. He was killed by a bomb tossed at him as he drove in his carraige through Saint Petersburg. His successor, Alexander III, a horrified witness of his father's death, responded, as had Nicholas I to the Decembrists, by an orgy of revenge and repression, a flood of ever more reactionary decrees and laws. Nevertheless, it was during the 1880's that the Russian revolutionary movement, with a tradition almost as old as that of tsardom itself, came face to face with the autocracy, surfaced in Russian history, and began an increasingly successful attempt to wrest control of that history from its former masters. But before examining the origins and progress of the Russian revolutionary movement, it might be well to generalize briefly about the kind of society, emerging from centuries of tyranny, within which that movement arose.

First of all, the absolute autocracy of the tsars had no parallel in European history since the time of ancient Rome. Western kings and emperors might exercise tremendous personal power; but this power had to contend variously with the power of the Roman Catholic Church, the power of the feudal hierarchy of the lesser nobility, the power of emerging merchant classes, and the power of neighboring, rival kings. Even during the darkest ages of feudalism, no Western sovereign ever exercised the kind of absolute power over his serfs that the tsars of Russia enjoyed. As late as the middle of the nineteenth century, article four of the "Fundamental Laws" of Russia read:

"To the Emperor of all the Russias belongs the supreme autocratic power. To obey his commands not merely from fear but according to the dictates of one's conscience is ordained by God Himself."

The catechism of the Russian Orthodox Church, the only printed material most peasants were ever likely to encounter, read:

"Question. What does religion teach us about our duties
to the tsar?

"Answer. Worship, fidelity, the payment of taxes, service,
love and prayer—the whole being comprised in the words,
worship and fidelity."

Russian peasant society, based on the strength of the family
within the local village, had always been strictly patriarchal;
the ultimate patriarch was the tsar, referred to as "Our Own
Dear Father," or "Father in the Flesh." Absolutism in Russia
was not in the Western tradition, not even in the tradition
of such powerful monarchs as Charlemagne, Louis XIV, or
Napoleon; it was in the tradition of the East, the tradition of
the Byzantine emperors and of Genghis Khan.

The apparatus through which the tsar exercised his absolute
power also had no real parallel in Western Europe. With a
nobility that had remained crushed and dependent since the
days of the Mongol invasions, no delegation of authority
through the aristocracy was possible. The tsar ruled through
an immense bureaucracy and a huge police force, both personally responsible to him alone. Nicholas I said, "Russia is
not ruled by me, but by my forty thousand clerks." Aristocratic landowners might be petty tyrants on their own estates,
might use or abuse their serfs as they wished; but they were
subject to the *immediate* personal and absolute authority of
the tsar expressed, if he so wished, through the lowliest of his
clerks, the most obscure of his public officials.

Russia for centuries then, could be likened to one immense
personal estate, utterly owned and controlled by a single man.
So long as that estate produced the taxes, services, defenses,
worship, and glory necessary to its owner, there could be but
little impetus on his part to change it. Only the fear of rival
pretensions on the part of neighboring foreign powers could
induce the tsar grudgingly to "reform" their domains. But
even these reforms, as we have seen, were designed primarily
to preserve and extend the central autocracy. Universities
were established to produce more competent technicians;
railroads, telegraphs, and other internal improvements which
were to come so late to Russia were designed to more efficiently control and protect the tsar's sixth of the world;
emancipation of the serfs was undertaken in the hope of
establishing a more personally involved, more literate base
for the tsar's armies and to further weaken the hereditary
power, however slight, of the land-holding aristocracy; the
establishment of manufacturing on any large scale was per-

mitted only after the middle of the nineteenth century and was, in the first instance, directed to the production of better arms and armaments.

Thus, at the time of Alexander II's assassination, there existed in Russia no middle class worthy of the name. Between the tsar with his governing apparatus of clerks and police and army on the one hand, and the vast masses of illiterate peasantry on the other there was no real power. The vacuum between tsar and peasantry was filled partially only by impoverished nobles and those intellectuals who, trained at the universities, had perforce been exposed to Western ideas and whose discontent and frustration arose precisely from their realization that they had no means of expressing or applying these ideas to their closed world.

It will be seen then, that without *revolution* there was no possibility of *evolutionary* change in Russia, for there existed neither the economic-social class to force evolutionary change nor the social framework within which it might take place. Change could come only as the gift of the tsar—a gift that the naive peasantry continued to await from the hands of the "dear little father." Or it could come through the complete destruction of tsardom. If the tsar's power was shattered there would remain in Russia only the power of the peasantry —hopefully led by the intellectuals. What of the industrial workers? It was true that during Alexander II's reign these had increased in number to about 1,000,000; but they were scattered among the large cities of Saint Petersburg, Moscow, and Kiev, and in any event, compared to Russia's vast population (150,000,000 during the late nineteenth century) were too small a group to be effective. But how were Russia's intellectuals to reach the illiterate peasant masses? Various small groups of university students had made such attempts in the past, even going so far as to adopt peasant costumes and attempting to work in the fields, only to be ignored and mocked by the newly liberated serfs. Feeling themselves very much alone, confronted by absolute power, early Russian revolutionists turned to the weapons available to isolated individuals and small groups—conspiracy and terrorism. It was for this reason that they welcomed the theories of Bakunin.

Absolute secrecy, absolute devotion, absolute ruthlessness —these were the ingredients of revolutionary conspiracies in nineteenth-century Russia. These were the ingredients of the student-intellectual conspiracy known as *Narodnaya*

Volya, the People's Will, whose members perished by the
score on tsarist gallows and were sent by the hundreds to
Siberian exile in return for their continuing attempts to kill
Alexander II—attempts which were crowned with success
when one of the few survivors of the conspiracy managed
to blow the tsar up in his carriage in 1881. Typically, this
act, far from arousing the peasant masses from their grum-
bling slumbers, was viewed by many peasants not as an act
by revolutionaries, but as an assassination probably carried
out by nobles and landlords outraged by the tsar's emancipation of the serfs! The *Narodnaya Volya,* already all but
shattered by their losses incurred in previous assassination
attempts, passed out of existence under the savage reprisals
exacted by Alexander III for his father's murder; but their
traditions of secrecy, devotion, ruthlessness, and absolutely
centralized control of members was to survive and, in large
measure, inspire the thinking of later revolutionaries. Their
overall theory, which held that in semifeudal Russia only the
peasantry represented a potentially revolutionary force, continued to be embraced by the majority of Russian intellectuals
and became the central conviction of the Social Revolutionary
party which was to be formed late in the nineteenth century.

One of the early members of the *Narodnaya Volya* who
disagreed both with their program of individual terror and
their assumptions about the peasantry was Georgi V. Plekhanov. He and certain of his followers had disassociated
themselves from the terrorist group before the murder of
Alexander II. In searching for a more realistic lever with
which to move Russian society, they had come upon the
works of Karl Marx. It was Plekhanov who first applied the
theories of *Capital* to Russian conditions, and in 1883, the
year of Karl Marx's death, Plekhanov and Pavel B. Axelrod
founded the first Russian Marxist political group, The League
for the Emancipation of Labor.

It may come as something of a surprise to realize that while
the tsarist police hounded and **per**secuted Social Revolutionaries and other groups who sought to ally themselves with or
represent the peasants, they at first accepted Marxism as a
legal doctrine; *Capital* was published openly in Saint Petersburg, evidently having satisfied the state censor. But on
further reflection, police toleration of the early Marxists only
reflected the realities of the situation and the problems of
Plekhanov and his associates.

For if Marxism was a revolutionary theory of the establishment of socialism, then it represented almost no threat to the autocracy. If the working class was to lead the revolution and establish a dictatorship of the proletariat, where was this Russian working class? All but nonexistent. If the bourgeoisie were to have so organized the means of production as to have won absolute state power, brought about utter social alienation and apocalyptic economic crises, where was this Russian bourgeoisie? All but nonexistent. In fact, where were these "means of production" in the Marxist sense of highly organized factories, mines, mills, distribution networks, etc.? Also all but nonexistent in nineteenth-century Russia.

On the other hand, the police might well have seen Marxism as a theory which, prophetical fervors aside, actually described the emergence of capitalism from feudal society. Then it would not only have been tolerable, it might even have been welcome. For, as we have seen, the tsarist autocracy itself was busily attempting to establish and organize capitalist means of production within Russia during the last decades of the nineteenth century. This process, it was true, was undertaken solely for the sake of preserving tsarism from its external as well as its internal enemies. And under the iron hand of Alexander III Russian capitalist development was to be completely controlled by and dependent upon the government. It was, in fact, to develop not as "free enterprise," but as state capitalism; the private ownership of the means of production was simply to be a mask for absolute government control. Thus the tsar's government could accept the basic tenet of Marxism—that the means of production must be owned or controlled by the state. Marx had foreseen this coming about as the result of revolution from below; the tsarist autocracy was engaged in bringing it about by decree from above. Substituting "state" for "working class"; "bureaucracy" for "bourgeoisie"; "dictatorship of the autocracy" for "dictatorship of the proletariat" we find that many of the essentials of Marxism seem to apply equally well to the aims of Alexander III.

In all probability of course, the tsarist police did not trouble themselves with these theoretical considerations (neither did the Marxists), and the League for the Emancipation of Labor was soon to enjoy the same kind of savage repression that all other opposition groups experienced at the hands of the tsarist government apparatus. The point is made here only in order to emphasize the wide gulf which existed between Marxist theory and Russian reality during the 1880's. It was no wonder that Marx and Engels remained unsure about Russian Marxism; Plekhanov, Axelrod, and their associates themselves remained unsure. Marxism had been designed not only as an explanation of certain historical developments but as a means of intervening in history, as a key to fit certain historical locks. Before it could hope to fit the lock of Russian history it would have to undergo important modifications, and these modifications were to be provided by a new generation of Russian revolutionaries which emerged into the stifling atmosphere of tsarist absolutism during the last decades of the nineteenth century.

Chapter Six

THE MAKING OF A REVOLUTIONARY

> Society can never think things out:
> It has to see them acted out by actors,
> Devoted actors at a sacrifice—
> the ablest actors I can lay my hands on.
>
> —*God to Job,*
> in Robert Frost's "The Masque of Reason"

On March 1, 1887, sixth anniversary of the assassination of Tsar Alexander II by the *Narodnaya Volya,* seven young men, students of the University in Saint Petersburg, were caught by the police as they prepared to explode a bomb outside the tsar's winter palace. It quickly developed that this aborted attempt was strictly the work of amateurs (the conspirators were all just out of their teens) and that behind the would-be terrorists there existed no organization, only memories of the defunct terrorist group, *Narodnaya Volya.* Nevertheless, Tsar Alexander III was so frightened by this reminder of his father's bloody end that he directed that four of the youthful students be hanged. Despite the admitted frankness with which the youths defended themselves in court and the selflessness of their motives, their pitifully isolated conspiracy would hardly have been remembered in history were it not for the fact that one of the executed defendants was a young man named Alexander Ulyanov. His sixteen-year-old brother Vladimir, when he received the stunning news of Alexander's arrest and execution, is reported to have said, "That means, then, that Sasha couldn't have acted in any other way." Though probably apocryphal, the story reflects the thoughtful reserve that was already to be noted in young Vladimir, even in 1887, many years before he adopted his famous pseudonym, Lenin.

The brothers Ulyanov (Vladimir was born on April 22, 1870) grew up in a provincial district capital, Simbirsk, which was far from Moscow and even farther from Saint Petersburg. Their family life was essentially middle-class, their father being Inspector of Schools for the province and entitled to be addressed "Your Excellency." Their mother, of Russo-German extraction, was a Lutheran and although their house was a happy one, it had some of the austerity of Protestant strictness about it. The children were expected to do well in school, and they did. Alexander won many medals for scholarship and Vladimir, a few years behind him, showed the same intellectual brilliance and serious attention to his studies. Since their father had died in 1886, the execution of Alexander a year later made Vladimir the head of the family, thrusting a man's responsibilities onto his shoulders.

Alexander's death wrought some profound changes in Vladimir's outlook on life. Until his father's death he had been dutifully religious; now he discarded his religious training entirely. The stigma of being the brother of a would-be assassin of the tsar closed off Vladimir's path to respectability; his normal career, which might have been that of a lawyer or an educator, was now beset by official suspicion. And if the execution of his brother developed in Vladimir a profound and lasting hatred of tsarism, it also taught him to hold liberals in contempt. For when his mother journeyed to Saint Petersburg in a frantic and fruitless attempt to save her son's life, none of the respectable, middle-class liberal friends of the Ulyanov family (they had been many) were willing to accompany her on the trip; they were all too frightened to associate with the family.

Vladimir graduated (at the head of his class) from the local Simbirsk high school soon after his brother's execution. But when he applied for entrance into universities at Saint Petersburg and Moscow, he was abruptly turned down. Finally the authorities grudgingly allowed him to enter the University of Kazan where he started to study law. But within a few months he was arrested by the police for having taken part in a student demonstration. He had been neither among the instigators nor the leaders of this demonstration, merely a bystander. But his name, Ulyanov, associated with his brother's deeds, brought expulsion from the university. It was just after this event that Vladimir first read some of the works of Karl Marx. Soon he joined an informal (and secret) group of students who gathered from time to time to study "the social question."

Partly from fear of what Vladimir's association with an illegal study group might bring, partly in a desperate attempt to find some other career for her son, Vladimir's mother bought a farm near Samara. But as a farmer Vladimir was not a success. Years later he recalled to Krupskaya, his wife, "My mother wanted me to engage in farming. I tried it, but I saw that it would not work: my relations with the peasants got to be abnormal." By this, the future Lenin meant that his experience (he spent three years on the farm at Samara) of exploiting peasant labor as a landowner was repellent to him. Nonetheless it taught him much about rural conditions and the pressing problems of the peasantry. In any event, his career as gentleman farmer was ended in May 1889 when, after years of pleading, his mother finally wrested permission from the authorities for her son to study for a law degree. Even so, he was not permitted to enter a university (his presence might contaminate other students), but had to study as an "outside" student at the University in Saint Petersburg. Characteristically, he learned the four-year course in less than a year and then passed his examinations with the highest possible marks. He returned to practice law in Samara (the police would not permit him to practice in either Moscow or Saint Petersburg), but there he spent as much time studying Marxism as he did in earning a living. And it was there that he first read the writings of Georgi Plekhanov.

But Vladimir Ulyanov's conversion to Marxism was not a swift process. His awakening to politics and his radicalization had been prompted by the execution of his brother; but that brother had died a hero of the *Narodnik* (People's or Populist) movement, not of the Marxist movement. The *Narodniks*, the inheritors of the same traditions and theories that had given rise to the *Narodnaya Volya*, while not as yet organized into a nationwide party, comprised the great majority of Russian radical intellectuals. To accept the import of Alexander Ulyanov's martyrdom meant to accept, to a certain extent at least, the validity of such *Narodnik* beliefs as that Russia was destined, through the instinctive socialism of the Russian peasantry, to lead the world to socialism without ever having to pass through the stage of capitalism; that individual acts of terror were legitimate means of social struggle—both conceptions being absolutely anathematic to orthodox Marxists. It was not until 1891–1892 that Vladimir's essential differences with his *Narodnik* associates in Samara came to the surface, and it was from that time that his conversion to Marxism may be considered final.

For in those years famine swept over Russia. The earth turned to dust and grain withered in the fields. Thousands of peasants took to the roads searching for food; thousands more simply squatted down in their village streets to die of starvation. Cholera, typhoid, and typhus spread fearfully. In Samara, as in other Russian cities, the radical intelligentsia, while denouncing the "medieval" incompetence of a government which could not even organize the distribution of such food as was available, busied itself with help and "relief" projects for the starving peasants. The question that arose was whether this aid should take the form of cooperating with government authorities or, as Plekhanov urged from Switzerland, should be used as part of the revolutionary struggle against that government. Many *Narodniks* and most of the liberals thought that the famine might be a lever in the liberalization of the regime. Vladimir Ulyanov and an increasing circle of his friends in Samara preferred to follow Plekhanov. In the event they were proved right; the liberals, far from ingratiating themselves with the tsarist autocracy, were held up as scapegoats by government officials (charges of profiteering in grain supplies were brought against them) and looked upon with indifference or outright hostility by the suffering peasants. Charity as an effective social engine simply did not work in Russia at the end of the century.

But the famines of 1891–1892 marked a turning point not only in Vladimir Ulyanov's attitudes, they marked a turning point in the views of very many Russian radicals. For this there were objective reasons beyond famine. First of all, the pace of Russian industrialization, though still far behind that of Western nations, had now reached the point where it posed an increasingly effective alternative to peasant socialism; Russian capitalism (largely state capitalism) was coming of age. Between 1877 and 1897 the production of textiles doubled and the production of metals tripled. In 1897 there were more than 600,000 workers in textile industries alone; the Russian working class long sought for by Marxists was rapidly coming into existence. It began to appear more and more unlikely that Russia would be able to escape that capitalist development which Marxists held to be essential before a meaningful socialist revolution could take place. Secondly, as Vladimir had learned from his experience as a farming landlord, the abolition of serfdom had led to a growing differentiation among the peasantry. Some were becoming rich; some remained poor; some were sinking into even deeper poverty and despair. They were far from the homogeneous, idealized "peasantry" upon which the *Narodniks* counted. Furthermore, this differentiation was just what Marxism predicted. This fact, too, was becoming apparent in the last decade of the nineteenth century.

Finally, and perhaps of decisive importance to the development of Marxism inside Russia, the closing decade of the century saw a revival of socialist vitality throughout Europe. The French working class, recovering from the terrible wounds of 1871 was once again organizing its forces through both trade unions and socialist political parties; in 1891 the German Social Democrats eliminated those Lassallean features of their program which had caused Marx to denounce the Gotha proposals nearly twenty years earlier. In Britain the trade union movement, organized into the Independent Labour party, was busily organizing the vast masses of unskilled laborers and preparing a political program that went beyond better wages and shorter hours. In 1889 the revitalized socialist organizations of many European countries set up a new International Congress. Claiming to inherit the traditions of Marx's defunct First International, it called itself the Socialist and Labor International Congress, and is referred to generally as the Second International. Georgi Plekhanov, on behalf of the Russian delegation, addressed the founding meeting of the new International with these words: "In Russia, political freedom will be gained by the working class, or it will not exist at all. The Russian Revolution can only conquer as a working-class revolution—there is no other possibility, nor can there be." To the representatives of the powerful German Social Democratic party and the strong French socialist parties, these words must have seemed no more than an orthodox Marxist truism. But as a description of the emergence of a Marxist viewpoint among Russian revolutionaries enmeshed in an abnormal social structure, Plekhanov's words were electrifying to his followers inside Russia. Their emerging doctrines had resounded with all the prestige of a great international organization to amplify them; it is hardly too much to say that Plekhanov thus converted an entire generation of Russian radical intellectuals to Marxism.

Vladimir Ulyanov's study of Marxism, begun while he was in Kazan and continued in Samara, was all-consuming. He read everything written by Marx or Plekhanov that he could lay hands on. He even learned German so as to be able to read *Capital* in the original. From friends and libraries and government publications he gathered all the statistical material he could about Russia's economic development; he read the economic dissertations of liberal and *Narodnik* theorists; he applied Marxist theory to all this material in the spirit of a devoted, perhaps fanatical, disciple. "Marxist philosophy," he later wrote, "[is] a solid block of steel, from which you cannot eliminate even one basic assumption without abandoning objective truth, without falling into the arms of the bourgeois-reactionary falsehood." Vladimir Ulyanov, graduated in the school of Marxist theory, and prepared to enter his role of revolutionary, emerged from that provincial Russia where he had spent the first twenty-three years of his life as Lenin, a conspiratorial name he was to adopt a few years later, but one which will be convenient to use from now on as a description of a man who had made himself, as had Marx before him, into an instrument of history.

At the beginning of 1894 Vladimir went to Saint Petersburg where he plunged into the debates of a Marxist study group and met his future wife, Nadezhda Krupskaya, a Marxist intellectual who had been devoting herself to the education of workers. At first scornful of the "gradualist" tactics implicit in this attempt to educate the very few workers who could be persuaded to attend study classes, Vladimir soon realized that he had as much to learn from the workers as they from him. Through close questioning he was able to learn much about the actual, as opposed to the theoretical, conditions of the Saint Petersburg workers in their rapidly industrializing society. He learned, too, how to "talk the workers' language"; to formulate their immediate demands succinctly and forcefully and yet express them within the framework of Marxist theory. He summed up his attitude towards the workers' study groups in a leaflet he circulated among Saint Petersburg Marxists: "The role of the intelligentsia is to make special leaders from among the intelligentsia unnecessary."

In 1895 Vladimir suffered an attack of nerves (the doctors diagnosed pneumonia!). Partly to recuperate, but primarily to get into touch with Plekhanov, Axelrod, and the other exiled leaders of the Social Democratic party (as the Russian Marxists called themselves soon after the founding congress of the Second International), he journeyed to Switzerland. He made an excellent impression on Plekhanov and Axelrod —even though, at that early date, certain theoretical differences were already emerging between the viewpoints of the older Marxist leaders and their new disciple. What seemed to trouble Axelrod most was Lenin's attitude towards the liberals. It was quite proper for a Marxist to denounce liberals in those Western countries where capitalism had already been established, Axelrod pointed out, but to criticize Russian liberals was to criticize the proletariat's indispensable allies for the founding of the capitalist system without which no socialist revolution could proceed. Lenin, in awe of the legendary exiles, the men who had for so long been the leaders and teachers of the Russian Marxist movement, did not press his point; they in turn, having existed so long in isolation from events and followers inside Russia, welcomed the new arrival. When he returned to Russia in October 1895, he carried seditious pamphlets in the false bottom of his suitcase. He traveled to Moscow, Vilna, and other cities and for the first time, the exiled leaders in Switzerland began to receive reports from Russia that indicated the growth of a real and solid organization.

Lenin had returned to Saint Petersburg just as the first wave of great industrial strikes broke over that city. Demanding such primitive reforms as receiving pay at regular intervals (Russian industrialists were often in the habit of withholding wages for months, sometimes for an entire year) the textile workers and the metal workers were out on the streets. Lenin immediately began to prepare leaflets for distribution among them and tried to organize an underground newspaper to be called *The Workers' Cause*. But the tsarist police had been on Ulyanov's trail ever since his return from Switzerland. In December of 1895, just three months after his return, the police sprang their trap: Lenin, Krupskaya, and almost all the other members of the newly formed Saint Petersburg Social Democratic group were arrested. Lenin, and later, Krupskaya, were sentenced to Siberian exile for three years.

Siberian exile, under the tsars was a peculiar form of punishment. There were few guards—prisoners often traveled by themselves to their destination and were required only to report their presence weekly to local authorities; furthermore, they were permitted to move freely within very restricted areas. They could work, get married, set up a household—Lenin and Krupskaya were married shortly after her arrival in Lenin's exile district. The prison walls of Siberia were its vast distances and frozen wastes; the "punishment" was isolation among a handful of barely literate peasants and the very primitive conditions under which exiles, like natives, were forced to live. Under these circumstances it was not surprising that Siberian exile became the training camp and school for Russian revolutionaries. They corresponded with each other, and, through various chemical invisible inks, with comrades back in Russia. Occasionally they were able to meet. They read, studied, and pondered. Lenin himself maintained so voluminous a correspondence with the underground movement throughout Russia that even while in exile his reputation and prominence as one of the new leaders of Russian Marxism steadily increased. He found time too, to write a book, *The Development of Capitalism in Russia,* which was to remain the major theoretical work of his lifetime. In it, through detailed analyses of hundreds of statistical and theoretical reports, Lenin advanced his thesis that industrial capitalism in Russia had already advanced far enough to make a socialist revolution practicable, and that the growth of agricultural capitalism among the emancipated serfs had grown sufficiently to completely undermine the old *Naródnik* hope of a peasant-socialist revolution. The Russian proletariat was coming of age, claimed Lenin, while the Russian peasantry was undergoing a transformation—not unlike that which had overtaken the French peasantry after the Revolution of 1789—into a mixed class of small and large landowners and agricultural laborers. Lenin recognized, however, that capitalism in Russia was growing as state capitalism; the independent bourgeoisie were, and would remain, a pitifully small, inept, and powerless class. A revolution in Russia, led in the first instance by the city proletariat and supported by the poorest, landless peasants would directly confront the state itself. Although it might, from time to time "utilize" elements of the liberal bourgeoisie, there could be no question of the revolution "allying" itself with this all-but-non-existent class.

It was in Siberia, towards the end of his exile there, that Lenin learned of the first important theoretical split within the world Marxist movement—the revisionist theories of Eduard Bernstein. The impact of Bernstein's book, *Evolutionary Socialism* (a copy of which reached Lenin in Siberia in 1899), was tremendous throughout Europe. Bernstein himself was the literary executor of Engels (who had died in 1895) and a leading light of the mighty German Social

Democratic party. Furthermore, it appeared to many socialists that his criticisms of the Marxist classics were highly realistic.

For by the end of the nineteenth century, economic, political, and social conditions in Western Europe had changed profoundly. Since 1870 there had been neither great wars nor large-scale revolutionary upheavals in Europe. The sudden expansion of Europe overseas, the imperialistic conquest of Africa and much of the Far East combined with the era of railroad building and a growing armaments race to provide a period of prosperity. It seemed that the Marxist predictions of falling profits, deepening economic crises, social alienation, wars, and revolutions were simply not being borne out by events. Monopoly profits were rising, economic crises were fewer and recovery from them swifter, was only the faintest cloud on the European horizon, and, above all, the working classes of Europe, far from becoming ever more alienated, had formed themselves into socialist parties with ever-growing influence in political affairs. In France the socialist movement had split into several sectarian parties but by 1899 socialist influence had risen so high that a prominent socialist leader, Alexandre Millerand, was offered and accepted a seat in the essentially middle-class French cabinet. He was the first socialist ever to hold important government office. In Germany the Social Democratic party, legalized at last, could count its votes in the millions, its deputies to the Reichstag by the dozen. In England various socialist leaders were gradually winning support from the labor unions for programs that went beyond immediate gains; in 1893 labor and socialist leaders were able to found the Independent Labour Party. Also in England in 1884 evolutionary socialist thinkers (of whom Sidney Webb and George Bernard Shaw soon emerged as the most prominent) had founded the Fabian Society. Taking its name from that of a Roman general famous for his gradualist tactics of wearing down the enemy, the Fabian Society sought to influence the English labor movement to demand progressive *reforms* rather than dream of revolution.

Bernstein had, for many years, been the London correspondent of a leading German socialist newspaper, and his views were heavily influenced by Fabianism and the practical bread-and-butter approach of English labor to social problems. In his book, *Evolutionary Socialism* (published in 1898), Bernstein denied the Marxist dogmas. Looking over European conditions, Bernstein pointed out that the working classes were better off, the middle classes were growing, and the contradictions between classes were growing less, not more acute. In actuality, for all their fiery speeches, the German Social Democrats had become simply another political party devoted to gaining political power through constitutional means; why not admit as much? Beyond that, Marxism also failed philosophically. Insisting that Marxism was a "science" was, at best, irrelevant; certainly as a theory it provided little moral motivation. What was needed, Bernstein felt, was a new standard of morality which would not exclude some classes, as Marxism did, but would rather include *all* elements of society. Under such a moral standard the essential solidarity of the entire human race could be reaffirmed; and as moral consciousness gradually grew so, too, would socialism gradually grow.

Bernstein's theories found support among Russian socialists. A certain Mrs. Kuskova, applying Bernstein's analysis to Russian conditions, drew up a document which Lenin ironically called "the Credo." In it she pointed out that the development of democracy and industrialism in the West had enabled the proletariat to conquer a share of political power; indeed, the Western working classes had found it easier to go into politics than to build trade unions. But in Russia, against the stone wall of tsarist absolutism, the only path open to the growing proletariat was, in fact, the attempt to organize trade unions. There could be no talk of political action in a nation where politics was forbidden. The Russian working class would have to turn to trade unionism and learn to support the Russian bourgeoisie in political questions.

Lenin received Bernstein's theories with indignation; when he learned that Bernstein's revisionism had found followers in Russia his indignation turned to contemptuous fury. Through correspondence with other exiles he sought to combat the Bernsteinian heresy, and when Karl Kautsky, a German socialist leader brought out a book castigating *Evolutionary Socialism* in withering terms. Lenin greeted it so enthusiastically that he translated it into Russian within two weeks! In fact, although Bernstein's theories split socialist parties throughout Europe, the most prominent socialists and the most powerful socialist parties (including Bernstein's own German Social Democratic party) quickly denounced "revisionism." And yet Bernstein had raised questions which orthodox Marxists found difficult to answer and which they find difficult to answer even today. For basically, Bernstein's revisionism was rooted in a central Marxist contradiction:

the old question of "will" versus "inevitability." If Marxist historical analyses were correct, then socialism must inevitably emerge; why make its emergence the occasion of hatred and class warfare? If, on the other hand, there was nothing inevitable about the emergence of socialism, then the human "will" which was to create a socialist society would be much more profitably employed, practically speaking, in winning whatever gains it could, even if this meant working with and through liberal, middle-class politics. Those in Russia and the West who tended to rely on Marxist inevitability were soon dubbed "economists," both to describe their reliance on developing industrialization to produce the prerequisite conditions for socialism without the need for agitation or revolution, and also to describe their programs which, in Western European countries took the form of trade unionism and "gradualist" political activities.

But for Lenin the idea that the human will was to be suspended while history developed along "inevitable" lines, was an anathema. He could conceive of no moral system which could embrace both him and the tsar; talk of "solidarity" between the oppressed and their oppressors on any human level whatsoever was sheer nonsense. Worse than that, it was an insidious undermining of revolutionary will. Thus, objectively, no matter what the professed intentions of "revisionists" or "economists" might be, they were actually more dangerous enemies of the revolution than tsarist autocracy itself and all its police agents. To Lenin matters were very clear. The Marxist classics were holy books containing absolute truth. This truth was the principal weapon with which a revolution must be armed in Russia. Those who tried to blunt this weapon were mortal enemies. Lenin did not consider himself a Marxist theoretician; indeed, he left the demolition of Bernstein's theories to such as Karl Kautsky in the West. Instead he looked upon himself as a Marxist disciple, teaching Marxist truth in such a way as to arm his followers. His objectives were not theoretical but practical, and he bothered his head with theory only insofar as it might be necessary to advance his practical goals. His violent reaction to Bernstein's work and the emergence of the Russian "economists" and their "Credo" was rooted not so much in theoretical controversy as it was in a very personal distaste and impatience with those whose views threw new stumbling blocks in his path.

Now the isolation of Siberian exile really began to play

on his nerves. He had to endure his solitude and relative helplessness in the knowledge that the newly emerging Russian Social Democratic movement was already splintering, being misled by "opportunists," as he called them. He grew restive, nervous, irritable as the months dragged on, with all the frustration of a man conscious of his own powers but incapable of using them. For the experiences of his life and his tireless study of Marxism and Russian conditions had not only equipped him with the ability to transform words— Marxist words—into weapons, they had also made the man himself into a weapon. At last in February of 1900 Lenin's term of exile came to an end. He hurried at once to Geneva, Switzerland, to rejoin Plekhanov and Axelrod, his head bursting with plans. The weapon, loaded and very dangerous, was now to be loosed into the mainstream of European politics.

Chapter Seven

BOLSHEVISM EMERGING

> History has confronted us with an immediate task
> that is more revolutionary than all the immediate
> tasks that confront the proletariat of any other
> country. The fulfillment of this task, the destruc-
> tion of the most powerful bulwark, not only of
> European but no less of Asiatic reaction, places the
> Russian proletariat in the vanguard of the interna-
> tional revolutionary proletariat.
>
> —*Lenin*

When Lenin arrived again at Geneva in the spring of
1900, he was able to present to Plekhanov, Axelrod, and the
other older leaders of the Russian Social Democratic party,
an organization plan which was intended at once to unite,
strengthen, and purify the party both within and without
Russia. This plan centered around his proposal that the
émigrés publish a newspaper to be called *Iskra* (the Spark)
which would inform, explain, and channel socialist ideas.
The newspaper would be printed abroad, but it would be
smuggled into and throughout Russia by chains of secret
agents who would smuggle it into factories and cities. *Iskra*
would help to fuse the scattered local socialist groups into
a nationwide organization while assuring that theoretical
direction remained in the hands of the exiled leaders. Of
even greater importance, the agents who smuggled *Iskra*
across frontiers and past the tsarist police would themselves form the basis of an organization which could be
developed into a centralized conspiratorial party which, by

its secretive nature and mastery of underground techniques, could resist police persecution.

Plekhanov agreed to serve on the editorial board of *Iskra,* along with Lenin, Axelrod, and others, provided it was understood that the older man would retain a final say in editorial policy. Lenin agreed to this with mental reservations about the future. Already he was beginning to sense that a gap was opening between his own generation of revolutionaries and the older generation represented by the Geneva exiles. This unacknowledged rift in opinion illuminated an essential quality of Lenin's thinking. Plekhanov was a thoroughgoing Marxist theorist, indeed the dean of Russian Marxists. To him, no less than to Lenin, Marxist thought was holy scripture. But Plekhanov tended to emphasize the "inevitable" historical processes described by Marx, whereas Lenin emphasized the Marxist "will." Plekhanov held as an unalterable article of faith the conviction that Russia would not escape the traditional Marxist pattern of bourgeois-democratic revolution, developed capitalism, and socialist revolution. Lenin, while paying lip service to this classical Marxist view, was always seeking indications, ways, and means of short-circuiting this "inevitable" process through the action of the informed and dedicated will. And in the vast mass of classical Marxist literature both men could easily find "scripture" to back either view.

Thus while *Iskra* was, to Plekhanov and the other editors, simply a revolutionary underground newspaper, to Lenin it was a weapon with which he would combat not only anti-socialist views, but also all deviations from what he considered to be orthodox Marxism within the party. It was not to be so much the voice of a political party as the means of creating such a party; the agents who transmitted *Iskra* inside Russia would themselves emerge as the framework of that party—its leaders and watchdogs.

In the fourth issue of *Iskra,* Lenin published an article entitled "Where to Begin." A year later this same article, considerably expanded, appeared as a pamphlet of 160 pages entitled *What Is To Be Done?* which contained almost all the ideas on politics that have later been called "Leninist." Adherence to its views was to become the touchstone separating "hard" socialists from "soft." The keynote of *What Is To Be Done?* was to be found in the quotation from Lassalle with which Lenin adorned its title page:

"Party struggle gives a party strength and life . . . a party becomes stronger by purging itself!" Whom did Lenin intend to purge? All Bernsteinian revisionists, all lingering *Narodnik* peasant-socialists, all "economists," all socialists who were unprepared to discipline themselves into the most zealous and dedicated revolutionaries. He insisted on the necessity of "unifying" the nascent Russian party; but by "unification" Lenin meant exclusion of all those who were not prepared to unquestioningly accept the views of the *Iskra* editorial board.

Turning his attention to the growing Russian trade-union movement, Lenin insisted that left to itself trade unionism would inevitably degenerate into bourgeois politics. The working class had neither the time nor the educational background to comprehend socialist thought on its own. This thought must be propagated within the working class by dedicated socialists. Thus Lenin's proposed political structure emerged: Only the proletariat could lead Russia into revolution and socialism; only a dedicated, secretive, and conspiratorial group of socialist intellectuals could lead the proletariat itself; and only the leadership of this group of socialist intellectuals (that is, only Lenin) could direct the tightly organized socialist vanguard in its tasks. He wrote:

> I assert: 1. That no movement can be durable without a stable organization of leaders to maintain continuity; 2. that the more widely the masses are drawn into the struggle and form the basis of the movement, the more it is necessary to have such an organization and the more stable it must be; 3. that the organization must consist chiefly of persons engaged in revolution as a profession; 4. that in a country with a despotic government, the more we *restrict* the membership of this organization to those who are engaged in revolution as a profession . . . the more difficult it will be to catch the organization . . .

To socialists who complained of the lack of democratic principles in Lenin's proposed organization scheme, he replied witheringly. How could one have democratic principles without free publicity and free elections? But if socialist leaders were to so expose themselves they would immediately be arrested by the tsarist police. How were uneducated workers to decide delicate but vital questions of socialist theory by majority vote? These were, after all, questions of Marxist science, and only Marxist scientists with the requisite background could decide them. Of course workers were to be educated and advanced into the ranks of the socialist leadership as rapidly as possible; but this would require time and, in any event, it was highly unlikely that more than a mere handful of workers, given the conditions of their daily lives, would ever find the time and economic freedom to master Marxist principles while struggling for their daily bread. "Think it over," Lenin admonished ". . . and you will realize that 'broad democracy' in party organization, amidst the darkness of the autocracy and the domination of the police, is nothing more than a *useless and harmful toy*."

In the summer of 1903 Lenin's ideas were put to the test at the second Congress of the Russian Social Democrats held in Brussels and, after the Belgian police intervened, in London. Here an incredibly complex and intricate battle was fought over the question of whether the Social Democratic party was to be organized along broadly democratic lines or along the totalitarian lines advocated by Lenin. In the end, after bitter debate, Lenin's views prevailed by just two votes. On the basis of this rather shaky evidence he claimed for his followers the name *"Bolsheviks,"* which meant "majority," while leaving to his opponents at the Congress the title *"Mensheviks"* or *"minority."* In reality, then, as later, it was the Mensheviks who were in the overwhelming majority within the Social Democratic party. This became apparent a few months later when Lenin's carefully stage-managed victory at the Second Congress collapsed. Led by Plekhanov, the Mensheviks were able to reverse the decisions of the Second Congress, forcing Lenin to resign from *Iskra.* He was assailed as a potential dictator, an autocrat, an extremist, a party splitter. And indeed, he found himself isolated with but twenty-two followers among the Social Democratic delegates. But he welcomed this isolation for now it was apparent to him who were the real hard-core revolutionists and who the opportunists within the party. He published a defense of his position entitled *One Step Forward, Two Steps Back* in 1904. "It would be," he wrote confidently, "criminal cowardice to doubt for a moment the inevitable and complete triumph of the principles of revolutionary Social Democracy, proletarian organization and *party discipline.*" "Of such stuff," Plekhanov observed, "are Robespierres made."

At the Brussels-London Congress where Lenin had won his fleeting majority, there had been present a brilliant young man from the province of Kherson, on the Black Sea. Nearly ten years younger than Lenin, Lev Davidovich Bronstein was born in the tiny hamlet of Yanovka on November 8, 1879. The Bronsteins were Jews who had managed, in the face of recurrent fits of tsarist anti-Semitism, to amass some land—about 650 acres, and become successful farmers. In fact, old man Bronstein (as the local peasants called him) was a *kulak*, a rich peasant, who owned the only gristmill in the area. Although Tsar Alexander III, as part of his general program of repression, reinstituted many of the anti-Jewish laws and restrictions which his father had relaxed, the Bronsteins, living far from the city ghettos, suffered no more than harassment. The elder Bronstein was quite unreligious; his son would grow up an atheist.

Lev Davidovich went to school in Odessa, the teeming Black Sea port which had originally been founded by French émigrés and was notable for a cosmopolitan atmosphere. Lev Davidovich would later write, about tsarist anti-Semitism: ". . . it was lost among all the other phases of social injustice. It never played a leading part—not even a recognized one— in the list of my grievances."

What certainly did play a leading part in Lev Davidovich's growing consciousness of social inequality was what he observed of the relationship between the local peasants and his father who employed some of them. Just as a mild indication of what this relationship was, it may be pointed out that the peasants were never given meat to eat unless they made a silent protest by congregating before the Bronstein house and *lying down on their faces*. These were the "free" peasants Alexander II had liberated from serfdom, and their lot was no worse in Yanovka than anywhere else in Russia.

Lev Davidovich displayed outstanding ability at the Odessa school and, an already growing talent with words. "In my eyes," he later wrote, "authors, journalists, and artists always stood for a world that was more attractive than any other world, a world open only to the elect." He started a school magazine in Odessa and devoured Russian literature at the libraries. Almost inevitably he was drawn into the company of radical students and began reading Populist (*Narodnik*) and Marxist writings. As he came to understand the long-standing dispute between *Narodniks* and Marxists he sided with the *Narodniks*. Perhaps, coming from a rural background, he was more willing to see possibilities in the cherished *Narodnik* dream of peasant socialism. Nevertheless, it was in the cause of city workers that Lev Davidovich received his first revolutionary baptism. With a handful of other young men (he was just eighteen), in 1897, he attempted to organize the electrical workers of Odessa into an all-but-nonexistent group he was pleased to call the South Russian Workers' Union. Within a few months the tsarist police caught up with the leaders of this semiimaginary union. Lev Davidovich was sentenced to four years' exile in Siberia.

There, nearer Alaska than Moscow, as he observed, the young exile first seriously applied himself to the study of Marxist economics. He read *Capital* and also Lenin's *Development of Capitalism in Russia*. Later he received smuggled copies of *Iskra* and read Lenin's *What Is To Be Done?* He found himself in complete agreement with Lenin's theory of a highly centralized, conspiratorial party organization; in fact, he had written an essay setting forth the same views which was circulated among the Siberian exiles. When Lev Davidovich finally managed to escape from Siberia in 1902 (hidden beneath the hay of a peasant's cart) he was a confirmed Marxist and, as he thought, a Leninist. In that same spirit of irony which was to illuminate his writings later, Lev Davidovich chose for his underground name that of one of his tsarist guards, Trotsky. It was under the pseudonym Leon Trotsky that Lev Davidovich Bronstein would trace, like a meteor, a brilliant and self-consuming swath through the Marxist heavens.

Trotsky made his way to Switzerland and then to London. His writing ability and fiery personality won him quick recognition among the Russian exiles. He was invited to contribute articles to *Iskra* and professed himself one of Lenin's disciples (to Plekhanov's annoyance). Lenin, living at the time with Krupskaya in London, took Trotsky on a walking tour of the great city. "From a bridge," Trotsky later recalled, "Lenin pointed out Westminster and some other famous buildings. I don't remember the exact words he used, but what he conveyed was: 'This is their famous Westminster,' and 'their' referred, of course, not to the

English but to the ruling classes. This implication, which was not in the least emphasized but, coming as it did from the very innermost depths of the man and expressed more by the tone of his voice than by anything else, was always present, whether Lenin was speaking of the treasures of culture, of new achievements, of the wealth of books in the British Museum, of the information in the larger European newspapers or, years later, of German artillery or French aviation. They know this or they have that, they have made this or achieved that—but what enemies they are! To his eyes, the invisible shadow of the ruling classes always overlay the whole of human culture—a shadow that was as real to him as daylight."

This observation of Trotsky's, while a good example of the quick perception of human character and ability to describe delicate nuances of thought which were to make his books modern classics, is important for quite another reason. Observe that Lenin, accurately described in that passage, has really succeeded in making himself an objective instrument of history. Himself a product of bourgeois background and education, Lenin is completely outside his own class. He does not display hatred or anger at the owning classes; on the contrary, he is able to admire their handiworks in the certain knowledge that one day the proletariat will fall heir to them. Lenin, as we have seen, has emphasized the "will" of man in the making of history, rather than the "inevitability" of Marxist processes. But that "will" as expressed in himself, is the will of an *impersonally* dedicated historical instrument. And this was to emerge eventually as the greatest single difference between Lenin and Trotsky.

For Trotsky, a literary artist of the very first rank (which Lenin certainly was not), was never able to submerge his personality within his conception of history. Indeed his idea of history was slightly but decisively different from Lenin's. Lenin saw history as the expression of human will—a will which would "inevitably" body forth a socialist society as objective factors changed. But he did not ascribe to history, as Marx had tended to do, any sort of super-existence beyond and above the human will. Trotsky, on the other hand, goes far beyond Marx in unconsciously elevating history to the rank of a supernatural force. History, for Trotsky, rewards, punishes, blames, and urges men on in their struggles like Jehovah in the Old Testament. And since this conception of history is, of course, subconscious with Trotsky (as a determined materialist he would never admit that he had replaced God with history), it tends to find expression both in his life and his writings as a confusion with his own aims and objectives. Edmund Wilson has summed up the difference between Lenin and Trotsky by pointing out that while Lenin identified himself with history, Trotsky identified history with himself.

It was almost inevitable then that Trotsky, despite his reverence for Lenin, would immediately go about establishing an independent position for himself within the Social Democratic party. It seemed a personal necessity to him then and later to maintain both an independent viewpoint and an independent power base within the socialist movement. When the fierce struggle between Bolsheviks and Mensheviks erupted at the Brussels-London Congress, Trotsky took a position independent of both factions. Later, when Lenin found himself isolated within the party, Trotsky bent his energies to attempting to reconcile Mensheviks and Bolsheviks—a reconciliation that would always be impossible for Lenin. Yet, during the great Russian revolution of 1917, Trotsky would become Lenin's chief lieutenant, and his independent ideas would make an important modification upon the body of Leninist thought which became known as Bolshevism.

If we have gone into some detail regarding the subjective development of the thought of Lenin and Trotsky it is because, despite Marxist insistence on the relative unimportance of the individual, without them there would never have been a coherent body of thought conveniently labeled Bolshevism. We have seen that Bolshevism, which may be defined as Leninist Marxism, emerged as a pragmatic *political adaptation* of Marxist theory the objective of which was to bring about a socialist revolution in Russia. But Bolshevism did not spring full-grown from the brains of Lenin or, later, Trotsky; it was deeply influenced in its development by objective events also. It is time now to return to these historical events.

Tsar Alexander III died in 1894. Although he had, through the most savage repression, effectively maintained the autocracy, his robust health was undermined by constant fear of revolutionary terrorists. He died at the relatively young age of fifty as he had lived—virtually a prisoner of his terrors, surrounded on his country estate by massive cordons of secret police. In 1896 his son was crowned Tsar of All the Russias as Nicholas II. A slight, handsome young man, Nicholas was utterly unfit to maintain the iron-handed rule of his dead father. Those who were able to observe the new tsar closely were almost unanimous in remarking on his lack of brains or character. Later, the notorious religious charlatan Grigory Rasputin who insinuated his way into the very bosom of the royal family would observe that the tsar "lacked insides." Yet, from the very first, Nicholas displayed one simple, overriding ambition—to transmit absolutely unaltered to his descendants the vast prison-estate called Russia which he had inherited. Suspicious of men more talented than himself (most were), obsessively certain of his divine rights, Nicholas's will to rule could express itself as little more than peevish cunning. One of his ministers, Count Sergei Witte, was later to write: "I wish it, therefore it must be—that motto appeared in all the activities of this weak ruler, who only through weakness did all the things which characterized his reign—a wholesale shedding of more or less innocent blood, for the most part without aim."

Nicholas was encouraged in his limited abilities by his tsarina, Alexandra, a German princess he'd married in 1894. She was a devout convert to the Russian Orthodox Church and given to superstition. When, after giving birth to four daughters, she was finally able to present Nicholas with a male heir to the Russian throne, it soon developed that the young boy had inherited haemophilia, the dread "bleeding sickness" which afflicted many European royal families. In her concern to preserve her son's health, Alexandra turned to every sort of quack doctor and bogus holy man, submitting to their advice and, in turn, passing on their "wisdom" to her husband. Eventually a disreputable Siberian mystic, Grigory Rasputin, whose powers apparently included hypnosis, was ensconced in the royal palace. So great was his power over Alexandra (and, through her, over Nicholas) that this drunken libertine was able to dismiss government ministers, appoint his own creatures to power, and decide questions of national policy!

How did this ruling family appear to the Marxists? It may be instructive to see how Marxist analysis, in the hands of one of its ablest theoreticians, Leon Trotsky, may be applied to a problem of history. The problem: Did it really matter what kind of man Nicholas was? Was the Russian Revolution, when it came, really influenced in its course by the personality of the last tsar? And was Nicholas's character (or lack of it) an expression of something individual to him, or part of his "inevitable" historical "role"?

Trotsky, in his *History of the Russian Revolution,* compares Nicholas to both Louis XVI and Charles I (both of whom, it will be recalled, lost their heads to earlier revolutions). Using quotations from and about each of these three monarchs he illustrates how amazingly alike they were in character, personality and intellect, although separated by thousands of miles and hundreds of years:

> The scripts for the roles of Romanov and Capet [writes Trotsky] were prescribed by the general development of the historic drama; only the nuances of interpretation fell to the lot of the actors. . . . They were both, chiefly and above all, the last-born offspring of absolutism. . . .
>
> You might object: if Alexander III had drunk less he might have lived a good deal longer, the revolution would have run into a very different make of tsar, and no parallel with Louis XVI would have been possible. . . . We do not at all pretend to deny the significance of the personal in the mechanics of the historical process, nor the significance in the personal of the accidental. We only demand that a historic personality, with all its peculiarities, should not be taken as a bare list of psychological traits, but as a living reality grown out of definite social conditions and reacting upon them. As a rose does not lose its fragrance because the natural scientist points out upon what ingredients of soil and atmosphere it is nourished, so an exposure of the social roots of a personality does not remove from it either its aroma or its foul smell.

The foul smell, in any event, of the last of the Romanovs became extremely pungent during the opening years of the twentieth century. Unlike his father, who had been more or less content to confine his tyranny to Russia, Nicholas dreamed of military adventure and conquest. With expansion to the west barred by the military-industrial power of Germany, expansion to the south barred by English-French support for the tottering Ottoman Empire, Nicholas continued to pursue the ancient Russian policy of colonizing in the East. There his forces were opposed only by vast distances, impenetrable mountain chains, semibarbaric nomad tribes, and, on the shores of the Pacific, the weak and decaying power of the crumbling Chinese Empire. While British, French, German and American economic imperialisms (backed up when necessary by military force) were carving out vast "spheres of influence" within the prostrate Celestial Empire, Russia secured virtual domination over the Chinese province of Manchuria and sought to extend its power into the "hermit kingdom" of Korea. The impulse for this aggression was economic; at stake were Asiatic markets, Pacific port cities such as Darien and Port Arthur, and the raw materials of eastern Siberia. But for Nicholas and his fanatically religious wife, the Russian "mission" of bringing or imposing Christianity upon the Asiatic "heathen," was at least as important, probably more so, than material considerations. So upon a rationally explicable chain of historic events, Nicholas imposed his own brand of irrational stubbornness and superstition, which had much to do with the resultant disaster.

For Russian ambitions in the Far East ran head-on into Japanese imperialistic dreams in that area. Having already won one war against the Chinese Empire in 1894, Japan saw the fruits of her victory now seriously endangered by Russian expansion into Manchuria and Korea—areas Japan had marked out as her own spheres of influence. Negotiations between Japanese and Russian diplomats to attempt to resolve these problems were constantly undermined by Nicholas's obstinate faith in the crusading mission of his armies in Asia. So on February 8, 1904, in a surprise attack not dissimilar to one they would make thirty-seven years later, Japanese forces under the command of Admiral Heihachiro Togo fell upon the Russian fleet and city at Port Arthur. Within hours Russia's Far Eastern Fleet was destroyed, within days Japanese infantry was pouring into Korea and Manchuria, and within a few months the entire Russian position in the Far East had become untenable. When, in a spirit of blind gambler's folly and reliance upon divine intervention, Nicholas ordered Russia's ill-equipped, ill-led and ill-trained Baltic Fleet on a fourteen-thousand-mile voyage around Africa to Pacific waters, Admiral Togo dispatched the fleet (at the Battle of Tsushima) within a few hours.

At the peace conference, sponsored by President Theodore

Roosevelt at Portsmouth, New Hampshire, in September 1905, Russia emerged with relatively lenient terms considering her decisive defeat. But these included the loss of Darien, Port Arthur, and control of Manchuria as well as elimination of Russian influence in Korea. Yet the collapse of Nicholas's dreams of Asiatic domination was far from the most serious result of the Russo-Japanese War. For that war created a revolutionary situation in Russia itself.

Demoralized soldiers trickling back from the fronts along the line of the trans-Siberian railroad brought tales of military disorganization, official cowardice and corruption, mass slaughters and capricious surrenders on an all-but-unbelievable scale. Surviving Russian sailors who had seen their comrades perish by the thousands through bureaucratic incompetence and royal whim told their stories in port cities from Odessa to Saint Petersburg. And these seeds of bitter rebelliousness fell upon fertile soil. The Russian workers, whose miserable daily life had been made even more intolerable by wartime speed-ups, food shortages, and price hikes, and whose friends and brothers had perished in scandalously mismanaged battles, began a series of massive strikes in Saint Petersburg, Moscow, and Odessa.

Ironically, the organizational framework for these strikes had been provided, not by the revolutionary movements (although Social Democrats and *Narodniks* were both active in them) but by the tsarist police! In an attempt to forestall socialist penetration of the Russian workers' movement, the tsarist bureaucracy had itself organized trade unions. In the west such unions would have been called "company unions," and have been understood to be under the domination of the company ownership, responsive to corporate needs. In tsarist Russia, however, where, in the final analysis the autocracy itself was the "company" it was the state itself, through its police power which organized, infiltrated and dominated these "unions."

One of the police-instructed agents who developed a remarkable following among Saint Petersburg workers, was a Russian Orthodox priest named Father Georgi Gapon. Father Gapon, however, deeply religious and appalled by what he had learned of working-class life, took his position of leadership among the workers seriously. In January 1905 the Saint Petersburg metal workers went on strike for four days. When this massive strike bore no fruit, Father Gapon wrote a letter to the tsar: "Sire! Do not believe thy ministers! They are cheating thee in regard to the real state of affairs. The people believe in thee. They have made up their minds to gather at the Winter Palace tomorrow at 2 P.M. to lay their needs before thee. . . . Do not fear anything. Stand tomorrow before the people and accept our humblest petition. I, the representative of the workingmen, and my comrades, guarantee the inviolability of thy person. Gapon."

The naïvete revealed by this curious letter was not confined to Father Gapon. We have seen how the patriarchal relationship between the Russian masses and their "dear father tsar," had developed over the centuries. That relationship had proved one of the chief stumbling blocks to the attempts of revolutionaries to educate Russian workers and peasants. This stumbling block was now to be kicked aside by the tsar himself.

On January 22, 1905, two hundred thousand workers and their families, led by Father Gapon, trudged silently through the freezing streets of Saint Petersburg, carrying icons and religious banners and pictures of the tsar to assemble before the winter palace. In his hand Father Gapon carried their petition—a humble request for the eight-hour day, a minimum wage of one ruble (fifty cents per hour), no overtime, and the calling of a constituent assembly to draft a constitution for Russia. But when this mighty throng reached the Winter Palace, Nicholas was not there. He had hastily removed himself and his family to his palace at Tsarskoye Selo. Behind him he left a reception committee of policemen and Cossacks. These, perhaps panicked by the immense throng before them, opened fire directly into the crowd. Five hundred men, woman, and children were killed, many hundreds more wounded. The crowd dropped their icons and religious banners and fled screaming and bloody through the streets. Behind them they also left the last of their illusions about the tsar.

Making his way to Finland, Father Gapon wrote again to Nicholas: "The innocent blood of workers, their wives and children, lies forever between thee, O soul-destroyer, and the Russian people. . . . Let all the blood that has to be shed, hangman, fall upon thee and thy kindred!" Having dispatched this letter, Father Gapon went to Switzerland where he urged Plekhanov, Lenin, and other of the exiled revolutionaries to act at once. This spectacle of a deeply religious Russian Orthodox priest who had been a police agent, turning now to revolutionary Marxists for inspiration, was a small example of what now took place all over Russia on a gigantic scale: the radicalization of the Russian working class. The military and domestic disasters of the war with Japan, combined with the massacre which was to go into Russian history as "Bloody Sunday," convinced enormous segments of that working class that the pamphlets, smuggled issues of *Iskra*, and words of Social Democratic agitators were correct. There could be no compromise with tsardom, nor could the workers rely upon any leadership that was not their own. They had to take matters into their own hands— and, in 1905, they did.

The revolutionary exiles, excited by news of general strikes, peasant uprisings, and military mutinies in Russia, impatiently tried to get home. The first to succeed was Trotsky. Arriving in Saint Petersburg early in 1905, he found the city already largely under the control of striking workers. He at once asserted his leadership and, with both Bolshevik and Menshevik agents, hastily organized *soviets* (councils) of workers in factories and shops which in turn elected representatives to a central Saint Petersburg Soviet. In Moscow, Kiev, Odessa, and other cities, Bolshevik-Menshevik-led soviets also soon appeared. Everywhere they disputed power with the tsarist autocracy. Nor were the workers and their Social Democratic leadership alone in their struggles.

The old *Narodnik* populist circles which looked forward to peasant-led socialism in Russia had in 1904 organized themselves formally into the Social Revolutionary party. They remained bitterly opposed to the Marxist principles of the Social Democrats, whether Bolshevik or Menshevik, but, in 1905 found it possible to cooperate with them in the attempt to destroy tsarism; there were enough revolutionary tasks for everyone, no matter of what political persuasion. At the same time, the slowly and weakly developing Russian middle classes had organized a political party which went so far as to demand a constitutional convention (looking toward a constitutional monarchy on the English model). They called themselves Constitutional Democrats, *Cadets* (in Russian: Kadets) for short. Both of these groups supported the general strikes aimed against the autocracy.

Nicholas II, his throne tottering beneath him, began to

make concessions. There would be a constituent assembly; the legal code would be overhauled; certain land-reform programs would be instituted; a *Duma* (representative assembly) would be tolerated; amnesties would be decreed. And, while he made promises, the tsar gathered together whatever reliable forces he could find—the police, certain military regiments, the Cossacks—to strike a blow against the revolution. Satisfied with Nicholas's promises, the Cadets soon withdrew their support of the city soviets whose power now began to dwindle in divisive debates. Trotsky, president of the Saint Petersburg Soviet pressed for further revolutionary action (he attempted to undermine the tsarist financial structure by having the workers make a "run" on the Saint Petersburg banks), but found himself more and more a general without an army. For the workers, worn out by the privations of the war and the months of revolutionary struggle, seemed increasingly content to believe the tsar's promises.

By now Lenin and Krupskaya and other exiled leaders had also made their way back to Russia. Lenin assumed the presidency of the Moscow Soviet, attempting to instill in it his own uncompromising spirit of struggle. But in Moscow as in Saint Petersburg, the threatening tidal wave of revolution gradually ebbed. It was hastened in this process by the blows that Nicholas now felt able to deliver. Loyal regiments and Cossacks appeared in the streets of the capitals; artillery was turned on the workers' districts and the police began to arrest revolutionary leaders. Trotsky was caught in Saint Petersburg and once again sent into Siberian exile; Lenin and Krupskaya escaped back to Switzerland just one step ahead of the police. The soviets were disbanded and the Russian working class would once again retire sullenly into its social prison, waiting now to see whether Nicholas would keep his promises and, if he did, whether those promises would effect any difference in their lives as Russian liberals assured them they would.

The events of 1905 made a tremendous impact upon the theories and ideas of Russian revolutionaries of all persuasions. The Social Revolutionaries, observing the relative ease with which the autocracy had isolated, defeated, and decapitated the workers' uprisings in the cities, became even more convinced that a socialist revolution in Russia could only base itself upon the peasantry. The working class, they pointed out, had shown itself too weak to succeed—as was to be expected in a nation only just beginning to emerge into capitalist industrialization. The Mensheviks, who had taken an active part on the city soviets, were much impressed by their own failings. It had been revealed, when they attempted to administer political power in the capitals, that both they and their working-class followers lacked the bureaucratic skills, the administrative knowledge to successfully guide events and rule a great nation. This only reinforced the central Menshevik conviction which was that revolution in Russia could only be accomplished by adhering to classical Marxist principles. First, time would have to be allowed for the development of capitalist industrialization. This would produce and strengthen a Russian middle class (which, they pointed out, had already found a voice in the Cadet party) and give the working class much needed time for further political and social education. The middle class would win democratic reforms; indeed they had won some very important concessions already. Only after a decisive development of capitalist industrialization and democratic government would it be time to move toward a socialist revolution. Any premature attempt to organize one could only lead, as 1905 painfully proved, to disaster for the workers. Furthermore, now that the tsar had promised democratic reforms, it ought to be possible to organize a Social Democratic party in Russia on a legal, open basis, thus making the Bolshevik conception of a closed, conspiratorial, dictatorially centralized party plainly unnecessary, even counterrevolutionary.

Trotsky, who, it will be recalled, had taken a position independent of both Bolsheviks and Mensheviks, reached different conclusions from the experience of 1905. Having been in the middle of events, having witnessed the revolution grow, struggle, and subside beneath his hand, as it were, he now developed the theory of "continuous revolution" which was to be his central contribution to Marxist thought. Briefly, this theory held that, given the peculiarities of Russian development, a revolution in its opening phases might as well proceed as a capitalist-democratic uprising against the semifeudal autocracy, but that it could continue, as broader and broader classes of the population were drawn into the struggle, to impose a socialist direction upon events. Thus the power transferred into the hands of the capitalist middle classes and richer peasants in the early phase of the revolution would gradually be wrested from them by the working class and the poorest peasants as the revolution progressed. Indeed the power would be forced into their hands by the inherent contradictions of the revolution itself. The French Revolution had been stifled by the bourgeoisie as soon as it had achieved bourgeois ends. But a century of industrialization had intervened between 1789 and 1905, and the next revolution, even in backward Russia (which, Trotsky insisted, was more highly industrialized than many realized) could not be so stifled because the working classes were now infinitely more powerful and politically advanced than they had been at the close of the eighteenth century. Furthermore, their intervention would assure that the peasantry would not be turned into a lower middle class of small landowners who could then be used for counterrevolutionary purposes. Later, as we shall see, Trotsky was to expand this theory of "continuous" or "permanent revolution," into an internationalist view of historical development that would provide his strength in 1917–19 and his weakness in 1924–30.

For Lenin and the Bolsheviks, 1905 taught lessons that were as much practical as they were theoretical. Once again, the desertion of the Cadets, once the tsar had made sufficient promises, only seemed to underscore Lenin's conviction that liberals could never be relied upon. The lack of impact of the many scattered peasant uprisings seemed again to prove the hopelessness of expecting the basically disorganized and semiliterate peasantry to lead the way to revolution. The ineffectiveness of the soviet administration in the capitals only proved again that the working class must be led by revolutionaries trained and educated in their tasks. The fact that the tsar had been able to muster regiments to put down the rebellions demonstrated that no revolution could succeed unless the army had first been won over to the cause. The relative ease with which the autocracy had been able to disrupt, demoralize, and capture the revolutionary leadership proved conclusively the need for organization, organization, and still more organization. Spontaneous leadership could never succeed; discipline and centralized control were essential. On the other hand, the patience and heroism of the workers in their struggles, the massiveness of their intervention, and the fact that they had come remarkably close to winning state power, reinforced the Bolshevik contention that it would be possible to proceed at once to a socialist revolution without the necessity of establishing the forms of capitalist democracy.

It will be seen, then, that each of the revolutionary groups that participated in the revolution of 1905 drew from their experience conclusions which reinforced their own preconceptions. Each was certain that events had proved them right; but as to which of them actually drew the proper conclusions, only future events could tell.

Chapter Eight

BOLSHEVISM TRIUMPHANT

> If a war threatens to break out, it is the duty of
> the working class . . . to intervene in favor of its
> speedy termination and to do all in their power to
> utilize the economic and political crisis caused by the
> war to rouse the peoples and thereby to hasten the
> abolition of capitalist class rule.
>
> —*Rosa Luxemburg*

Since the establishment of the first Communist government
in Russia in 1917, it has been a general rule that no Com-
munist regime has ever come to power in any country
without the *immediate* circumstance of international war.
The Russian Communist government followed the ravages
of World War I; the imposition of Communist regimes in
Eastern Europe in Poland, Rumania, Hungary, Bulgaria,
Yugoslavia, Albania, and Czechoslovakia followed the devas-
tation of World War II; the triumph of Communism in
China and Korea followed the Pacific phase of the Second
World War; the establishment of Communist regimes in
North Vietnam, briefly in Indonesia, and almost haphazardly
in Cuba has been one of the results of the Cold War. There
have been, of course, other important immediate circumstances surrounding this phenomenon—not to mention more
basic circumstances. But in every case the older society was
first destroyed or undermined by wars—wars of imperialist
aggression, before Communist governments were able to win
power. In some cases, for example, those of Poland, Czechoslovakia and Hungary it is possible to state that communism
would almost certainly not have triumphed had Nazi German

129

aggression not first destroyed the power, economics, and society of these nations. In the case of China it is possible to argue that even if communism had eventually triumphed, its route would have been infinitely longer and more complicated had the Japanese warlords not first caused an upheaval in Chinese society.

But this, of course, is hindsight. For Lenin and other socialist leaders in Europe during the years 1906–1914, the approach of war (which they foresaw with remarkable clarity) presented problems which threatened to wreck the entire Socialist movement. These problems were anxiously discussed at conferences of Second International leaders, and debated furiously within individual socialist parties; but they were never satisfactorily solved.

Lenin devoted almost all his energy during these fateful years to effecting a decisive split within the Russian Social Democratic party. He was determined to force the Menshevik faction into isolation, determined to rule or ruin the party. And this policy, which was a natural outcome of his views on what a revolutionary party ought to be, was bearing fruit. The Bolsheviks, led by Lenin and such new associates as Maxim Litvinov, Lev Kamenev and Grigori Zinoviev, were steadily winning power among Social Democratic circles within Russia. They had a new newspaper now, *Pravda* (truth), which served not only as a propaganda weapon (its illegal circulation in Russia was about 40,000 copies) but also, as had the original *Iskra,* as a focal point for underground organization. And *Pravda* was in the hands of the Bolsheviks. When other socialist leaders tried to impress upon Lenin the need for complete unity of all socialist parties in the face of gathering war clouds, he resolutely turned aside their suggestions. He would accept unity among Russian Social Democrats only on the basis of their complete acceptance of his program and leadership—that is, if they all became Bolsheviks.

Although Lenin could not bring himself to believe in the imminence of European catastrophe, the decade between the Russian Revolution of 1905 and the fateful year 1914 was actually the sunset of the nineteenth-century bourgeois world. Germany, France, England, Austria-Hungary, and Russia were all engaged in feverish arms races and military preparations; each international crisis brought the great powers closer to the brink of war; the General Staffs of Europe were planning—for exactly what, none of them could be quite sure. The complicated Balkan Wars of 1911, 1912, and 1913 turned that area into a tinderbox awaiting only a spark. The spark was provided by the assassination of the Austrian crown prince at Sarajevo on June 28, 1914. Within weeks all of Europe was seized by war fever.

To understand the response of European socialists to this crisis, it is necessary to review, briefly, the development of some of the individual socialist parties. The prime question facing them, from about 1895 on, was whether or not they should take part in their various national governments— governments which were dominated by capitalist parties. Many felt that to engage in the politics of parliamentary democracy was to voluntarily disarm working-class movements. Yet the major European Socialist parties, even the mighty German Social Democratic party, the party of Marx and Engels, were all, as we have seen, participating in bourgeois governments by 1905. In England various splinter Socialist groups, guided both by trade-union leaders such as James Keir Hardie and by the theoreticians of the Fabian Society, had formed a loose amalgamation in 1893 known as the Independent Labour party. Exerting growing pressure on both the older bourgeois parties, Liberals and Conservatives, the I.L.P. soon elected members to Parliament and the threat implicit in its burgeoning power forced basic changes in the British structure of government, such as the abolition of the House of Lords' absolute right of veto over legislation. By 1914 it was already clear that the Labour party was on its way to eliminating the Liberal party, and to directly contesting power with the Conservatives.

In France the socialist movement, despite fitful attempts to unite, remained split into a bewildering profusion of groups which finally, after 1900, regrouped into two rival organizations: the Socialist party of France and the French Socialist party. At issue among the various factions was, again, the question of whether or not socialists could join a national government. The issue was settled in 1905 when the two parties amalgamated into the Unified Socialist party under the leadership of Jean Jaurès. A growing bloc of socialist representatives joined the Chamber of Deputies and socialists were even to be found in the government ministries.

The German Social Democratic party, accepting the tenets of Bernstein's revisionism, despite their "orthodox" Marxist oratory, had been heavily represented in the Reichstag since the turn of the century. But the severe limitations of democratic forms within the German constitution ensured that they would never be faced with the problem of actually joining one of the kaiser's ministries. Social Democratic spokesmen such as Karl Kautsky and Karl Liebknecht, supported by the fiery Polish socialist Rosa Luxemburg, might maintain their Marxist orthodoxy, their militant stance; but the German Party as a whole was, by 1914, deeply enmeshed in the essentially bourgeois politics of evolutionary socialism.

The inescapable logic of circumstances which forced all these socialist parties away from Marxian visions of apocalyptic revolution was everywhere the same. If they were to win mass support for their programs, the parties must establish themselves at the head of working-class movements. But the working classes, with the growth of trade unionism, were much more interested in bread-and-butter issues such as the eight-hour-day and better wages, factory inspection laws, than they were in theoretical socialism. Furthermore, in England, France and, even in a limited sense, Germany, the political forms through which these modest demands could be won already existed in the form of parliamentary democracy. Socialist parties would therefore be forced to use these forms to win these gains if they hoped to hold their mass membership. Otherwise other groups, other leaders, by granting immediate reforms, might drain the labor movement of all revolutionary energy.

Only the Russian socialists, in Europe, escaped these problems. They escaped them simply because despite the promises of Nicholas II after 1905, Russia remained an absolute autocracy. True, a Duma (parliament) had been elected in 1906 in which the Cadets won the largest number of seats. But when these middle-class liberals respectfully drew up a list of proposed reforms for submission to the tsar's government, they were informed that their proposals were simply "inadmissible." When this produced angry speeches in the Duma, Nicholas sent troops to disperse that annoying institution. And this was the pattern that parliamentary democracy was to follow in Russia during the brief period in which it was tolerated. From time to time the tsar would assemble a Duma to rubber-stamp his decrees; the Duma, even though composed overwhelmingly of conservatives, could not stomach the government's policies; and Nicholas would again dissolve it. Despite all this, the Menshevik faction of the Social Democratic party favored participation in the Duma. In fact, just before 1914 they even succeeded in electing a handful of deputies to this all-but-moribund institution. This, of course, only increased Lenin's wrath against them.

A more serious obstacle to Lenin's program was to be found in the reformist policy of Prime Minister Peter Stolypin, called by Nicholas to head the government in 1906. Stolypin inaugurated a program of selling state-owned land to the peasants on easy credit terms with the aim of creating that very class of small landowning peasants whose immunity to revolutionary appeals had frustrated every French revolution since the first one. Lenin recognized the danger of Stolypin's plans, admitting "If this program [of land reform] should continue for a long period of time . . . it might force us to renounce any agrarian program at all. It would be empty and stupid democratic phrasemongering to say that the success of such a policy in Russia is impossible. It is possible!"

The problems posed by the emergence of even so limited a reform movement as represented by Stolypin were resolved, however, on September 14, 1911, when the prime minister was assassinated (probably by a secret police agent) while attending, with the tsar, an opera in Kiev. Thereafter Nicholas turned again (undoubtedly with considerable relief) to government by "cronies" and religious fakers such as Rasputin. It was with this "leprous court camarilla" as even one of the grand dukes described it, that the autocracy sought to deal with the nation's problems.

Among these problems, the most salient was the tremendous pace of industrialization in Russia between 1905 and 1914. During those years Russia's industrial production approximately doubled. At the same time, since the establishment of industry occurred so late, that industry, taking advantage of western experience, was remarkably advanced. Thus while in the United States at that time, industrial enterprises employing more than 1,000 workers accounted for only 18% of the American labor force, in Russia such enterprises accounted for more than 44% of the total labor force. Furthermore, although the working class remained a distinct minority within the nation, out of a population of 100,000,000 it accounted for 25,000,000 people (wives and children included)—no small number. This working class, constantly recruiting new members from the peasantry, was concentrated in Saint Petersburg, Moscow, and a handful of other big cities. And just as the working class was concentrated, so too, was the capitalist ownership of industry—not only concentrated but very highly organized. Much of Russian industry was foreign financed, controlled, and owned. Russian industrialization in fact represented to a surprising degree a sort of economic colonization on the part of French, British, and German finance capital. Thus, while the Russian working class expanded in numbers and advanced in self-consciousness, there was no real corresponding development of a Russian middle class. Capitalism in Russia remained the prerogative of the very few—the government bureaucracy and foreigners.

It may be remarked here that to orthodox Marxists, the development of industrial capitalism and a capitalist farming system in Russia would have been welcome as a sign of progress on the "inevitable" path of feudalism-capitalism-socialism. One of the basic distinctions between Marx's view and that of Lenin is that to the impatient Russian revolutionary, the "inevitable" emergence of a landowning middle-class farming population represented not progress but a vital threat to revolutionary development. Between 1905 and 1914 Lenin devoted much time to a consideration of the problem and the role of Russia's peasantry. His conclusions were typically realistic: A proletarian revolution in the big cities could only succeed by enlisting peasant support with the slogan, "land to the landless." But such a revolution would have to take place while there still remained sufficient numbers of the "landless" for such an appeal to be effective. Thus the pace of proletarian revolution would have to measure itself carefully against the pace of peasant uprisings and seek to wrest final state power at the moment of greatest peasant rebellion. Thereafter the ruling proletariat would have to once again take the land away from the peasants to prevent their emergence as a potentially counterrevolutionary landowning middle class—that is to say, change the peasant into a working-class land-laborer.

It will be seen then, that in grappling with the problems of Russian society, Lenin, even before 1914, had arrived at many of the conclusions which were to form the basis of policy of the coming Bolshevik regime. But there was one further step in the development of Leninism without which it is doubtful the Bolsheviks would have mustered the confidence to act. This step was a result of the outbreak of war in Europe in August 1914.

Socialists of all the major European parties had predicted war, in a vague way. They had discussed what to do to prevent it or use it if it came. One of the central tenets of Marxism was the international solidarity of the working class. It was unthinkable that, at the bidding of capitalists, workers of any nation should be enlisted to kill their brothers. But what practical steps could be taken to avert catastrophe? At several hastily summoned international Socialist conferences during the agonizing summer of 1914, various measures were proposed—the most obvious and potentially effective being a mighty general strike to be called in any nation which went to war. But, pointed out the German Social Democrats, if we were, through a general strike, to hamper our nation's war effort, it would only ensure the triumph of the backward autocracy of tsarist Russia. In international terms this would represent a setback for the European working class. And, said the French Socialists, likewise, were we to undermine the French war effort, this would only ensure the triumph of Imperial Germany—and the kaiser's victory would be a victory of reaction over democratic progress. *But what if all should strike at once?* It was when this solution was discussed that the inherent weakness of the politically enmeshed post-Marxist European socialist parties became apparent. Having partaken of the bourgeois parliamentary political game, the socialist parties of Europe had become hopelessly infected with middle-class, nationalist views. Brought to the precipice of revolutionary action, the German Social Democrats had to admit that for all their parliamentary strength, they could not count on the unwavering support of the German working class in what would surely develop as a civil war in Germany. Russian Socialists (represented mainly by Mensheviks, Lenin paying but little attention to these emergency meetings) pointed out that they were simply unprepared to guarantee the effectiveness of a general strike in the face of the tsarist absolutism. The French socialists, though generally more willing to act, were already participating in the French government which felt itself threatened by German militarism; they spoke continuously of German aggression, making but little distinction between the kaiser and the German working class.

Some socialists of all nationalities rose above nationalist

suspicions. They included Jean Jaurès of France, Karl
Kautsky and Karl Liebknecht of Germany, Rosa Luxemburg
of Poland, Plekhanov of Russia. But aside from Jaurès, none
of these were in actual control of their various party
apparatuses, and Jaurès was assassinated by a royalist
fanatic just as France slipped over the abyss into war. In
the event, the socialists proved themselves as nationalistic
as their capitalist enemies. The German Social Democrats
obediently voted to support the kaiser's war effort; the
Russian Mensheviks lined up behind the tsar; the French
Socialists patriotically enlisted to defend their homeland. It
was revealed that in a showdown between socialist theory
and nationalist historic actuality, Socialists thought of themselves first as Germans, Frenchmen, Russians, Austrians—
and only secondarily as part of an international brotherhood
of workers.

The capitulation of the European socialist parties to the
drumbeats of patriotic fervor in 1914 came as a stunning
surprise to Lenin. At first he thought that reports of
socialist support for the war efforts of the various nations
must be government propaganda. But his disbelief soon
turned to cold fury, and this fury prompted him into the
investigations and speculations which were to form one of
his most important books, *Imperialism: The Last Stage of
Capitalism*, published in neutral Switzerland in 1916.

In this remarkable work Lenin offered a reassessment of
capitalism as of 1916, when, he held, it had passed into
forms which Marx could not have foreseen. Calling the new
capitalism "monopoly capitalism" Lenin pointed out that
monopoly had largely replaced competition within the
capitalist structure. It was no longer then a question of
capitalists devouring each other in the mad scramble for
diminishing profits. No, profits had increased through the
imperialistic exploitation of backward areas of the world,
and these profits had become concentrated in the hands of
fewer and fewer finance capitalists in the most developed
countries. Furthermore, since monopolies had become so
gigantic, they now dominated national political life. Therefore
they were able to instigate governments to serve their needs by
engaging in forceful imperialism abroad. This imperialism may
be described as "national exploitation" where an entire nation
has become a "collective capitalist" and exploits other
countries as the individual capitalist exploited his workers.
The Marxist competition between individual capitalists has

thus become a competition between nations; and it is this competition which has produced war. Thus the struggle for a socialist revolution has become a struggle between nations as well as between classes. On one side stand the capitalist nations, primarily England, France, Germany, and the United States, on the other stand the colonial countries, which must include Russia, since Russian industrialization is but a masked colonialism of foreign finance capital. A revolution then, in one of the colonial countries, cannot hope to succeed without the support of a revolution among the capitalist countries, otherwise the capitalist nations will simply suppress it through force of arms. *A Russian socialist revolution must base its ultimate hopes, and measure its progress against socialist revolutions in Western Europe.* But may such revolutions be expected? Yes, because despite the now-apparent corruption of the socialist parties of Western Europe, the world war is creating the objective conditions for such revolutions. Monopoly capitalism and imperialism are the highest stages of capitalism and have at last dragged mankind into the pit of universal destruction and killing. The awful experience of war is rapidly educating the European working classes to the essential truth that they are but cannon fodder to their greed crazed capitalist masters. Thus the world war brought on by imperialism will end as civil war, class war in which no one can doubt that the now-trained and militarily equipped working classes (who, after all, form the majority of the national armies) will triumph. *A Russian socialist revolution may well signal the opening of socialist class warfare in all the warring nations—and if Bolsheviks can win power in Russia, they will not have long to wait before they receive the massive, essential support of Western European socialist revolutions.* And this support will not only ensure the immediate victory of Bolshevism in Russia, it will also ensure the rapid and relatively painless socialist development of Russia as Western socialist nations make available their technology, industry and "know how," to a fraternal socialist state. Thus the objective conditions of the "inevitable" Marxist progression from feudalism through capitalism to socialism already exist—provided only that one takes an internationalist view.

In *Imperialism* Lenin very typically fuses Marxist "inevitability" with Marxist "will." That is, the coming socialist revolutions in Western Europe are assured by the march of history as illuminated by this study of its highest and final capitalist phase, while the socialist revolution in Russia remains to be made, guided and won by a *willful* program of revolutionary action.

Yet when the revolution first broke out, during the beginning of March 1917, neither Lenin nor any of the other exiled leaders, whether Bolshevik, Menshevik or Social Revolutionary, were prepared for it. They were as stunned by the onrush of events as was the tsarist autocracy.

It began on March 8 (International Woman's Day) with demonstrations by thousands of Saint Petersburg housewives protesting the newly introduced bread rationing. On following days they were joined by almost all the industrial workers of the capital. Huge crowds numbering hundreds of thousands took to the streets and battled the police. Even those ancient subduers of the people, the Cossacks, refused to intervene. When army regiments were ordered into action, they joined the revolutionary mobs. Within days the tsarist power in Saint Petersburg was broken, Nicholas had abdicated, and a revolutionary government had taken over. So rapidly and seemingly spontaneously did all this happen that many observers failed to discern the objective conditions which made it possible. Yet these conditions must be understood if the later, Bolshevik revolution is to be comprehensible.

Basic to the entire situation was the war. The ramshackle tsarist bureaucracy was simply not able to cope with the demands of modern war. Russian armies were sent into action pitifully underequipped and badly led. Russian soldiers died by the hundreds of thousands, then by the millions, sacrificed to the incompetence of the autocracy and the undefined (to them) ambitions of Russia's ruling classes. Retreat followed retreat, disaster piled upon disaster until widespread military mutiny became inevitable. At the same time the domestic economy of the country verged upon complete collapse. While workers in the cities suffered slow starvation from mismanaged rationing and distribution, they were treated to the spectacle of wild profiteering on the part of the aristocracy and the small middle classes. In the countryside the peasants felt the effects of this catastrophic war in the form of government commandeering of their crops and the drafting of their sons, brothers, and husbands for the army.

When the workers of Saint Petersburg finally rose, the army regiments Nicholas ordered into the streets against them were no longer the professional soldiers of 1905 but rather the peasant and worker draftees of 1917—men who were disinclined to shoot down their relatives and even less inclined to defend a government which would sooner or later ship them off to the slaughterhouse warfront. Furthermore, the workers themselves were no longer the overoptimistic and untrained mobs of 1905; between Russia's first revolution and her second, the Russian working class had been heavily propagandized and disciplined by Bolshevik and Menshevik agents while the peasantry had been ceaselessly agitated by the Social Revolutionaries. Finally, it must be pointed out that very large sections of the middle classes and the tsarist bureaucracy itself were prepared to aid the revolution in hopes that by controlling it they might prevent the worst "excesses."

The revolution of March 1917 produced a paradoxical "dual power" in Russia. The official government power supposedly rested with the Duma and a Provisional Government responsible to the Duma. But the workers in Saint Petersburg, Moscow, and other cities organized soviets which, while coexisting with the Provisional Government, exercised real power. The workers and soldiers would accept the authority of the Provisional Government only insofar as that authority was supported by the soviets. The fact that the soviets themselves did not proceed at once to assume all state power in Russia reflected the basic split in Russian Social Democratic thought.

The earliest soviets in the capitals were hastily assembled amalgams of local leaders in which Mensheviks predominated. The Menshevik theory that a Russian revolution must first establish the forms and conditions of capitalist democracy before socialism could triumph lay at the root of the matter. Actually holding the power, the soviets attempted to thrust it into the hands of the liberal middle classes thereby, so they thought, willfully carrying out one of Marxism's central theories. They were, in effect, holding the revolutionary masses in check, hoping to limit the revolution to the establishment of democratic forms and a free-enterprise capitalist industrial system. Later would be time enough, through democratic procedure, for the socialist parties to try to win power. But this attitude on the part of the Mensheviks (and many of the Bolsheviks), however orthodox in a Marxist sense, did not correspond to Russian realities.

The workers, soldiers, and peasants of Russia had risen

against the tsarist autocracy to win peace, bread, and the land. The soviet-supported Provisional Government, which succeeded that autocracy, could give them none of these things. It could not give them peace because, as middle-class liberal Russian politicians saw it, Russia was still an ally of Britain, France, and the United States in a world war against Germany. Should Russia make peace with Germany she would be prostrating herself before the savage ambitions of the German militarists and, most probably, suffer allied intervention to boot. And with a desperate war in progress, the Provisional Government saw no way to institute such reforms as the eight-hour day and wage hikes. As for a redistribution of the land to the peasantry, this would entail seizure of middle-class property and, most probably, open the floodgates to an endlessly savage peasant civil war. In short, Russian moderates and liberals could not accede to the basic demands of the nation's revolutionary masses without undermining their own economic position. So while they talked vaguely of the calling of a Constituent Assembly which would draft a democratic constitution for the country, they postponed immediate basic reforms.

Lenin returned to Russia in April 1917 with the aid of the German government which hoped that his presence there would serve to further confuse and undermine Russian resistance. From this fact, and also because it was later discovered that from time to time the Bolsheviks received money advanced by German agents, many have attempted to demonstrate that Lenin was a German spy and his policies shaped by the needs of the German government. This was untrue. Other Russian parties, such as the Mensheviks and Cadets received money surreptitiously from the British, French, and American governments; as for Lenin's attitude towards the kaiser's Germany, he lived in daily expectation and hope of a socialist revolution in that country.

Immediately upon arriving in Saint Petersburg, Lenin began hammering away at his principal theses: All state power must be assumed by the soviets; the Bolsheviks must place themselves at the head of the developing peasant revolution and help the peasants to simply seize the land; opposition socialist parties such as the Mensheviks and Social Revolutionaries must be exposed as objective allies of the middle classes; immediate peace must be made—peace at almost any price. Many of Lenin's Bolshevik followers were appalled by this program. What of the immediate tasks of revolutionary administration, what of the Provisional Government, what of the Constituent Assembly? "We don't need any parliamentary republic," Lenin insisted, "We don't need any bourgeois democracy. We don't need any government except the Soviet of Workers', Soldiers', and Peasants' Deputies!"

And through the following months, while liberal Provisional Governments came and went, amid various plots and counterplots and abortive attempts at counterrevolution, Lenin and the Bolsheviks (joined now by Trotsky who, having hurried back to Russia at last made his peace with Lenin's faction and assumed tactical leadership in Saint Petersburg) clung to their extremist policies. How could Lenin have been so certain he was right?

First of all, he was willing to make immediate peace with the detested German militarists because he felt sure that no matter how severe the terms they might impose, the settlement would soon be swept away in the imminent socialist revolution which would soon break out in Germany. This same socialist revolution would sweep over England and France and effectively prevent their intervention in Russian affairs. As for the immediate demands of the industrial workers for bread, better wages, better working conditions—since the Provisional Government could not meet these demands, they could only be achieved by *revolutionary* activity. Likewise the peasant demand for land could only be met by a deepening and widening of the revolution. The peasants were, in any case, already seizing the land, and unless the Bolsheviks led them and used this moment of greatest revolutionary activity among the peasantry, they would soon be confronted with a counterrevolutionary class of small landowning farmers that would be fatal to the further socialist revolution. Lenin said, "We are not charlatans. We must base ourselves only on the consciousness of the masses. . . . Our line will prove right. All the oppressed will come to us. . . . They have no other way out."

Lenin proved absolutely right. It is idle to speculate about the various turns the revolution might have taken. Only the Bolsheviks offered the Russian masses a program which promised immediate relief to a suffering which had become intolerable to them. Thus when, on November 7, 1917, the Bolsheviks, under the tactical direction of Trotsky, seized state power from the inept hands of the Provisional

Government, there was but little bloodshed and sparse fighting. The Bolsheviks had already won large majorities in the Saint Petersburg and Moscow Soviets; the regiments, the industrial workers, and the peasantry were overwhelmingly prepared to accept Bolshevik leadership. The Bolshevik revolution in Russia was accomplished not in those few days in November—it had been accomplished all during the eight months which separated the first from the second phase of the revolution of 1917. As Trotsky observed: "The bourgeois classes had expected barricades, flaming conflagrations, looting, rivers of blood. In reality a silence reigned more terrible than all the thunders of the world. The social ground shifted noiselessly like a revolving stage, bringing forward the popular masses, carrying away to limbo the rulers of yesterday."

Chapter Nine

FROM LENIN TO STALIN

> Enemies are gleeful that fifteen years after the revolution the soviet country is still but little like a kingdom of universal well-being. . . . Capitalism required a hundred years to elevate science and technique to the heights and plunge humanity into the hell of war and crisis. To socialism its enemies allow only fifteen years to create and furnish a terrestrial paradise. We took no such obligation upon ourselves. We never set these dates.
>
> —*Leon Trotsky*

In the days immediately following the Bolshevik revolution, *Pravda*, the party newspaper, declared: "They wanted us to take the power alone, so that we alone should have to contend with the terrible difficulties confronting the country. . . . So be it! We take the power alone, relying upon the voice of the country. . . . But having taken the power, we will deal with the enemies of the Revolution and its saboteurs with an iron hand. . . . We will give them the dictatorship of the proletariat. . . ."

The statement was not quite accurate. It was certainly true that most Mensheviks and Social Revolutionaries would in no way cooperate with the new Bolshevik regime, which they felt must collapse very shortly. But some among the Mensheviks, and a group of so-called Left Social Revolutionaries tried to talk the Bolsheviks into basing their power on a coalition of socialist groups and parties. To those who suggested this, Trotsky, at a Congress of Soviets held even while Bolshevik patrols were still arresting members of the old Provisional Government, shouted, "No, a compromise is no good here . . . to all who make like proposals, we must say, 'You are pitiful isolated individuals; you are bankrupt; your role is played out. Go where you belong from now on—into the rubbish can of history!' "

This was not mere rhetoric. Confident in the historical logic of their position and in the support of the vast majority of peasants, workers, and soldiers, the Bolsheviks assumed absolute state power in Russia—alone. Lenin, addressing that same Congress of Soviets after the Winter Palace fell, said simply, "We shall now proceed to construct the socialist order." He immediately proposed that peace be made, private land ownership abolished, and that a government composed exclusively of Bolsheviks (with a few Left Social Revolutionaries at first) be established. These measures were at once adopted. Lenin became president of the All-Russian Congress of Soviets; Trotsky became commissar for Foreign Affairs. Decrees and laws flooded out of Saint Petersburg in a torrent. Banks and all industrial enterprises were nationalized; the merchant marine was nationalized; the stock exchange was abolished; the right of inheritance was abolished; gold was declared a state monopoly; all government debts were declared null and void; the criminal courts were replaced by revolutionary tribunals in which any citizen could act as judge or lawyer; the old strict marriage and divorce laws were swept away; church lands were seized and religious teaching forbidden in the schools; the old Russian calendar was discarded in favor of the Western calendar; the Russian alphabet was modernized; all titles of rank or aristocracy were disallowed; conservative newspapers were suppressed "temporarily."

But although Lenin and the Bolsheviks acted as if they were in absolute control of the nation, this was far from the case. In the provinces bloody struggles between Bolshevik-dominated soviets and more conservative groups now erupted. The Ukraine, seeing in developing chaos a chance to establish an independent nation, organized a separate government. Various of the former tsarist generals began to raise independent military units of the disaffected and to negotiate with agents of the Allied powers for support. Within a matter of weeks after the Bolshevik seizure, Russia slid into a bloody civil war. Under various pretexts, British, French, Japanese, and American troops all intervenced in the ensuing struggle. As the tsarist armies dissolved through mass desertion, the Bolsheviks could meet this mounting flood of threats only through the creation of a new army. This new Red Army was to be commanded by Trotsky and, after three years of fighting, was to emerge victorious. Nonetheless, Bolshevik Russia was to lose the former tsarist domains of Poland, Finland, Latvia, Estonia, Lithuania, and portions of Rumania.

Peace with Imperial Germany, the peace of Brest-Litovsk by which Russia temporarily lost one third of its European land, most of its industrial power, and a quarter of its population, was signed after much wavering and discussion on March 3, 1918. The harshness of its terms would, Lenin felt, soon be nullified by the coming socialist revolution in Germany. Yet this blow to the Allied war effort (very many German divisions were now freed to mount a new assault on the Western Front) convinced the British, French, and American governments that they had been correct when they refused to recognize the new Bolshevik regime in Russia.

It is not our purpose here, however, to trace the details of the chaotic civil war and war against Allied intervention which now ensued. Rather more instructive would prove an analysis of how successfully Lenin and his associates were able to apply their theories to the immediate needs of governing Russia.

The Bolsheviks who seized power in 1917 had made themselves into just the kind of highly disciplined, centralized, conspiratorial party that Lenin had desired. It seemed then that his prescription for organization had proved to be the correct one. Theoretically this highly disciplined party was now at the head of the working class and peasantry and would act on their behalf in imposing a dictatorship of the proletariat. What this meant in practical terms was illustrated by the Bolshevik reaction to the Constituent Assembly which met in Saint Petersburg on January 18, 1918. This Assembly, which was supposed to draft a constitution for Russia, had been the goal and dream of almost all Russian revolutionaries for a century. Elections to it, held after the Bolshevik seizure of power, returned a majority of Social Revolutionaries (58%) and a minority of Bolsheviks (30%) with a scattering of Mensheviks and Liberals. Holding that the representation in the Assembly did not accurately reflect the feelings of the masses, the Bolsheviks dispersed it at the points of bayonets—just as the tsar had often dispersed the old Duma. It appeared then that the "dictatorship of the proletariat" was to be expressed as the dictatorship of the Bolshevik party; and that, in turn, due to the organization Lenin had long since developed for it, meant the dictatorship of the party leadership which was now the government of Russia. This dictatorship soon armed itself with a new secret police (the dreaded *Cheka*) and began executing and imprisoning its enemies. Apologists have held that this was inevitable, given the chaos and civil war that wracked the nation. Possibly. But it was even more inevitable, in fact, certain, given the entire history and development of Lenin's political policy. The Bolshevik party that came to power in Russia had, organizationally, no built-in means for democratic expansion, no built-in method of arriving at decisions on the basis of free discussion. Instead it had a tradition of centralized, dictatorial leadership—and that tradition was all it could bring to bear when faced with the problems of actually governing Russia.

But all of this was to be temporary, in view of the fact that socialist revolution would now sweep the West and enable the Russian Bolsheviks to relax their stern measures as they received international support and aid. What of Lenin's predictions in *Imperialism?* In fact a socialist revolution did break out in Germany in November 1918, bringing an end to the German war effort as well as the kaiser's government. Furthermore, a wave of socialist sympathy for the Russian revolution soon made itself felt in France and England, although in neither country did anything remotely resembling a socialist uprising take place. So in part, at least, Lenin was proved right. The Treaty of Brest-Litovsk was swept away and forgotten, and the Allied nations soon found that public opinion would support no further intervention in Russia. In that sense it may be said that socialist feeling in the West helped to preserve the infant soviet state from conquest. But "socialist feeling" in the West remained just that—a sympathy expressed by working-class parties. The German socialist revolution was quickly suppressed by the German Army, a Hungarian socialist revolution ended in bloody repression. By the end of 1919 it became apparent to Lenin and his followers that while they would be left alone to rule Russia, they could expect no aid, economic or otherwise from Western lands.

It will be recalled that Lenin had attempted to get around the iron Marxist insistence that communism could emerge only in the most advanced industrial nations by elevating the Marxist view to an international level. Russia could be considered, *in toto* as part of a European proletariat; when the other European working classes, ignited by the spark of the Bolshevik revolution, should win power, then it would be seen that communism could prevail in Russia as a part of an all-European communist order emerging from a highly industrial continent-wide society. When the proletariat in the rest of Europe failed to seize power, Russia found itself an isolated, underindustrialized, dictatorially ruled communist state, attempting to maintain itself not according to Marxist predictions, but *in spite of them*.

With the Russian economy in ruins as the civil war ended in 1920, and no hope apparent of industrial aid from the West, Lenin developed a strategy for economic survival which he called the New Economic Policy. This would provide for continued absolute domination by the government of large essential industries such as steel, coal, oil, the railroads, etc., but would allow a certain amount of "free enterprise" on the lower levels of the economy, especially in agriculture. What Lenin was proposing, in fact, was not dissimilar to the old tsarist economy: state capitalism supplemented by individual capitalism. Only by this tactical retreat, this concession to the ancient human motives of personal ambition and private profit did Lenin see any immediate hope of restoring the Russian economy. But the retreat was to remain tactical—political control was exercised ever more tightly by the Bolshevik state apparatus, and when the Russian economy should have restored itself, there was little doubt that all concessions to private enterprise would come to an end. By 1922 Lenin had even gone so far as to invite foreign investment in Russian industry! A trickle of foreign capital and foreign technicians began to flow into Russia.

Whether Lenin, with his highly pragmatic outlook, would ever have modified his Marxist views in the light of experience was, however, to remain unknown. In 1923 he suffered a stroke, and on January 21, 1924, he died. Winston Churchill, a bitter enemy of the Bolsheviks later declared, "He alone could have found the way back to the causeway. . . . The Russian people were left floundering in the bog. Their worst misfortune was his birth . . . their next worse, his death." But neither the Russian people nor history can accept this evaluation as true. Few today, among either the friends or the enemies of the Soviet state would dispute the justice of the renaming of Saint Petersburg, the city of Peter the Great, Leningrad, the city of Lenin. Vladimir Ulyanov had accomplished the historical task he had set for himself; he had overthrown the tsarist autocracy. The intellectual weapons he employed in this task were, as we have seen, developed over many years by many men in many countries. Lenin and his associates were the first to open a historical lock with the key of Marxist theory. The fact that the door they swung wide open onto a vista far different from the one they expected should in no way detract from the importance of this fact.

The mantle of leadership was not to descend from Lenin to any of his oldest or erstwhile closest followers, but rather to a former editor of *Pravda,* a man of little theoretical skill but vast ruthlessness, Joseph Stalin.

Joseph Djugashvili (pronounced *Jugashvili*) was born in the tiny Georgian village of Gori, on December 21, 1879. Russian Georgia is a trans-Caucasian area bordering on Iran and Turkey and was, at the time of Djugashvili's birth, a museum of peoples and cultures. It had long been the crossroads for migrations and invasions from Asia into Europe and from the north into the Middle East. Many languages were spoken there (Djugashvili's first tongue was Georgian, he did not learn Russian until he was ten years old) and, in the face of tsarist oppression, the various peoples (one might almost say "tribes") clung to their ancient native ways.

Joseph's father, Vissarion Djugashvili was a poor peasant who, losing his small plot of land, became a factory worker and died when Joseph was eleven. His mother, a devoutly religious Russian Orthodox sent young Joseph to a religious school when he was nine years old. When he was fifteen he enrolled at the Tiflis Theological Seminary in order to prepare for the priesthood. Tiflis was the provincial capital of Georgia and there, for the first time, Joseph seems to have come into contact with revolutionary student circles. He seems to have been an apt pupil, both of religious and Marxist dogmas; he seems to have been expelled from the Seminary in 1898 for political activities. That year, or perhaps a year later, Djugashvili seems to have joined an underground Social Democratic activist group and begun to agitate among factory workers and peasants in the region.

If the above paragraph repeats the word "seems" several

times it is because at present it is all but impossible to sift historical fact from historical fancy in the early career of Joseph Djugashvili. For when this man became head of the Soviet Union, years later, he and his underlings undertook a rewriting of his personal history, a falsification of records and documents, a strong-scale purge of any who might remember the truth. The entire huge Soviet government apparatus was turned to the task of "creating" a suitable personal history for Joseph Djugashvili which has all but obliterated the true facts.

In any event, it is certain that on May 1, 1901, he was involved in a workers' strike and parade. Police and army units fired upon the demonstration and began arresting its leadership. Djugashvili escaped to his native Gori where he hid out for nearly a year. But he was finally found and arrested in 1902. He was imprisoned for many months and then sentenced to a three-year term of exile in Siberia. But on January 5, 1904, Djugashvili succeeded in escaping. Soon he reappeared in Tiflis, Batum, and other towns of Georgia.

The Georgian Social Democratic party at that time was one of the strongest in all Russia and, though it was dominated by Mensheviks, Lenin's Bolshevik faction was growing rapidly. The splits and internecine conflicts of the exile leaders in Switzerland and at the various Congresses in London and Brussels were not of much interest in faraway Trans-Caucasia. In Georgia Mensheviks and Bolsheviks worked in apparent harmony. It was not to be until 1913, on the very eve of the First World War, that the Bolshevik faction was to break loose—and many of the local Bolsheviks (Djugashvili among them), when they flocked to Saint Petersburg following the first March Revolution, enthusiastically supported the first Menshevik-dominated Soviet, much to Lenin's annoyance.

When Joseph Djugashvili returned from exile to Georgia he married a peasant woman named Ekaterina Svanidze by whom he had a son. But two years later, in 1906, Ekaterina died. A political associate of Djugashvili's attended her funeral and records: "When the modest procession came to the cemetery gate, [Djugashvili] firmly pressed my hand, pointed to the coffin and said, 'Soso, this creature softened my stony heart. She is dead and with her have died my last warm feelings for all human beings.' He placed his right hand over his heart. 'It is all so desolate here inside, so unutterably desolate!' "

This tale, like so many of the memories of Djugashvili's early years may or may not be true. But it accurately predicts the kind of man Djugashvili was to become. Shortly thereafter he was to adopt his conspiratorial name of Stalin (man of steel).

Stalin, although a tireless organizer and agitator, took no leading role during the Revolution of 1905—indeed he first met Lenin only after the stormy events of that year. What seems to have attracted Lenin most about the young Georgian was his fanatic devotion to the Bolshevik party machine; he was an "apparatchik" par excellence and could be depended upon to carry out any task, provided only the Party (i.e. Lenin) demanded it. It was well that Stalin was capable of such loyalty, for the tasks set for him by Lenin beginning about 1908 were dangerous in the extreme.

The entire question of financing Bolshevik activities had long wracked the Social Democratic party. Contributions from members could only be extremely modest; donations from wealthy liberal patrons were fitful. To Lenin and his followers it seemed reasonable that funds should simply be "expropriated" from Russian banks and industries—that is, stolen. The Mensheviks and a majority of Bolsheviks protested against this method of fund-raising. Lenin, seeming to go along with the majority, actually secretly encouraged those of his followers who were bold enough to continue their armed robberies, the moneys going into the Bolshevik faction's treasury, rather than into the coffers of the Social Democrats. It was Stalin's fortitude and ability in directing these armed robberies which first won him Lenin's admiration. On several celebrated occasions, armed bands of Georgian Bolsheviks succeeded in robbing huge amounts of money from local banks, industrial payrolls, and even Army paymasters.

In 1913 Stalin was arrested and again sent into exile in Siberia. Liberated by the Revolution in March 1917, he hurried to Saint Petersburg. There he took over direction of *Pravda* and, until Lenin's return from exile, preached a program of moderation and cooperation with the Mensheviks and other Socialists in the Saint Petersburg Soviet. When Lenin hammered home his April Theses, upon his return, Stalin obediently reversed his position. But as late as September 1917 he opposed Lenin on the feasibility of an immediate Bolshevik take-over. Once again, when Lenin insisted the time had come to strike, Stalin changed his mind and supported the October Bolshevik uprising in party debates.

After the Bolshevik Revolution, Stalin, undoubtedly because of his non-Russian origins and his experience in the trans-Caucasus, was appointed Commisar of Nationalities in the Soviet Union. From this position he was able to build up a personal following among Bolsheviks far from the main cities, who became used to following orders signed *J. Stalin*. Later he was appointed general secretary of the Communist party—a post for which his fanatic devotion to party bureaucracy admirably fitted him.

The picture which now emerges of Joseph Stalin is one of a man of undoubted courage and determination, but with little imagination and almost no personal theoretical capabilities. It is a picture of a man who has chosen the revolution as his profession, the picture of the perfect bureaucrat. And as the perfect bureaucrat, in the days following 1917, of the consolidation of Bolshevik power in Russia, by serving the party he served himself. A ruthless administrator with a capacious appetite for detail, he used the burgeoning government bureaucracy to build for himself a personal following among bureaucrats as uninspired but as devoted to the acquisition and administration of power as himself. When, following Lenin's death in 1924, a struggle for leadership commenced, Stalin had little difficulty in using his party "machine" to secure power for himself. Slowly, over subsequent years, he exiled or murdered almost all of the Old Bolsheviks who might have contested his supremacy. Trotsky, for example, was driven into foreign exile at the end of the twenties and, when this failed to silence him, he was murdered by a Stalinist agent in 1940.

But it is not really necessary to seek the seeds of totalitarian dictatorship in the personality of Stalin. We have seen that the Bolshevik party (it was renamed the Communist party in 1920) was organized as a totalitarian apparatus. If Lenin's personal restraint and political good sense mitigated its tyranny during the years of his leadership, there was no built-in guarantee that a successor might not wield the party like a weapon to gain absolute personal power. Years before, Trotsky had warned: "The organization of the party will take the place of the party; the Central Committee will take the place of the organization; and finally, the dictator will take the place of the Central Committee." This was exactly what happened—and it would undoubtedly have happened no matter who succeeded in winning power after 1924.

The transformation of the Leninist revolutionary dictatorship into a permanent party and personal dictatorship in Russia depended not only on the inherent tyrannical aspect of party organization, but also on objective exterior factors. Prime among these was the fact that the socialist revolutions which Lenin had so eagerly awaited in the West never transpired. True, as we have seen, socialist power in Western Europe was sufficient to prevent the military strangulation of the infant Soviet state by capitalist countries. But it was not sufficient to provide the industrial aid, to furnish the international industrial base upon which the Russian revolution, according to Lenin's revision of Marx, ought to have depended. Thus Russia, after 1917, found itself both ruined and isolated. Lenin had attempted to resolve the problems of revitalizing Russian industry through his New Economic Policy, through a tactical retreat into small-scale capitalism at home and tentative cooperation with capitalist industrialized states abroad. Stalin, however, declared that Russia would have to "build communism in one country." To follow Lenin's New Economic Policy might open the way for Russia to slip back into capitalism; to liquidate the New Economic Policy would be to alienate foreign capital.

So be it! Stalin declared. A communist Russia would industrialize itself with the capital available—the labor power of the Russian people. Like all good Marxists, Stalin devoted not a little time to reinterpreting Marx and Lenin in order to find theoretical support for his position. His principal work along these lines was *Foundations of Leninism,* a massive book he published after Lenin's death. The unimaginative, dry, and repetitious text (in which the catechismical training of Stalin's years at the Seminary in Tiflis is evident) enshrined certain of Lenin's teachings as dogma—just as Lenin had enshrined Marx. But Lenin's teachings had been largely political, so such tactical conceptions as party discipline and centralized organization now became universal and permanent theoretical laws.

Basically, Stalin held that all things and phenomena are interrelated. Furthermore, all things are in evolutionary flux toward a higher degree of organization. This evolutionary flux develops in "leaps" as the result of sudden accumulations—that is to say, a quantitative difference makes a qualitative difference. This conception, derived from Hegel, may be stated simply as the observation that if sufficient numbers of things, events, people, are accumulated, then the nature of the individual thing, event, person, undergoes a change. Thus, for example, an individual's personal reactions may elude prediction. If the individual is part of a large crowd, his reactions become statistically more predictable. If the individual is part of a huge crowd—say a nation— statistically his reactions become completely predictable. Objectively he is no longer an individual, simply a pre- dictably responsive number in a vast accumulation of numbers. The very "quality" of being an individual thus changes. Furthermore, he personally feels himself changed in his individual nature from what he was in isolation to what he has become in a vast mass. Applying this to eco- nomic events, Stalin could point out that Russian industrial- ization, up to a certain point, would simply make of the nation a farming society armed with industry; but beyond that certain point of industrialization Russia would change its very nature as it became an industrialized society that also undertook agriculture in order to feed itself.

It will be seen that Stalin's views were admirably suited to form the theoretical basis of a ruthlessly exploitive and manipulative society in which individuals, no less than industries, were to be whipped into their new roles accord- ing to preconceived notions of their natures and necessities in the mass. Those who resisted would, by definition, become enemies of society—that is, of the state. They might think of themselves subjectively as loyal, if critical citizens; ob- jectively their "obstructionism" would be high treason.

Having established himself in power through the murder or exile of those older associates of Lenin who would not cooperate, Stalin, in 1927, began to reshape Russia in his own image. His solution to the agricultural problem, to the scarcity of food, was the industrialization of agriculture, its mechanization through the introduction of machinery. But such mechanization could only be carried out efficiently on a large scale, collectively. Therefore he reduced some 25 million individual peasant farms to 200,000 collective farms. The peasants, who had just won their land a few years before, resisted their transformation into agricultural laborers on state property by burning their fields, killing their livestock, and even fighting pitched battles with police and Army units sent to enforce the new decrees. Stalin's response was to starve, kill, and exile all who opposed his plans. It has been estimated that between 1927 and 1929 no less than 5 million peasants were killed through military action or enforced starvation, and another 10 million deported to the icy wastes of Siberia. Not since the time of the Mongol Khans had such wholesale massacre descended on the Russian land.

Russian workers found themselves as regimented as Russian farmers. They were tied to their jobs as completely as the old serfs had been tied to their masters' estates. Inefficiency on the job, absenteeism, were classified now as treason and could be punished by exile to Siberia or incarceration in one of the many dreadful labor camps established by Stalin's secret police. This reign of terror was supplemented in the mid-thirties by an incentive program known as the "Stakhanov Movement." Named for a worker (Stakhanov) who had overfulfilled his production norms, the program offered better rations, higher pay, medals, and even, on occasion a trip to Moscow to shake hands with the top government officials, to workers who exceeded their expected daily output.

Beginning in 1928, Stalin introduced the first of a series of Five-Year Plans for the expansion of Russian industry and the mechanization of Russian agriculture. Typically, Stalin found his first plan amid the dusty files of the old tsarist regime. Sprucing it up and claiming it for his own, he used it not only as a means of rationalizing Russian economy, but also as a political weapon in his rise to absolute power. During the thirties Five-Year Plan succeeded Five-Year Plan (sometimes overlapping) with bewildering rapidity. By the beginning of World War II three had been put into effect. The first Five-Year Plan concentrated on the construction of new factories, hydroelectric stations, and transportation networks; the second on improving labor productivity by rationalizing production methods; the third was intended to coordinate the growth of mechanized agriculture with the new needs of an emerging industrial society, but it failed. One of the reasons it failed was because by 1937, when it was introduced, Russia lay in the grip of widespread terror as Stalin instituted his Great Purges.

Actually the purges may be said to have started when the Leningrad Party Leader, Sergei M. Kirov, an old associate of Lenin's, was assassinated on December 1, 1934. It was later to be revealed that Stalin was an accomplice in this murder. He used it as an excuse to begin the systematic murder, imprisonment, and exile of anyone and everyone who might pose even the most remote threat to his personal power. Almost all the Old Bolsheviks, the men and women who had struggled with Lenin and Trotsky to make the revolution, were executed by the secret police. All those newer members of the Communist party in Russia who might conceivably have supported the Old Bolsheviks were in turn arrested and either shot or exiled. Fully half of the top leadership of the Communist party and of the Soviet government was wiped out between 1934 and 1939. In 1937 the Great Purges extended to the Red Army and Navy; 75,000 officers were executed, among them the top commanders of the armed forces. Then the terror reached factory managers, technicians, collective-farm directors, professional men such as lawyers, doctors, artists. In the end no one could tell how many people perished in Stalin's purges— estimates run from 500,000 to 5 million—but the psychological scars of these years of terror are still evident in the attitudes of Soviet citizens to this day.

Of what were these many thousands of victims accused? Basically, of high treason. The details of the accusations varied, but they centered around charges of conspiracy to undermine or overthrow the Soviet state. In several "show trials" put on for the benefit of domestic and foreign observers, victim after victim "confessed" to having plotted with Trotsky, Wall Street, the German General Staff, International Bankers; any suitable or unsuitable group, for the destruction of the Soviet regime. The world was appalled to see and hear some of the most important Soviet leaders cringe in open court and admit themselves guilty of the most improbable crimes—crimes which sometimes could be easily shown to be utterly imaginary. And the world wondered. Why did these men, who must have known they were doomed to death anyhow, debase themselves by reciting litanies of self-accusation before the world and posterity?

There were several reasons. Some hoped, by cooperating with their executioners, to save their families from persecution; others broke down under continuous and savage police brutality; still others, however (and these were the most enlightening cases), evidently felt that even by offering themselves as cooperative sacrifices to Stalin's terror they could still serve communism. For it must be remembered that many of these men, especially the most powerful, had devoted their entire lives to the establishment of the Russian

Communist state. To admit to themselves that the ideal for which they had suffered and struggled all their lives had turned into a tyranny far worse than the old tsarist autocracy would have been to rob their lives of meaning.

Decades later, after Stalin's death, Soviet leaders were to publicly state that the dictator had been insane. This was undoubtedly true. The Great Purges bear all the marks of a desperate paranoid fantasy. But to ascribe all the suffering, the terror, the blood to the deranged mind of Stalin begs several vital questions. How was it possible, for example, that a madman could rise to the leadership of the Russian Communist party and the Soviet government? How was it possible that Communist party officials and government employees could cooperate for so many years with a man far advanced in paranoia? How was it possible that the Russian people, who had demonstrated such perseverance and courage in the overthrow of the tsarist regime, could fail to rise again against this newer and infinitely more savage tyranny?

The answers to these questions lie at the root of the Bolshevik revision of Marxism and in the sources of Russian history. Marx had predicted a socialist revolution upon highly developed, capitalist industrialization and the rise of a powerful bourgeoisie. Without either of these elements the new Soviet state had to create an industrial society in a matter of decades. The lack of capital, managerial skills, and technical ability was made up for by the brawn and blood of Russian workers and farmers. It was they who were sacrificed to the forced industrialization of the Soviet Union. Marx had foreseen the emergence of powerful socialist parties which would be drawn from and place themselves at the head of organized working classes, working classes which would form the vast majority of the citizens of any given nation. But the Russian Bolsheviks, lacking a majority, highly developed working class to begin with, had created their party as a dictatorial apparatus which would not only lead, but unquestioningly direct the Russian proletariat and use it as a tool, not only to overthrow tsarism, but also to suppress the peasant majority in Russia. Under Russian circumstances, the "dictatorship of the proletariat," which meant the dictatorship of the Communist party and, eventually, the dictatorship of the single most powerful individual in that party, threatened to become a permanent way of life. Marx had looked forward to the "withering away of the state" when socialism should have been achieved. His "dictatorship of the proletariat" was only meant to be a transitional phase. But in Russia, the state, in its political, economic, and social aspects had first to be created before anyone could so much as dream of its "withering away." And in creating that state, Stalin, no less than the entire Communist party, found himself thrown back on the methods of tsarist tyranny—made infinitely harsher by the baleful lights of a "scientific" approach.

And the vast masses of the Russian people—peasants for the most part, lacking education, lacking any tradition of freedom, lacking any experience of free political activity, oppressed for centuries by poverty—were not (as Marx had foreseen they would not be) prepared for the establishment of free, democratic institutions within the tsar's former empire. Enough for them that factories sprouted, that schools opened, that the old masters had been routed; the new master was the state, but they were constantly assured that they ultimately controlled the state. The self-proclaimed goal of the Communist regime was the production of a new "Soviet Man," one who would be, presumably, fit to enter the paradise of socialism. To this ideal every human distinction was to be sacrificed until it appeared that "Soviet Man" was to be no more than a robot extension of the huge, self-sustaining government bureaucracy.

Later we will examine in greater detail both the structure of Soviet society and the success or lack of it with which it has approached its goals. Here it suffices to point out that under Stalin the Russian Revolution came to its inevitable end. As Feodor Dostoyevsky, the great nineteenth-century Russian novelist had predicted of a Russian revolution, "Starting from unlimited liberty, it will arrive at unlimited despotism."

Part Three

THE GIFT OF TONGUES

Chapter Ten

EXPORTING THE REVOLUTION

> Is everything that is gathering force, underground,
> in the dark, in the night, in little hidden rooms out
> of sight of governments and policemen . . . is all this
> going to burst forth some fine morning and set the
> world on fire?
>
> —*Henry James*

The Second International, it will be recalled, fell to pieces in 1914 over the question of whether or not socialists would support the war efforts of their various nations. The leading socialist parties of Europe, the French and the German, had succumbed, like their bourgeois enemies, like their governments, like the human race, to the passions of nationalism and patriotism. Likewise the Menshevik section of the Russian Social Democratic party, and even a few Bolsheviks, had followed the lead of Plekhanov and the older leaders in rallying to the cause of Russian victory in World War I. Lenin and a small band of the most devoted Bolsheviks, stunned and enraged by this continentwide betrayal of socialist principles found themselves very much isolated in their uncompromising antiwar position. Lenin, characteristically, sat down and composed *Seven Theses Against the War* in which he briefly extrapolated his views from *Imperialism* to expose the ignoble motives of World War I and in which he proposed to turn the "war of imperialist brigandage" into civil, class war throughout Europe. But, as always, Lenin's prime concern was with how the war could be made to serve the interests of the revolution inside Russia.

But Lenin's Bolsheviks were not the only socialists in

Europe to oppose the war in a serious way. The German
socialists, Karl Liebknecht and Rosa Luxemburg, spent many
months in jail during the war, and leaders of several European socialist parties met twice, once in Zimmerwald and
once in Kienthal (both in neutral Switzerland) to discuss
measures for ending the mass slaughter. These leaders represented only small fractions of their national parties—and
Lenin promptly split with them over the most obscure
differences. Yet it was to the antiwar socialists of Western
Europe that the Russian Bolsheviks turned in the dark days
of 1918 and 1919 in an attempt to spark off that European
socialist revolution without which they still believed their
own was doomed to failure.

A distinction between socialists and communists might well
have been apparent much earlier—it could be based on the
differences between Lenin's tactics and strategy and those of
his Menshevik opponents; or it might have been established
on the basis of those who accepted Bernstein's revision of
Marx and those who did not. But the founding of the Third
International in Moscow during the first week in March
1919 is generally accepted as the most convenient occasion
on which to introduce a permanent distinction. Socialists
and communists both based their ideologies on the teachings
of Marx and Engels; both believed in the communal ownership of the means of production, etc. But henceforth the
word communism would acquire a much more specific
meaning; it would mean the acceptance of Marxist doctrines
*as modified, explained, and manipulated by Lenin and his
heirs.* Eventually, communism as an ideology would be all
but indistinguishable from an apology for the day-to-day
needs of specifically Russian foreign policy.

Only thirty-five delegates (hand-picked by Lenin) attended
the founding congress of the Third (Communist) International, and of these only five came from outside Russia. But
their presence served Lenin's purpose, which was to establish
an organization (it would be called the Comintern) which
could claim allegiance from the more radical sections of
foreign socialist parties. The Comintern was to function, in
the first instance, as an instrument through which separate
Bolshevik, or as we shall call them from now on, Communist
parties might be established in European countries in opposition to the older socialist parties. It was also to function
as an instrument through which Russian advice, direction,

agents, money, and arms might be supplied to foreign communist parties to help them in their revolutionary work.

This work was of the highest possible urgency to Lenin's government as World War I came to an end. The Russian revolution was to have been, in Leninist theory, the signal for European-wide socialist revolutions. Without those revolutions the Russian leaders were sure that their own cause would fail; yet they saw their hopes dashed even given the propitious conditions of chaos which engulfed postwar Europe. The fate of the German Communists was typical.

The more radical of the German Social Democrats, those who opposed any aid to the kaiser's war effort, had either been jailed or had gone underground during the war. But as Germany went down to defeat, these radical socialists, under the leadership of Karl Liebknecht and Rosa Luxemburg, established the Sparticist League—an organization which came to be regarded as the foundation of the German Communist party. When the kaiser abdicated on November 9, 1918, on the advice of the German General Staff, political power in Germany was fractioned. Part of it fell into the hands of the regular majority German Social Democratic party; a smaller part fell into the hands of the Sparticists. The balance of power between these two groups was held by the General Staff and its retreating, but not completely disorganized field armies. While Social Democratic leaders Philipp Scheidemann and Friedrich Ebert proclaimed a German Republic from the balconies of the Reichstag in Berlin on that fateful November 9, the Sparticists, about a mile away were proclaiming a German Soviet Republic from the balconies of the former Imperial Palace. The General Staff, choosing the lesser of what appeared to it twin evils, decided to support the Social Democrats. Accordingly, an agreement was secretly made between the General Staff and Provisional Government President Ebert. On January 10, 1919, regular German Army units entered Berlin and began rounding up Sparticists. Hundreds of workers were shot during what came to be known as "bloody week" in Berlin. Karl Liebknecht and Rosa Luxemburg were captured and brutally murdered by officers of the Guards Cavalry Division. Their deaths momentarily weakened the German Communist party, but by no means signaled the end of the struggle.

In March 1919 the newly established state of Hungary adopted a Communist government under the leadership of an ex-Russian prisoner of war, Béla Kun. A few weeks later, in April 1919, German Communists established a separate Soviet Regime in Bavaria. Both of these revolutionary attempts were quickly suppressed; the Hungarian by Allied-supported Rumanian troops, the Bavarian by German Army units and irregular veterans' groups which were the spiritual forerunners of the Nazis. Thus by the spring of 1919 it became apparent that Communist revolutions were not going to succeed in Western Europe. At the Third Congress of the Third International, held in Moscow in 1921 (and attended by hundreds of delegates from all over the world, in contrast to the First Congress), Trotsky declared: "History has given the bourgeoisie a fairly long breathing spell. . . . The revolution is not so obedient, so tame, that it can be led on a leash, as we imagined."

Yet Lenin, faced by the collapse of revolutionary hopes in Western Europe, was still convinced that the capitalist states would never permit the new Russian Soviet government to survive. The Allied intervention on behalf of anti-Bolshevik forces during the Russian Civil War in 1918 and 1919 seemed to support this view. War weariness and immediate political problems at home might divert capitalist attention from Communist Russia for the moment; eventually the ring of capitalist enemies of the Soviets would strike. Although the bastions of capitalism in the West had proven themselves too strong for frontal attack, as the German and Hungarian experience demonstrated, perhaps there yet remained some "weak links," in the chain of bourgeois power?

Lenin had already postulated, in *Imperialism*, the theory that capitalism had become an international force exploiting, in Africa and Asia, an international proletariat. Capitalist power in the twentieth century was then dependent upon imperialism and colonialism. The submerged nations of the world were, then, the "weak links" in the capitalist chain. And these were the areas to which communists must devote their principal energies. Even if revolution could not be immediately fomented in colonial lands, continued unrest and turmoil there might well keep the capitalist nations sufficiently off balance to prevent their attack on the Soviet homeland.

Thus after 1921 the Soviet program of exporting communist revolution to other countries took on two different aspects. In the capitalist countries of Europe and North America, communist parties were established or, where they existed, brought under Russian control with the long-range purpose of radicalizing labor movements, destroying opposition socialist parties, self-educating members in the rigors of revolutionary struggle, agitating publicly for foreign policies which would benefit Soviet Russia, and fomenting as much political turmoil as possible in those lands with established parliamentary procedures. But in the colonial or submerged nations of the world, especially in India and China, communist parties were established with the overriding short-term aim of encouraging struggles for national liberation. It was recognized that colonial lands were not theoretically prepared for socialist revolutions—those might come later. For the moment communist parties were to ally themselves with *nationalist* forces of whatever economic, political, or social persuasion in the first of all revolutionary tasks— the winning of national independence from imperialist exploitation.

Coordinating and directing the worldwide communist efforts would be the Comintern, a permanent bureau of the Third International, with headquarters in Moscow, supplying agents, instructions, money and, at times, arms to the various foreign parties. The deadly seriousness which which the Comintern took its role is reflected in a resolution adopted by its Executive Committee in 1922: "We are the deadly enemies of bourgeois society. Every honest communist will fight against bourgeois society to his last breath, in word and in deed and if necessary with arms in hand. Yes, the propaganda of the Communist International will be pernicious for you, the imperialists. It is the historical mission of the Communist International to be the gravedigger of bourgeois society. . . ."

The Leninist policy (vigorously supported by Trotsky, with his theory of worldwide permanent revolution) was later to be characterized by many as "internationalist," as opposed to Stalin's policies which were called "nationalist" because they seemed to subordinate foreign communist revolutionary activity to the necessities of preserving socialism within Russian borders. But the motives behind Lenin's "internationalism" were primarily nationalist; his overriding intention remained to protect socialism in Russia by attacking capitalism abroad. Nor did Stalin's "nationalism" deter him from using the Comintern even more vigorously than had Lenin. A more useful distinction might be to point out that Lenin's hopes for success in the exportation of communism, while by no means neglecting practical support for foreign communist parties, depended primarily on his theoretical analysis of Marxist world history. To him, communist revolutions abroad remained "inevitable," with or without Russian aid. But Stalin, especially in his later years, so far from having confidence in the "inevitable" triumph of Marxist theory abroad, preferred to base his hopes on much more material advantages—such as the presence of the Red Army.

Communist parties now came into being all over the world. Always they were founded by native radicals, not Russian agents; but always they fell under the immediate domination of the Russian Communist party through the Comintern. In England the Communist party remained small and ineffective; protest and agitation there continued to be funneled through various splinter socialist groups and, of course, the Labour party and the trade unions. In France and Italy important Communist parties were established, but the Italian party was soon driven underground by the advent of Mussolini and fascism. In Spain the Communist party, though boasting a brilliant leadership, remained much smaller than the Anarchist Associations founded many decades before by Spanish followers of Bakunin, and when Trotsky was driven into exile by Stalin, splintered between Stalinist and Trotskyite branches. Communist parties were also established in Asia (China, India, and French Indo-China), in the United States and in a few Latin American nations. With the exception of the Chinese party, all of these remained small and ineffective until after World War II.

The establishment of communist parties abroad was achieved, under Lenin and the Comintern, by the splitting of older socialist parties; the most radical members in the several countries adopted Lenin's organization plan and set themselves in opposition to other socialists much as the Bolsheviks had fought the Mensheviks in the Russian Social Democratic party. Communist parties competed with socialists for the allegiance of intellectuals and workers during Lenin's time, but not until Stalin became master of Soviet Russia did foreign communist parties turn to attack other socialist groups as their first and most hateful enemies.

The open warfare waged by communist parties throughout the world against socialists of all persuasions from 1926 to 1934 would seem both suicidal and inexplicable without an understanding of the problems, both objective and personal, faced by Stalin during those years.

Stalin, described by those who knew him best and longest, was a man consumed both by vanity and a lust for power. He demonstrated immense capacity for patience, ruthlessness, and dissimulation and a genius for political tactics. But he was also a man keenly aware of his inferiority compared to the brilliant intellects who had founded and dominated the international socialist movement for many years. He had come late to the struggle against tsarism, and, until after the revolution, had remained an obscure "practical" worker. While Lenin and, to a certain extent Trotsky, could exercise profound influence over communist parties throughout the world through the respect commanded by their theoretical contributions to Marxist thought, Stalin realized that his own domination of the international socialist and communist movement would depend on fraud and force —the two political tactics he understood best. Was it important to him that he dominate foreign parties, even after he had made himself absolute dictator of Soviet Russia? Yes, because Stalin never forgot how a veritable handful of isolated intellectual exiles had successfully overthrown one tyranny. To his dying day he seems to have remained fearful that his rivals within the international communist movement might succeed in using against him the moral and political force of socialist opinion outside Russia to bring about his overthrow. Therefore it was not in Stalin's interest that any foreign Communist party achieve revolutionary success or win state power; that would only strengthen the hands of potential rivals. Yet, as the titular head of the Russian party and the Comintern, Stalin had always to pose as the architect of worldwide communist revolution, if only to ensure his continuing control of foreign Communist movements. The tortuous policies and political disasters to which this basic contradiction led, are best exemplified by the debacles of the communist parties in Germany and Spain during the late twenties and thirties.

It was at the Sixth Congress of the Third (Communist) International held in Moscow in 1928 that it was decided that the prime target of the German Communist party henceforth would be the German Social Democratic party— the ruling moderate socialists of the German Weimar Republic who, from now on, would always be referred to in Communist propaganda as "Social-Fascists." That this policy perfectly fitted Stalin's personal political needs was obvious; it would serve to weaken moderate German Socialists and, at

the same time, ensure the political stagnation of the German
Communist party (which could not hope to come to power
in Germany following such a line). But the new Comintern
directive to German Communists was also clothed in ideological justification.

According to the purest Marxist theory, a revolution
could only be carried out by a class—in capitalist lands, by
the proletariat. Of course all German political parties to
the right of the Social Democrats were self-proclaimed
bourgeois parties. Now the Social Democrats themselves
were accused of being in the pay and control of German
capitalists. Thus there was no question of a revolution being
possible in Germany (the bourgeois parties would hardly
lead a revolution against themselves) except under the
auspices of the German Communist party. All warnings that
Germany might suffer a *revolution from the right* were
brushed aside by Comintern theoreticians. The rise of militant right-wing parties in Germany, especially the rise of
the Nazi party after the economic depression that started
in 1929, was looked upon as insignificant in Moscow. Social
Democrats, Republicans, Royalists, Nazis—all were, from
the Kremlin's viewpoint, bourgeois parties representing German capitalism; none were really any worse or any better.
In fact, Comintern observers even appeared to welcome the
rise of Adolf Hitler's Nazis on the theory that they would
inevitably destroy not only the hated German Social Democratic party, but also, through their bungling, the entire
foundation of capitalism in Germany. When those two objectives had been accomplished only the German Communist
party would stand ready to pick up the pieces of German
society and forge a Soviet Germany.

During the years 1928–1933, the years which saw Hitler's
Nazis subvert and club their way to power in Germany,
the German communists, obedient to instructions from
Moscow, concentrated their political fire on the German
Social Democrats—the only political party which stood any
kind of chance of suppressing the Nazi movement. At every
political crisis point during this period, the German Communist party denied its support to the Social Democrats
and even, on occasion, supported the Nazis in hopes of
creating deeper disruption of the German political and
social fabric. German Social Democrats even appealed to
the Russian embassy in Berlin to order the German Communist party to help them in their losing and desperate

fight against the Nazis before it should be too late. But to all such appeals Stalin turned a deaf ear; the road to a socialist Germany, the Comintern was convinced, lay through the chaos that Hitler would surely bring.

It must not be thought that Communist party policy in Germany caused the advent of the Nazi regime; there were wider and more profound reasons for the emergence of Nazism in Germany. But German communists consistently undermined and opposed whatever slim possibilities presented themselves for effective resistance to Hitler. The penalty they paid for this tactical misconception was the total political and physical destruction of the German Communist party. Within months of his elevation to power in 1933, Hitler had broken the power of both Communists and Social Democrats in Germany; many thousands of members of both parties were shipped off to prisons and the sinister new concentration camps where they were ruthlessly executed. A mere handful of communist leaders escaped the blood bath in which their party was drowned; so effective was the Nazi terror that from 1933 until 1945 no communist organization worth describing, even underground, existed in Germany.

Behind the tactical errors forced upon the German Communist party by Moscow lay a much more important theoretical misconception. It had been assumed that the Nazis, although more violent and barbaric than other bourgeois parties, were simply an extreme expression of capitalist political maneuvering, not a revolutionary force. Indeed, since the Nazi party did not represent the German proletariat but rather the German bourgeoisie, how could it be a revolutionary party? But, in very vital ways, it was. The very word "Nazi," a contraction of "National Socialist" might have provided a clue. For while it was certainly true that Hitler's rise to power was welcomed and financed by top German industrialists and capitalists as a means of countering the socialist threat, his movement (insofar as its chaotic ideology could be reduced to any reasonable premises) represented a revolution against the capitalist structure of German society. The German economy, despite the occasional retention of figureheads, was to be utterly nationalized, so was the German working class. In effect, Hitler was introducing state capitalism to Germany. That this basic restructuring of the German state was accompanied by racial madness, military adventures, and all the insane para-

phernalia of Nazi rule, was coincident to specific German
history and Hitler's deranged mind. And there *was* a class
in Germany that would support this revolution from the
right—the class of the small bourgeoisie; the small shop-
owners, the lower classes of white-collar workers, small independent farmers, disgruntled intellectuals—all of whom,
in the crisis of the Great Depression which affected Germany
as deeply as any other country, saw themselves teetering on
the brink of economic and social disaster. Allied with German
capitalists who feared a socialist victory, with the German
military, and with millions of unemployed workers, these
groups provided sufficiently heavy mass-support to ensure
the National Socialist victory.

It seems to have taken Stalin at least two years to fully
comprehend the threat to Soviet Russia implicit in Hitler's
assumption of power in Germany. Perhaps, like so many
others, Stalin did not take Hitler's threats seriously at first.
But the creation of a rigidly totalitarian regime in Germany,
accompanied by German rearmament and by a constant
flow of Nazi propaganda insisting that the Slavs were a
"degenerate race" which would have to be enslaved and
exterminated to make room for German expansion to the
east, finally compelled Stalin to change his tactics. By 1935
it had become apparent to the Soviet government that Hitler
meant business, that Russia might soon be faced with a
major war.

Accordingly, at the Seventh Congress of the Communist
International held in 1935, the former policy of open warfare
against moderate Socialist parties throughout the world was
suddenly reversed. Communist parties abroad were now instructed to seek the friendship, not only of socialists, but
also of republicans, and democratically inclined conservatives
—of all political elements which might be enlisted in a
United Front against the spread of fascism. Communist
criticism of rival political parties was to be muted; unity in
the struggle against Nazism was to be the foundation of
communist policy. At the same time, Russian diplomacy on
the governmental level was directed toward an attempt to
forge alliances with the nations menaced by Nazi aggression.
A treaty of mutual aid was signed with France; diplomatic
relations were reestablished with the United States; Soviet
representatives at the League of Nations, headed by Maxim
Litvinov, made the air ring with denunciations of German,
Italian, and Japanese aggression.

But if Stalin saw his regime and Russia itself threatened by world fascism, he was not insensitive to the impact events abroad might make on his personal power. After all, it was by his insistence that the German Socialists and Communists, who might have been effective allies against Hitler, had been destroyed. Russian critics of Stalin's policies could now point not only to the famines of the twenties, to the various failures of industrialization schemes, to the excesses and rigors of his police-state apparatus; they could also point to a massive failure in foreign policy, a failure which had left Russia exposed and alone to confront a savage enemy. It was no mere coincidence, then, that the establishment of the United Front policy for communist parties abroad occurred just when Stalin began to institute his great purge trials, to submerge all potential critics of his regime within Russia in a bloodbath of unparalleled ferocity.

Western socialists and liberals, themselves frightened by the rise of fascism, and with but scanty knowledge of what was happening in the prisons and forced labor camps of Soviet Russia, saw in the new United Front policy not only the possibility of stopping fascist aggression, but also the first indications that the world communist movement might have relaxed its obstinate suspicions and hatred of all things bourgeois. They welcomed the United Front (and many hastened to join) as a reconciliation of sorts between the two branches of Marxist socialism which had been sundered by Lenin at the turn of the century. Socialist and Liberal opinion in the West was also favorably impressed by the new Constitution which Stalin promulgated for Russia in 1936—an outstandingly democratic document which had, of course, no effect whatsoever on the continuing Stalinist tyranny, but which was carefully calculated to impress both domestic and foreign critics of the Soviet regime. The enthusiasms generated by the apparent "softening" of communist policy and the establishment of the United Front were to receive their most important boost, however, from the extraordinary emotions generated by an extraordinary event—the Spanish Civil War.

In certain instructive ways, political developments inside Spain since the middle of the nineteenth century had been remarkably similar to those within prerevolutionary Russia. Like tsarist Russia, monarchist Spain had remained largely a peasant-based society with a very small middle class and a sterile aristocracy and monarchy. Like tsarist Russia, Spain

had begun to industrialize fairly rapidly after the turn of
the twentieth century. Furthermore, a marked similarity
might be noted between the effects of tsarism's disastrous
Russo-Japanese War of 1905 and monarchist Spain's equally
disastrous Spanish-American War of 1898. The revolutionary
and socialist groups in Spain reflected some of the same
contradictions within Spanish society that had been apparent
in the prerevolutionary Russian social fabric—but with one
important exception. In Spain there existed no large, well-
organized, and brilliantly led Bolshevik or Communist party
to dispute power with other socialists.

Just as Russian peasants had been represented by the
Social Revolutionary party, with its inheritance of the terror-
istic ideals of the *Narodnik* movement, so Spanish peasants
overwhelmingly placed their faith in an Anarchist movement
with many of the same ideals and with specifically similar
origins. It had grown under the inspiration of Mikhail
Bakunin, Marx's old enemy of First International days. The
industrial workers in Spain followed the leadership of several socialist parties of moderate intentions—not at all dissimilar to the Menshevik wing of the old Russian Social
Democratic party. There were, as there had been in Russia,
small and, as it turned out, relatively powerless middle-
class liberal parties. But, as has been pointed out, the Spanish
Communist party came into existence only after the Russian
Revolution. The party was established as a creature of the
Comintern, and after Stalin drove Trotsky into exile, it split
between Stalinists and Trotskyites with the Trotskyites in-
heriting a majority of the Spanish Communist following.

In 1931 for many of the same reasons which had prevailed in Russia (semifeudal agricultural conditions, misery
among the working class, impatience and dissatisfaction
among the tiny but vocal middle classes, a prolonged and
losing war in Morocco) the Spanish monarchy fell, to be
replaced, as had the tsarist autocracy, with a democratic-
socialist regime of moderate views. But as there was no
Communist organization of any real power in Spain, this
moderate government managed to prevail until July 1936.
At that time it was attacked, not from the left, but from
the right. Disgruntled army officers, the all-but-disestablished
Spanish Catholic Church hierarchy, the wealthy, dispossessed
aristocrats and monarchists and the followers of a native
Spanish fascist party, the *Falange* (modeled on the Italian
fascist party of Benito Mussolini) united in rebellion against

the Spanish Republican government and plunged Spain into
an incredibly fierce and bloody civil war.

Domestically, this uprising of reactionary groups inevitably
pushed the Spanish Republican government to the left. Republicans, socialists of all hues, anarchists, Trotskyites and
Communists attempted to subdue their bickerings and unite
to defeat a common enemy. The Communists, who had had
but scant representation in the Spanish *Cortes* (parliament)
offered, as might be expected, an extremely realistic and
practical program and example. Armed workers' brigades
were formed to fight under Communist leadership and among
those portions of the Spanish working class in which Communists had influence, rigid work-discipline was maintained;
special Communist long-term aims were subordinated to the
pressing need to defend the Republic. All of which con-
trasted with failures of organization, discipline, and ruthlessness among Anarchists and other socialist parties. Spanish
Communist leaders such as Dolores Ibarruri *("La Pasion-
aria"),* Juan Modesto, and Valentín González *("El Campe-
sino")* became famous not only in Spain, but throughout the
world.

But the rise of Communist influence in Republican Spain
was due primarily to massive Russian intervention. In the
very earliest days of the Civil War, General Francisco Franco
(leader of the fascist forces) had appealed for aid to Nazi
Germany and Fascist Italy. The Republican government
begged for help from France, England, and Russia. The
Germans and, especially the Italians, dispatched massive,
probably decisive aid to Franco; but the English and French,
fearful of provoking a second world war for which they
felt themselves unprepared, gave but scant support to the
Republic. Only Soviet Russia sent important supplies of
ammunition, tanks, planes, food, and "volunteers." And
since this Russian aid at various times spelled the difference
between the Republic's defeat or survival, the influence of
the Spanish Communist party (which never controlled the
Republican government) was bound to rise.

An even more spectacular example of worldwide communist aid to the Republic was the formation, under Comintern auspices, of International Brigades of volunteers to
fight against fascism in Spain. Raised by communist parties
throughout the world, about eighty percent of the volunteers were or became communists—the rest were socialists
and liberals of various descriptions. But all were idealists.

For these were the days of the United Front policy and, through the International Brigades, it seemed to many men of good will everywhere that at last a chance had come to strike a solid blow against the creeping evil of fascism. Eventually there were to be five International Brigades in Spain (including two American battalions, the Washington and the Lincoln) and over 40,000 men would serve in them. Well trained and well armed, under the command of able generals (many of whom later rose to prominence in the communist world—Marshal Tito of Yugoslavia, Premier Dimitrov of Bulgaria, Ulbricht of East Germany, and Togliatti, head of the Italian Communist party), the International Brigades more than once saved the Republic from disaster.

Stalin's decision to intervene on behalf of the Spanish Republic, and, through the Comintern, to mobilize communist and United Front aid around the world, was due to obvious calculations of strategy. By 1936, it will be recalled, he had already come to understand that he would undoubtedly one day have to face war with Nazi Germany. His entire United Front policy had been aimed at rallying international support for an anti-Nazi coalition which might provide Russia with allies when the dreaded moment came or might even conceivably wipe out the Hitler threat without full-scale war. If Spain went fascist it would mean that France, Russia's most obvious natural ally against Germany, would be surrounded by enemies. France might herself go fascist or, in any event be unwilling or unable to cooperate effectively with Russia should war come. Furthermore, by providing a physical as well as a moral outlet for anti-fascist opinion of all shades, Communist intervention in Spain might help bring domestic pressure to bear on the governments of Western Europe to ally themselves immediately with the Soviet Union to stop the spread of fascism. In all of this, it will be observed, there is no mention of any interest on Stalin's part in the Spanish Communist party—no such interest existed. The Spanish Party was, like the German Party before it, to be treated simply as an extension of Russian foreign policy.

Late in 1937, suddenly, and seemingly inexplicably, Russian intervention in Spain underwent a dramatic change. From that time on almost no Russian military aid was dispatched to the Republic; only economic aid continued. A short time later (in 1938) the Comintern, obedient to instructions from Moscow, withdrew the International Brigades. All of this was supposedly due to the fact that Russia, Britain, France, Italy, and Germany had signed a "Non-intervention Agreement" which bound them to stop taking part in the Spanish Civil War. But it was well known that this Agreement was meaningless; German and Italian intervention continued on a massive scale. Russia could well have found excuses to continue direct military support for the Republic. Yet although Stalin, through economic aid, hoped to keep the Republic alive (because its struggle continued to tie down important German and Italian forces), he refused it the means of victory. Why? Apparently for several reasons. First of all, Stalin seems to have genuinely feared that heavy Russian commitment in Spain might well lead to war with Germany and Italy. Secondly, Stalin had apparently concluded by 1938 that the Western democracies had no intention of seriously opposing Hitler but simply hoped to direct Nazi ambitions eastward against Soviet Russia—leaving Stalin to fight against Germany alone or make a separate deal with Hitler. Finally, it must be remembered that all during the Spanish Civil War, Russia was undergoing the agony of Stalin's bloody purges. All domestic Communist opposition to Stalin's tyranny was being ruthlessly stamped out. The idealistic fervor with which socialists and communists joined liberals to fight fascism in Spain might prove contagious; it might even transform itself into an important anti-Stalinist Communist power center abroad. A victory for the Republic undoubtedly would have meant a victory for those moderate elements within the worldwide Communist movement of which the Russian dictator lived in morbid fear. All of these reasons combined to change Stalin's mind about Spain and, when the Spanish Republic went down to defeat in 1939, Moscow's only reaction was to begin a systematic purge of any and all Russians who had been associated with its cause.

It will be seen, then, that from the triumph of Bolshevism in Russia, to the outbreak of the Second World War, exporting the revolution really meant no more than adding another weapon to the armory of specifically Russian national foreign policy. The revolutionary triumph of communism in other lands, which might have been welcomed by Lenin and Trotsky during the very early twenties, had actually become unwelcome to Stalin during the late twenties and thirties. The shock which came as an all-but-mortal blow to Com-

munist parties around the world when Stalin finally made
his deal with Hitler in 1939, was due to a basic misappre-
hension about what communism, at least in the Western
World, had come to mean. By the late summer of 1939,
when Stalin and Hitler signed that nonaggression treaty
which enabled Nazi Germany to embark on World War II,
communism in the West as an organized force had become
the totally supine instrument of a cynical, frightened, and
highly conservative dictatorship.

Chapter Eleven

COMMUNISM AND THE UNITED STATES

> Russia for a number of years has treated the United
> States as badly as she has treated England. . . . I
> should like to have been friendly with her; but she
> simply would not permit it. . . .
>
> —*Theodore Roosevelt*
>
> The emblem of the party shall be the crossed hammer
> and sickle, representing the unity of worker and
> farmer, with a circular inscription having at the top
> "Communist Party of the U.S.A." and in the lower
> part "Affiliated to the Communist International."
>
> —*Article 2, Constitution
> of the CPUSA, 1938*

The impact of communism in and upon the United States
is, and always has been, a mixture (often a confusion) of
domestic challenges and responses with the current state of
Soviet Russian-American relations on the international level.
This has been due not only to the fact that the Communist
party of the United States has always conducted itself as if
it were a suboffice of the Russian Ministry of Foreign
Affairs; it has also been due to the fact that many Americans,
even those highly placed in our government, have often
been unable to distinguish between the objectives of Russia
as a nation and the objectives of the world communist
movement as generated and controlled by Moscow. But for
this they can hardly be blamed, since the emergence of the
Soviet Union has brought new and absolutely unique problems to the field of international relations.

By and large, most Americans welcomed the first (February) Russian Revolution; they looked upon the tsarist autocracy as a detestable tyranny which embodied everything that was most hateful to American ideals. American money and smuggled arms had been contributed to Russian revolutionary movements as early as the 1905 uprising (about which Mark Twain remarked, "If such a government cannot be overthrown without dynamite, then thank God for dynamite."). And Woodrow Wilson, about to lead the United States into the First World War in which she would be allied to Russia as well as to Britain and France declared:

> Does not every American feel that assurance has been added to our hope for the future peace of the world by the wonderful and heartening things that have been happening within the last few weeks in Russia? . . . The autocracy that crowned the summit of her political structure, long as it had stood and terrible as was the reality of its power . . . has been shaken off and the great, generous Russian people have been added in all their naive majesty and might to the forces that are fighting for freedom in the world, for justice and for peace.

But it was precisely on this last point—the continuation of the Russian war effort against Imperial Germany—that the first misunderstandings between the United States and Russia were to arise. American policy, like that of Britain and France, concentrated all its efforts during the fateful summer of 1917 on an attempt to keep Russia in the war. Yet, as we have seen, the one thing that the Provisional Government, the liberals, moderate socialists, and Mensheviks could not do with any hope of success was to drive the shattered, demoralized, and revolutionary Russian armies back into the slaughterhouse shambles of the crumbling Eastern Front. It was upon this rock-hard problem of whether or not Russia could continue fighting, that the Provisional Government and even moderate elements in the Petrograd Soviet came to grief. Above all else, it was the Bolshevik promise to end the war that brought them the mass support they needed to win power in October 1917. This Allied policy towards Russia, however, was not based only on blindness to the reality of Russian conditions in 1917; it was based also on harsh necessity. For without an active Eastern Front it was doubtful whether the Allies in the West could hold out long enough against German military might to enable a massive American contribution to be made. In fact, with the Peace of Brest-Litovsk that ended Russian participation in World War I, the Germans were freed to shift heavy forces to the Western Front and, under the driving energy of Erich Ludendorff, came close to capturing Paris in the early months of 1918.

Whatever repugnance the American government and people may have felt for Bolshevik theory (and at first they felt little, for the simple reason that few of them had ever heard of it), the immediate practical reason for hostility to Lenin's new regime was that it had apparently betrayed its treaties of alliance and, by making a separate peace with the Germans, endangered the entire Allied war effort. If Lenin and the Bolsheviks had but little choice in the matter, this, even upon the governmental level, was but dimly understood. The fact was that no Russian government could have continued the war; but it was Lenin's which had to bear the onus, in Allied eyes, of ending it.

One immediate consequence of the Russian surrender to Germany was anxiety in Allied councils over what would now happen to the mountains of supplies, guns, and munitions which had been shipped to Russia and were piled high at the Arctic port of Archangel and the Pacific port of Vladivostok. What would happen to the thousands of German and Austrian prisoners of war held in Russia, and to the Czechoslovakian Legion, an army of former Russian prisoners of war which had been formed to fight against Austria-Hungary and liberate their homeland? Would not all this materiel, all these prisoners, be seized by the Germans and added to the German war effort? Would not the Czechoslovakian Legion now be destroyed by German forces? It was these fears which prompted the dispatch of American troops to both Archangel and Vladivostok in 1918.

The nature of the American intervention in Russia in 1918 and 1919 must not be confused with the nature of the British-French intervention to which it was largely subordinate. The British and French hoped not only to protect military stores, but hoped also, both by direct military confrontation and by supporting reactionary Russian elements during the Russian Civil War, to bring about the downfall of the Bolshevik government. The United States government, before, during, and after its dispatch of American troops to Russia specifically disassociated itself from this objective. Indeed, American troops in Russia in 1918 and 1919 were kept quite clear of any entanglement in the civil war then raging there. In the Far East it was due largely to the presence of American forces that the Japanese were thwarted in their desire to seize the opportunity to detach large portions of Siberia and the Maritime Territory from the fledgling Soviet state—a fact which contemporary Soviet leaders acknowledged gratefully but which more recent ones have seen fit to forget. And by the end of 1919 the small American detachments in Russia had all been withdrawn. Yet by that time the seeds of hostility between the United States and the Soviet Union had been planted so deeply that no American government would so much as recognize the Communist government of Russia for the next fifteen years. Why?

There were a tangle of reasons—many of them domestic. First of all, through the pronouncements of its leaders, the Soviet government immediately made plain its objective of inciting revolutions throughout the world, including the United States. Secondly, Lenin's government had not only denounced previous Russian treaties, but had also renounced all the debts incurred by the tsarist regime—a blow against many Americans who directly or indirectly had invested money both in private Russian industrial enterprises and in Imperial Russian State Bonds—not to mention the large public debt owed to the United States by the Russian government for wartime aid. This was an especially bitter pill for many Americans to swallow when they reflected that it was *after* the Bolshevik revolution, in 1919 and 1920, that Herbert Hoover's Food Relief Administration had distributed many millions of dollars' worth of American aid directly to the Russian people, greatly alleviating the widespread sufferings and famine that followed the close of the Russian civil war. Thirdly, Americans were deluged by the press with sensationalist propaganda about events in Russia. The Bolsheviks were painted as bloodthirsty ruffians, German agents, bewhiskered bomb-throwers, "nationalizers" of women, etc., etc. The reports of American observers on the spot, such as John Reed, a journalist whose *Ten Days That Shook the World* painted a highly sympathetic picture of the Bolshevik uprising, were drowned in the deluge of anti-Soviet verbiage. To Americans who had been overheated by the superpatriotism and intolerance generated by participation in World War I, the "Bolshevik Menace," quickly assumed a stature out of all proportion to its reality. A huge "red scare" swept the United States shortly after the war—officially fueled by Wilson's attorney general, A. Mitchell Palmer, who, during 1919 and 1920, instituted a hysterical program of shipping alien "radicals" out of the country without trial and imprisoning native ones. Under these circumstances, even if there had been no objective reasons for United States nonrecognition of the Soviet Union, any American government which attempted to deal realistically with the Russians would have risked domestic political defeat.

But the overall American reaction to the victory of communism in Russia—both on a governmental and a popular level—had roots which went deeper than hysteria and deeper than interpretation, correct or incorrect, of events many thousands of miles away. These roots are to be sought in the ways in which Americans themselves were attempting to cope with the problems posed by industrialization, urbanization and the growth of the power of capital at home. For however much Americans might view communism as a threatening foreign conspiracy, American radicalism and socialism were native, home-grown products with old historical sources in the United States.

The Civil War is traditionally and conveniently chosen as the Great Divide in American history between an essentially rural-agricultural and an essentially urban-industrial society. The early Utopian Socialist experiments in America, the Owenite communities, the Fourierist phalanxes, the idealistic farmer-artisan cooperative establishments, had been suited to a sparsely settled agricultural nation. They had failed mostly because of their rigidly idealistic views of human nature and because the overall society in which they were planted was simply too rich, too free, afforded too many opportunities, to require them. But between the flowering of Utopian Socialism in America and the post-Civil War era a great change had come over the country and the structure of society.

It may be of interest to note that during the Civil War, Karl Marx (who, with Engels wrote a series of articles regarding the war's development for the New York *Tribune*) viewed the United States government as the "highest" and most "democratically progressive" yet organized; after the Civil War he viewed the United States as the supreme bastion of reactionary capitalism. Be that as it may, it was certainly true that wartime demands gave a powerful impetus to industrialization in the North. So rapid and massive was

American industrialization after 1865 that by 1900 the United States had become the most powerfully industrialized nation on earth. Accompanying this phenomenon had been the speedy settlement of the West and the closing of the frontier; fueling it in great measure had been a tide of immigration that brought more than seven million Europeans to America between 1870 and the close of the century.

Industrialization in the United States was, in many ways, as ruthless and cruel in its social results as it had been anywhere in Europe. While the Carnegies, Rockefellers, Morgans, Vanderbilts, *et al.* amassed huge fortunes, indulged in "conspicuous consumption" (a disease not of the lungs but of the spirit), corrupted local, state, and even federal governments, and employed illegal practices to create and maintain their industrial and financial empires, workers subsisted on terribly scant wages, toiled twelve or more hours a day, lost health and sometimes life in unregulated factories and mines, and were housed in appalling slums. Marx's vividly dreadful picture of the English "Working Day" in *Capital* could, with almost no qualifications, have applied equally well to American conditions.

Until the late 1800's the Western frontier had acted as a safety valve for industrial discontent back East. If workers found their lives too intolerable, there was always the promise of land and opportunity in the Golden West. But most of the immigrants of the 1880's and 1890's lacked the means to make the westward trek; they stayed in the industrial centers of the East and Midwest. In any event, by 1890 the Golden West had lost most of its glitter for native as well as foreign-born Americans. Remedies for the economic and social miseries of industrialization would have to be found in social action, not escape.

A link in the transformation of American radicalism from pre-Civil War Utopian to Marxist socialist may be seen in the works of Henry George and Edward Bellamy—both Utopian in their way, but both concerned with changing society directly rather than through example. In 1879 Henry George published *Progress and Poverty*, a book in which he attacked the central problem posed by socialists: Why should the advance of the industrial revolution, which meant the advance of the means of producing more wealth, result in more and more poverty? George answered by arguing that all wealth ultimately depended upon the land, and since land is a commodity like any other, it tends to be increasingly monopolized by the rich. Furthermore, landlords tend both to charge excessive rents (thereby driving up profits while driving down wages) and to withhold land from use awaiting a rise in its value. To remedy this situation George proposed a "single tax" on land, to be based not on existing value but on potential value if the land were used efficiently. The tax would be so graded as to force landlords to either develop or sell their land, thereby increasing production and general prosperity. While not a socialist (he firmly believed in private property) Henry George's thesis made the basic socialist assumption that property must at least be socially controlled. His book sold millions of copies—becoming almost an American bible.

The success of *Progress and Poverty* was almost matched by Bellamy's *Looking Backward, 2000–1887,* published in 1888. In this novel Bellamy told of a nineteenth-century American who awoke from a prolonged hypnotic trance in the year 2000 A.D. to find himself living in a socialist paradise. By that time all business and industry had been merged into one gigantic trust that was owned and run by the people themselves. There was, of course, neither poverty nor crime nor sorrow in this socialist America. Although neither George's nor Bellamy's works had any immediate practical impact on American society (the conception of the "single tax" did influence later taxation legislation), they succeeded in awakening many middle-class Americans to the central fact that industrialization might require a conscious change in the structure of society.

This realization had long since come to American workers. As early as 1869 the first politically inspired general trade union had been formed (semi-secretly) and emerged as the Noble Order of the Knights of Labor, headed by Terence V. Powderly. The Knights of Labor accepted any and all workers, no matter what their skill or occupation. The idea was to form one big union as a means of directly confronting capitalist society and winning eventual worker-control of the means of production. Falsely accused of having instigated the Haymarket Riot in Chicago in 1886 (during which someone threw a bomb that killed a number of policemen), the Knights of Labor lost ground rapidly; membership dropped from 700,000 in 1886 to a mere 75,000 in 1893.

The Knights of Labor, early victims of "guilt by association" suffered from a general public suspicion regarding the objectives of labor unions which had only been inflamed

by the events in Haymarket Square. Many of the immigrant
European workers who were flooding into the United States
at that time came already convinced of any one of a number
of radical philosophies. New, and to many Americans, frightening words like *syndicalism, anarchism,* and *communism*
were being increasingly employed by radical and labor leaders. In fact it was through a general charge that the Haymarket affair was the work of "anarchists" that the Chicago
authorities were enabled to hang four (and imprison four
more) probably innocent workers.

The unreasonable fear with which many Americans
greeted new ideologies during the late nineteenth century
was grounded on more than a single riot; it stemmed from
a growing tide of industrial unrest that had commenced in
1877. In that year a nationwide railroad strike had brought
widespread violence in which mobs of workers fought
pitched battles with companies of armed Pinkerton detec-
tives. President Rutherford B. Hayes had been forced to
dispatch regular Army troops to Pittsburgh and Chicago to
restore order. But despite the fact that for the next fifty
years, almost inevitably, the full weight of local and federal
power (armed when necessary) was brought down on the
side of capital and against labor, agitation, strikes, and
sporadic outbreaks of fighting (usually provoked by employers as an excuse to call for state intervention) continued
and gathered momentum. There were more or less violent
strikes and lockouts in steel mills, mines, factories, and
western lumber camps all through the closing decades of
the nineteenth century. Sometimes labor's demands were
supported by disgruntled farmers, as during the Populist
Party movement during the 1890's. Generally labor found
itself isolated, its methods declared illegal by federal courts
and suppressed by federal force, its aims misunderstood
by the general public. Labor was, in fact, emerging as a
new class in American society, and if its definition as such
did not precisely fit the Marxist definition of "class," its
existence was to bring radical change to the nation's entire
social structure. How to succeed in forcing this change was
the subject of endless and bitter argument among labor
leaders and radicals for many years. Basically the question
was the same one which had afflicted labor and socialist
movements in Europe: Was labor to win its aims through
union-organized economic pressure or through direct political
action—and if through political action, was it to work for

reform within the democratic system or toward revolution in order to overthrow that system?

One answer to the question was advocated by Samuel Gompers, an English immigrant who brought to the United States much of the traditional antipolitical outlook of the British labor movement. In 1886 he organized the American Federation of Labor. Under his leadership the A.F. of L. was to organize unions on the basis of workers' crafts or skills. All carpenters would be organized into one union, for instance, all plumbers into another. Unskilled workers would not be accepted into A.F. of L. unions which would be hierarchically arranged with apprentices, journeymen, and masters somewhat on the model of medieval guilds. Furthermore, the A.F. of L. and its member unions would steer absolutely clear of any kind of political activity; their weapons would be strictly economic as would be their goals. The growth of the A.F. of L. was slow and sporadic, but solid. Its unions, comprising better-paid workers, were able to withstand prolonged strikes and to ride out recurrent depressions, but their exclusivity left the vast majority of workers unaided and untouched.

One of the earliest (and certainly the most notable) critics of the A.F. of L. organizational plan was Eugene Victor Debs. "Gene" Debs was born in 1855 and grew up during the great era of railroad building—he was, in fact, a locomotive fireman in his youth and became an officer of the Brotherhood of Locomotive Firemen, a craft union. Debs had witnessed the downfall of the Knights of Labor. He ascribed the failure of that organization not only to public hysteria but, more importantly, to basic flaws in its program. The idea of "one big union" to which all workingmen were to flock and which would, in turn, organize indiscriminate strikes against entire towns, or states, had the effect of uniting employers rather than dividing them and providing fuel for accusations of radical conspiracy against the Knights of Labor themselves. Furthermore, the all-embracing organizational plan of the Knights of Labor really meant no organization at all, since disparate groups of workers employed in many different occupations and including many different levels of skill could not readily submerge their differing backgrounds and immediate practical needs. On the other hand, Debs pointed out that the A.F. of L. organizational plan, by excluding the vast mass of unskilled workers, deprived the A.F. of L. craft unions of the mass support they desperately needed in order to win even limited, economic gains.

Gene Debs proposed a new kind of union—a vertical industrial union—which, while it would be limited to a particular industry, would include all workers in that industry, skilled or unskilled; all steelworkers, for example, or all railroad workers whether skilled engineers or ditch-diggers would belong to the same union. This industrial union concept was, many decades later, to provide the theoretical basis for the foundation of the Congress of Industrial Organizations (C.I.O.). Debs put the concept into practical effect in Chicago in 1893 when he founded the American Railway Union, the country's first industrial union. Limiting itself to economic weapons and goals, the A.R.U. grew rapidly. Although 1893 was a depression year in the United States, the union was able to win a strike against the Great Northern Railway Company in 1894. But in that same year it met disaster.

To counter losses incident upon the depression of 1893, the Pullman Sleeping Car Company, in 1894, discharged two thirds of its workers and radically cut the wages of the rest. When some of the men responded with a strike, all Pullman Company workers found themselves locked out. The fledgling American Railway Union thereupon decided to support the Pullman workers; its members refused to handle any trains which included Pullman cars. By late June 1894 more than one hundred thousand railway workers were on strike and railroad traffic west of Chicago was paralyzed. The Railway Managers Association, making common cause with the Pullman Company and hoping to provoke violence which would enable them to call for federal assistance and thereby break the American Railway Union, began adding Pullman cars to trains which did not ordinarily include them—even mail trains. With the excuse that strikers were interfering with United States mails, President Grover Cleveland dispatched Army units to Chicago, despite the bitter protests of both the mayor of Chicago and the governor of Illinois who pointed out that the strikers had not interfered with mail trains and had conducted themselves peaceably. As could be foreseen, the arrival of troops led to bloody rioting; this in turn enabled a local federal judge to issue an injunction (court order) declaring the strike a conspiracy in restraint of trade and therefore a violation of the Sherman Anti-Trust Law. When Debs refused to obey this preposterous order, he was jailed for contempt of court. Without his leadership the Pullman strike collapsed and, shortly thereafter, the American Railway Union went out of existence.

In his prison cell Gene Debs had time to reflect. He had seen that a peaceable strike to attain immediate, limited economic goals, had been crushed by the entire power of both capital and the federal government. The Marxist claim that governments, even in the most democratic capitalist societies were simply organized expressions of ruling-class power seemed amply demonstrated. Therefore if labor was ever to win its rightful place in society, it would have to undertake to change the very nature of society. Without political power labor could never win economic justice. Debs became a socialist. Emerging from prison in 1895 he joined the tiny, recently formed (in 1890) American Socialist party and quickly rose to leadership within it.

If we have gone into some detail regarding the steps by which Gene Debs became a socialist it is because this same path was trodden by many an American intellectual and labor leader at the turn of the century—a direct reaction to the brutality of capitalist industrialization of the United States and the apparent domination of all political machinery by capitalist interests. But although Debs and his followers recognized the need to change the basic structure of American society, they remained convinced that this could be accomplished within the framework of American democracy. The American Socialist party put forward candidates for local and national office who advocated peaceful change. Debs himself ran four times for the Presidency and even his imprisonment as a pacifist during World War I did not seem to undermine his basic faith in American democracy. The role played by the American Socialist party in the United States would, in European eyes, have corresponded to that played by Social Democrats in France or Germany—with the exception that the American socialists never enjoyed political power on any but the smallest local level.

Like its European counterparts, the American socialist movement was, from its inception, beset by factional quarrels and party splits. These generally reflected different degrees of militancy within the movement which, in turn, often reflected the influence of European immigrant groups, more embittered, more doctrinaire, more theoretically "advanced" than their American comrades. Several splinter socialist parties were formed around the turn of the century, of which the most important was the Socialist Labor party headed by Daniel De Leon. Born in 1852 on the island of Curaçao, De Leon emigrated to the United States in 1872. He was a fiery and doctrinaire Marxist and soon turned his considerable oratorical gifts to denouncing Debs's moderate program. De Leon attacked the whole idea of attempting to win political power through democratic processes—that was simply a sentimental illusion. He was, without realizing it, something of a Leninist, but with the very important qualification that he opposed any kind of violence. Yet how his revolution was to succeed without violence was never very clear. He proposed that workers be organized into giant industrial unions and that these, when strong enough, simply "take over" the means of production. Whenever his opinions alienated his followers, De Leon did not hesitate, in true Leninist fashion, to split the Socialist Labor party into even tinier fragments. Yet, on one occasion at least, he showed himself willing to cooperate with Debs (whom he generally characterized as "a traitor to the working class"). This was in 1905 when De Leon and Debs joined forces briefly to found a new labor organization, the Industrial Workers of the World.

Unfortunately, the I.W.W. soon repudiated both Debs and De Leon to follow more violent leaders. Preaching the old Knights of Labor idea of "one big union," the I.W.W. added "and one big strike." It looked forward to a hazy Armageddon in which all the workers in the entire country would join in one gigantic nationwide strike so huge and crippling that the entire structure of capitalist society would simply collapse. And until that time, "wobblies" (as I.W.W. members were called) would counter company, police, and government violence with violence of their own. Gaining strength in western mining towns and lumber camps, the I.W.W. used bullets and dynamite to advance its claims; and its members were savagely persecuted by authorities wherever they appeared. The movement lost much ground when its leaders opposed American entrance into World War I, and it disintegrated during the postwar "red scare" persecutions.

The splintering of the American socialist movement, the emergence of a leader such as De Leon (he died in 1914) and the phenomenon of the I.W.W.'s open industrial warfare were significant mainly as both a reflection of and a means toward the *radicalization* of socialist thought in the United States. When the news came of a successful Communist revolution in Russia in 1917, there already existed a very small but very militant minority of American socialists prepared to adopt specifically Leninist Bolshevik views. Accordingly, in June 1919 a National Left-Wing Congress of the Socialist party (completely divorced, of course, from Debs's American Socialist party) was held in New York City with the stated purpose of founding an American Communist party. Later that year, from September 1 to 7, Chicago saw two more conventions of groups that called themselves, respectively, the Communist Party of the United States and the Communist Labor Party. These two Chicago conventions were held at the behest of Gregory Zinoviev, one of Lenin's oldest associates and a high executive of the Communist International in Moscow. It was not until May 1921, however, that the two groups ironed out certain differences and, again upon instructions from the Comintern, united to form the Communist Party of the United States of America (CPUSA).

Thereafter American socialism was to be permanently split. The American Socialist party, under the leadership of Debs and, after his death in 1926, headed by Norman Thomas, continued to preach moderate socialist goals to be achieved through legal democratic processes. Though Socialist party strength at the polls remained slight (never rising above the 920,000 votes Debs won in 1920), as the century progressed, Socialist party programs won a sort of grudging intellectual respectability even among the most conservative Americans. By the time of his death in 1968 Norman Thomas could safely be claimed as an "elder statesman" by the American establishment.

The American Communist party, however, first under the leadership of William Z. Foster, later under the direction of Earl Browder, remained a captive not only of the Comintern (that is to say, Russian foreign policy), but of the most rigid Leninist-Stalinist theoretical concepts. Its organization, for example, followed the conspiratorial structure disguised as "democratic centralism" which had been devised by Lenin decades earlier to cope with entirely different conditions.

"Democratic centralism," in theory (both as originally propounded by Lenin and as later followed by the CPUSA) meant that party policy might be freely discussed on all levels of the organization, from bottom to top, and suggestions might be forwarded from lower to higher echelons. But decisions would be arrived at only by the top Party leadership, and once these decisions were made, every stratum of the Party was duty-bound to carry them out unquestioningly. Furthermore, every Party member was expected to bring himself to *believe* wholeheartedly in the validity of the most recent decisions and to support them unequivocally. Any objections to Party policy as finally handed down by the leadership would thenceforth be considered dangerous "deviationism" or outright treason to the Party.

The CPUSA, as organized in 1921 and reorganized in 1945, was built upon the basic organizational unit of the neighborhood club which was run by a club executive committee. A group of clubs in any given area would be organized into a section and controlled by a section committee. A group of sections would be controlled by a state or district committee. All the work of the state committee (and, in truth, of all committees on every level) would, in turn, be controlled by the national committee. Administration within the Party and the enforcement of leadership decisions were to flow from the top down; a national or section committee member could be sent at any time to lower-level organizations to state the Party policy and to discipline members who failed to adhere to it.

Thus, while in theory, "democratic centralism" did make provision both for a flow of new ideas and new leaders from lower to higher ranks, in practice, because of the absolute power wielded by the higher elements of the Party hierarchy, the CPUSA was an all-but totalitarian structure. And like all totalitarian structures it suffered severely from hardening of the arteries of interior communications. To rise in Party ranks meant that a member had to dedicate himself utterly to unquestioning loyalty to Party policy and to *every shift in Party policy* no matter what his previous personal views might have been. This obviously encouraged the advancement of time servers and bureaucratic political hacks within the Party. The advancement of a new idea or a question regarding Party policy opened the questioner to deep suspicion of heresy, and this effectively throttled the Party's intellectual life.

Aside from this publicly acknowledged structure, the CPUSA also, over the years, worked through "underground" channels—committees, individuals, groups, the Communist affiliations of which were unsuspected except to a handful of Party leaders. The strength and intricacy of this underground Party apparatus has been the subject of much debate, the intensity of which has fluctuated with the intensity of anti-Communist feeling in the United States and the fitful attempts of the American government to drive the Party out of existence. It is safe to say that during eras of intensive official persecution of the Party, the CPUSA's underground network assumes increased importance in the Party's life. It is also safe to say that due to its awesome inefficiency (it has always been riddled by police and F.B.I. spies) and to the objective conditions of American society, this underground organization has never represented the slightest real threat to American institutions.

Of greater interest have been the widely fluctuating series of "front" organizations through which the CPUSA has attempted, from time to time, to mobilize support for various specific goals. These "front" organizations have been public alliances with non-Communist groups or individuals (in which Communist influence is purposely muted) for the achievement of certain immediate ends. During the Spanish Civil War, for example, an entire kaleidoscope of "societies," "committees," and "congresses" were formed to enlist non-Communist support for the Spanish Republic. In that particular case, as in some others, American Communists were supporting a goal (the defeat of fascism) which commanded the respect and sympathy of a very broad band in the American political spectrum. Liberal and progressive non-Communist Americans flocked to join the many anti-fascist "front" organizations established through Communist initiative from 1936 to 1939. On the other hand, as soon as it became evident that any given "front" organization would always subordinate its proclaimed goals to both rigid Communist domestic policies and the shifting vagaries of Russian foreign policy, that "front" would lose its mass support. The only lasting effect that most Communist "front" groups have ever achieved (except for the radicalization of a very scant handful of those non-Communists who joined) has been to arouse distaste and suspicion among Americans for what would otherwise have been very worthy causes.

It must not be thought, however, that Communist domination of open "front" groups, even where Communists formed only a minority of both membership and leadership,

was due entirely or even primarily to conspiracy. The fact
was, that in many a good cause—support for the Spanish
Republic, the fight to build the C.I.O. and other trade
unions during the 1930's, the struggle for Negro and other
minority-group rights—Communists, due to their single-
minded dedication, were the most effective allies to be found.
They were the ones who showed themselves tireless in
ringing doorblls, passing out leaflets, organizing fellow
citizens, collecting (and contributing) funds to fight the
good fight. It took more than a few years for American
liberals and progressives to realize that despite the effectiveness of Communist participation in any given struggle, the
long-range objectives of the CPUSA were such as would
inevitably undermine any immediate joint undertaking.

And despite the fervor and energy with which American
Communists have attempted to achieve their goals in the
United States, despite the "front" organizations of the
1930's and 40's, the trade-union building of the Roosevelt
era, the establishment of newspapers and periodicals such
as New York's *Daily Worker*, the attempts to reach the
American student population through "Marxist Study"
groups, the establishment of an underground organization,
active participation in almost every liberal cause, despite
all of this, the history of the CPUSA from first to last has
been a history of abject failure. In 1919 the CPUSA boasted
68,000 members, in 1929 less than 10,000. During the worst
part of the Great Depression, in 1933, Party membership
reached 75,000, declined to 60,000 in 1948 and is presently
estimated at about 12,000. Even if, to these numbers, are
added supposed thousands of "secret" Communists and
communist-sympathizers, total membership in a nation with
more than 200,000,000 citizens remains pitifully small.

Of course Lenin's Bolshevik party was also a tiny minority
in Russia in 1917; the structure of the party, its semiconspira-
torial nature and its self-imposed rigid discipline do not
encourage mass membership. The CPUSA, like Lenin's
party, was intended to form a self-appointed *leadership* for
the working classes, not the following. Yet even if Communist party success in the United States be measured, not
by membership alone, but also by influence among broader
elements of the population, it will be seen that the Party
has been an abysmal failure. For example, Party influence
among trade unions, despite the zeal and bravery with which
Party members threw themselves into the union organizing

struggles of the Great Depression era, is today all but non-existent. And although the Great Depression itself, with its staggeringly deep and widespread economic and social misery provided an unparalleled opportunity to "radicalize" American opinion, Communist Party Presidential candidates during those years never received more than 100,000 votes in any election. For one final example—although the struggle for black equality is today the most crucial, radical, and potentially revolutionary movement within American society, Communist party advice, participation, and support have been brushed aside by almost all black militants as being, at best irrelevant, at worst, divisive and self-defeating.

The reasons for the failure of the Communist movement in America have been many. One of the most obvious has been the abject servility of the CPUSA's support of Russian foreign policy. From 1932 until the present time, American Communists have had to swallow, digest, and propagandize to their fellow Americans the most contradictory and wildly fluctuating policies as if they were, each in its time, absolute truth. During the Lenin era of hoped-for worldwide revolution, American Communists had to denounce all moderate socialists and liberals as "fascists." A few years later, during the time of Stalin's organization of popular fronts to fight fascism, these same socialists and liberals had to be hailed as noble allies. When the struggle against fascism no longer suited Stalin's immediate needs, the CPUSA was forced to defend his nonaggression pact with Hitler, the ex-arch enemy. While the Stalin-Hitler pact remained useful to Russia, American Communists had to loudly proclaim their opposition to the United States participation against Nazi Germany in World War II; but when Hitler invaded Russia in June 1941, they just as loudly called for immediate American intervention. During Stalin's lifetime he was hailed by American Communists as the most farseeing, selfless, and democratic of statesmen; but in 1956, after Soviet Premier Nikita Khrushchev's deflation of the Stalin myth, American Communists had to accept a Stalin who was a self-serving, murderous, anti-Marxist, partially insane tyrant. It is no wonder then that over the years thousands of American Communists have, sooner or later, found the diet of Party ideology simply undigestible and have disgorged their adherence to the Communist movement along with their faith in its independence or objectivity. To those Americans who have not been sympathetic to the CPUSA, its performance of these ideological acrobatics has been at once hilarious and deeply repugnant.

But the enslavement of the CPUSA to the needs and whims of Soviet Russian policies and leaders has not been the basic reason for its failure. That reason may be said fundamentally to be that the Marxist-Leninist-Stalinist theoretical dogma has proven itself irrelevant to the American experience and to American society. A few examples should suffice to demonstrate this.

The Marxist description of the emergence of capitalism from feudalism may be an extremely useful and accurate analysis, but no feudal society has ever existed in North America. The Marxist prediction of the inevitability of class warfare in capitalist societies assumes rigid class lines, but the United States has always been, and for the most part remains, an open, fluid society in which people cross these imaginary class lines with sufficient ease to prevent them from becoming real social obstacles. The Marxist conception of "class" itself seems irrelevant in a society in which workers enjoy a standard of living available only to the very rich in other lands, in which working-class strength expressed through trade unions has become immensely powerful, and in which social usage and historical tradition have always *denied that any man could be meaningfully defined by his economic status*. The Marxist conviction that wealth must, through monopoly, accrue more and more to fewer and fewer capitalists while ever broader segments of the population sink into ever deeper poverty has been refuted not only by the growth and spread of prosperity in the United States but also by the increasing social control exercised over accumulations of wealth. The Leninist argument that democratic processes are but a sham, that through them no real progress could be expected, has been undermined time and again by the notable success of various American reform movements—from Theodore Roosevelt's "Square Deal" through Woodrow Wilson's "New Freedom," to Franklin D. Roosevelt's "New Deal" and down to John F. Kennedy's "New Frontier." None of these were apocalyptic visions of either revolution or Utopia. All were very pragmatic efforts to restore economic and social balance to society and to further widen the nation's responsibilities to all its citizens. The fact remained, and it remained apparent to the majority of Americans, that if enough people demanded change, the forms of American political democracy (slowly, creakingly, grudgingly perhaps) provided sufficient means for them to win it.

All of which is not to say, of course, that Marxist thought was or is utterly inapplicable to American society. It is simply to demonstrate that American Communists have never succeeded in employing it to formulate a relevant understanding of American conditions or even a sensible program of political action. It will be recalled that *under certain conditions* Marxism has shown itself to be remarkably adaptable as a means of analysis and a prediction of events. Can American society usefully be defined as a total capitalist state confronted by an *international* working class? Does not the black minority in America constitute a true submerged class with a true class consciousness? Are American institutions growing so rigid as to be susceptible now to change only through violence? These and many other questions may be investigated with many analytical tools, of which Marxism is by no means the least useful. Later we will attempt to see if, within the framework of non-Communist Marxist thought, any useful insights into current American problems may be discovered. But for the present it my be sufficient to point out that when radical or revolutionary-minded Americans, black or white, attack American institutions as obstructive or irrelevant to current social problems and needs, they might as well (and most do) include the rigid, dogma-bound, bureaucratic, feeble, and fumbling American Communist party.

Chapter Twelve

THE TRUCE OF THE BEAR

> We are building communism in our country; but
> that does not mean that we are building it only with-
> in the framework of the Soviet borders and our own
> economy. No, we are pointing the road to the rest of
> humanity. Communism is being built not only inside
> the Soviet borders, and we are doing everything to
> secure the victory of communism throughout the
> world.
>
> —*Nikita Khrushchev*

Stalin's foreign policy was compounded as we have seen,
of a strange mixture of communist theoretical dogma, realistic assessment of Russian national needs, and a domestic
political insecurity so deep as to verge on paranoia. This
foreign policy, which had followed so tortuous a path from
the open hostility with which it regarded all capitalist states
during the 1920's to the attempt to cooperate with some
capitalist states against fascism during the 1930's to the Nonaggression Pact with Hitler's fascist Germany in August
1939, came crashing down around Stalin's head on June
21, 1941. On that day huge, mechanized German armies
overran the Russian borders to plunge the Soviet Union into
the bloodiest war in human history. During the next four
years almost one half of European Russia was to be occupied by a brutal enemy; more than one third of Russian
industry was to be destroyed and more than twenty million
Russians were to lose their lives. Yet up to and even beyond
the last minute, when Nazi tanks were already rumbling
across Russian fields, when Nazi bombers were already

pulverizing Russian cities, Stalin could not bring himself to believe that this dreadful calamity, so largely brought on by his own opportunism, was real. For vital hours after the onslaught began Russian armies remained without authorization even to defend themselves and Russian planes were refused permission to attack targets beyond the Soviet borders.

There were many reasons for this. Some were, evidently, personal (Stalin went into seclusion, leaving his nation almost leaderless for days); some were military (the great purges of the late 1930's had crippled the Soviet command staff; misinterpretations of battles in Spain had misled Soviet military theoreticians) and some—those which most concern us—were political. And these political miscalculations involved not only the practical politics of Russian foreign policy, but were also deeply influenced by communist theory. Even the signing of the German-Russian Nonaggression Pact, generally viewed as a coldly cynical triumph of practical opportunism over professed ideals was not without its basis in communist dogma.

The circumstances of the signing of the Nonaggression Pact were much misunderstood at the time and have been more beclouded by subsequent Soviet propaganda. The argument runs something like this: The Soviet Union, from 1934 to 1939 desperately tried to establish a coalition with the Western democracies for the defeat of fascism in Germany and Italy. Soviet Foreign Minister Maxim Litvinov repeatedly went before the League of Nations to plead the cause of a United Front against Hitler and Mussolini. During the Spanish Civil War this Russian policy took on solid form in the shape of aid to the Spanish Republic both directly and through the Comintern. But all attempts to enlist the Western democracies into a common struggle against the German and Italian aggressors failed. Britain and France, through their policy of nonintervention in Spain only assured the eventual triumph of the fascist forces supported by Germany and Italy; such German aggressions as the reoccupation of the Rhineland, the seizing of Austria and the dismemberment and eventual swallowing of Czechoslovakia went unopposed by the Western powers. When Hitler began to exert pressure against Poland, to be sure, France and Britain "guaranteed" that nation against German aggression. But in the light of their failure to live up to previous obligations, especially in the case of Czechoslovakia, what

reliance could be placed on this paper "guarantee"? Furthermore, the Russians, both during the Czechoslovakian crisis
and during the Polish crisis had actively sought a military
alliance with the West. The Russians had proposed that in the
event that Hitler struck they would advance against the Germans in the east while Britain and France advanced from
the west thereby handing the German General Staff the
nightmare of fighting a two-front war. Even the mere an-
nouncement of such a Russo-Franco-British Pact, it was
held, would have stayed Hitler's hand if not brought about
the Nazi dictator's downfall. But all these Soviet proposals
came to naught. Even at the last minute, in late August
1939, the Franco-British negotiating team in Moscow demonstrated their countries' basic unwillingness to reach a
meaningful agreement with the Soviet Union. Why? Clearly
because the Western allies hoped that Hitler would turn
his giant war machine to the east and crush the Soviets—
with any luck the two totalitarian powers might destroy each
other. Therefore what other course was left open to Stalin
than to conclude a pact with Hitler, however detestable his
regime, in order to buy time to prepare for inevitable war?

Not only the Nonaggression Pact, but certain events which
immediately followed upon it were to be justified in this
way. The Russian invasion of Eastern Poland, coinciding
with the German invasion from the west; the Russian seizure
of the Baltic states of Lithuania, Latvia, and Estonia; the
Russian "Winter War" against neighboring Finland in 1939–
1940—all of these moves were later explained as having
been prompted by the necessity of gaining strategic space
and position to meet the inevitable Nazi onslaught.

Much of the foregoing may be admitted to be true. It
was true that the Western democracies, dominated by ap-
peasers and defeatists, failed to stand up to fascist aggression
in Spain, Austria, and Czechoslovakia. It was true that
Western leaders viewed with extreme distaste any sort of
alliance with Communist Russia. It was true that certain circles, both within and without Western governments secretly
hoped that the Nazis and Communists would destroy each
other. It was true that the strategic space seized from
Russia's neighbors during 1939 and 1940 was valuable
eventually against Germany (it is doubtful if Leningrad
could have been successfully defended otherwise). Yet these
are not the only truths to be considered in any assessment
of the origins of World War II.

First of all, Western appeasement of Hitler was not simply the product of a ruling-class conspiracy in England and France; it was a policy supported by the large majority of the English and French people who remembered only too well the sacrifices and horrors of World War I. Comprehending very little of the true nature of the Nazi regime and its aims, deeply involved in the domestic economic crisis of the Great Depression, vividly aware of their lack of military preparedness, neither Western leaders nor their peoples were prepared to sacrifice a generation to preserve Austrian or Czechoslovakian independence or the Spanish Republic. Secondly, if Western governments showed themselves reluctant to cooperate with the Soviet Union in any way, they were not without reasons for their behavior. The Soviet Union, through its spokesmen, had time and again proclaimed itself the mortal enemy of capitalist states anywhere and everywhere. All but open warfare against capitalist interests in the colonial world had been waged unremittingly by the Comintern. Native Communist parties loudly avowed their ultimate intention of overthrowing through revolution the capitalist governments of their countries. Thirdly, if a large body of public opinion in the West could discern but little difference between the Nazi and Soviet totalitarianisms this, again, had some foundation. While the full barbarism of Hitler's regime was not apparent until war broke out, many in the West were very conscious of the nightmare of enforced collectivizations, famines, purges, political prisons, and labor camps which decorated Stalin's Russia. Finally, the foundering of the attempted military negotiations with the Soviet Union in 1939 was based on Polish reluctance to allow Soviet forces to enter their country even to fight against invading Germans. They feared that Polish independence would suffer in that event. Had the Poles at that time understood that Hitler intended their total extermination as a people, they might have chosen the lesser evil. But that this lesser evil was quite real has been amply demonstrated, not only in the case of Poland, but in that of most of Eastern Europe by subsequent events.

Thus, if the behavior of the Western democracies during the agonizing 1930's fully contributed to the catastrophe of World War II, Soviet behavior was no less blameworthy. But while the Western nations fumbled and blundered their day to day course to disaster guided only by immediate necessities, Soviet policy was, in part at least, guided by Communist theory and dogma.

From the traditional Marxist-Leninist viewpoint, no meaningful distinction was to be made between such capitalist nations as Britain and France and the fascist powers, Germany and Italy. Fascism was only an advanced stage of capitalism—a stage into which history would eventually drive all capitalist nations. Marx also had postulated as "inevitable" an increasing series of wars between the capitalist nations; Lenin had clarified this in *Imperialism* as a desperate fight for markets and the exploitation of underdeveloped nations. War, therefore, between the fascist powers and the Western capitalist nations was only the fulfillment of these prophecies. While it behooved the Soviet Union to stand guard against being drawn into this insensate conflict or be damaged by it, there was little point in choosing sides. Just as the Western powers were presumed to hope that the twin tyrannies of Hitler and Stalin would devour each other, so Communists hoped that the twin imperialisms of Hitler and the Western capitalists would devour each other.

If Communist dogma blinded Soviet leaders to any distinctions between fascist nations and Western capitalist states, it also blinded them to political realities within the democracies. According to Marx and Lenin the political forms of democracy were but a continuing fraud, a sham behind which absolute control was exercised by the capitalists. The entire structure of a capitalist democracy was, in fact, simply the disguised expression of the class-will of the bourgeoisie. In some of the more highly industrialized and capitalized nations—such as Britain, France, and the United States— this class-will had been transformed into a national will. Therefore when Western political leaders referred to "public opinion" in their countries, when they pleaded that they could not adopt such and such a policy for fear that they would be voted out of office, Communists, especially the power-conscious Communists in Moscow, could only smile at such a transparent deception. The reality of political democracy was denied by Communist dogma; hence it was denied as a real, practical force in the affairs of democratic nations.

The immediate impact of adherence to Communist theories about the nature of capitalist democracies was very practical. Soviet negotiators could not believe that it would be politically impossible for British and French leaders to "force" the Poles to accept Russian intervention. The Soviet leadership could not believe that it would be politically impossible for the British and French to go back on their word to Poland, that the leaders of those countries could not so manipulate affairs that they could avoid war. It is interesting to note that the French and British declarations of war against Nazi Germany came as complete a surprise in Moscow as they did in Britain.

It would be speculation to assume any other chain of events than those which subsequently ensued. Had Stalin refused a pact with Germany would that have prevented Hitler's aggression? We know now that important German elements were prepared to attempt the overthrow of the Nazi regime if it dragged Germany into a two-front war. In the event that there was no pact, would the Western democracies have abandoned Poland, hoping that Hitler, with a free hand in the East would continue into Russia? Almost definitely not. The Western Allies would almost certainly have stood by their guarantee to Poland or faced a vast political upheaval at home. Suppose Stalin had maintained his neutrality while Hitler and the West went to war, refusing to guarantee Germany's eastern front but likewise refraining from the grab of Eastern Poland and the Baltic States. Would Russia's eventual military strength *vis-à-vis* Germany have suffered? We know today that it would not. The German war machine overran the Baltic States and Eastern Poland in a matter of hours and days; the time supposedly gained by the Nonaggression Pact did not prove sufficient to increase Russia's military preparedness in any meaningful way. On the other hand, the Nonaggression Pact and the subsequent invasions of Poland, the Baltic States, and Finland did much to lose Russia the friendship, influence, and trust that had been so painfully built up in the West during the period of the United Fronts.

It is not our purpose to trace in any detail the story of Russia in the Second World War, except insofar as that story has a bearing upon the development of Communism as a theory and a political fact of life. The war in Russia was not fought so much as an ideological struggle, but as the Great Patriotic War of the Soviet Union (its official title in Russian histories) in which every available propagandistic element from religion to chauvinism was enlisted, regardless of its theoretical Marxist validity. It was a war of Russians against Germans, not of Communists against fascists. Likewise, when Russia found herself allied with Britain, and, later, the United States, the alliance was between Russians, Englishmen and Americans, not between Communists and capitalists. And, finally, the heroic sacrifices and dogged fighting abilities of the people of the Soviet Union, which more than any other factor or combination of factors brought about the destruction of Nazi Germany, earned them the lasting gratitude of mankind as Russians, not as Communists.

Stalin, in order to assure the vitally necessary success of his alliance with the Western democracies, was prepared to throw overboard a large part of the Communist international apparatus. Communist parties in Britain and the United States were instructed to mute their attacks against explutocratic capitalist wolves now transformed into heroes of production and against ex-imperialistic oppressors now transformed into gallant allied governments. In 1943, as a gesture to placate those in the West with long memories, the Comintern was officially dissolved. Later in the war, at Allied conferences held in Teheran and Yalta, Stalin went so far as to declare his unwavering support for Chiang Kaishek's Nationalist Chinese government as opposed to Mao Tse-tung's Chinese Communist movement. It was not until victory was assured and World War II was reaching its end, that communism in theory and practical political fact began once more to assume importance in Russian foreign policy.

During the last months of 1944 and the beginning of 1945, vast Russian armies, having fought their way thousands of miles from Leningrad, Moscow, and Stalingrad, erupted over Russia's prewar borders in pursuit of their stricken enemies. As they drove triumphantly on to the capture of Vienna and Prague, their meeting with American troops on the river Elbe and their final conquest of Berlin, the Red Armies liberated almost all of Eastern Europe from the dreadful nightmare of Hitler's insane "New Order." The fact that this liberation was purely *incidental* to the final crushing of Nazi Germany (as was the Allied liberation of Southern and Western Europe) did not dilute the very real gratitude with which most Eastern Europeans greeted the Soviet forces. It was generally realized throughout Eastern Europe too, that in the future the national security of Eastern European nations would have to be linked with the strength of the Soviet Union. This was a geographical fact of life which the Second World War had made abundantly clear. It was further recognized that if national security depended on friendly relations with Russia, then the domestic political structure of Eastern European nations would have to be such as would not arouse Russian suspicions or hostility.

Before the outbreak of the Second World War, the social, economic, and political structures of such countries as Poland, Hungary, Rumania, Bulgaria, and Yugoslavia had been, to say the least, reactionary. All were countries with a large and badly exploited peasant majority. Some, such as Rumania and Yugoslavia, had been kingdoms; Poland had been an oligarchy of the very rich and the military; Hungary had been a dictatorship. It might well have been supposed that these countries were ripe for a Communist revolution in any event. But if they were, that revolution would have to be domestic, not imported, and Communist, not Stalinist. Many of the postwar political leaders of Eastern Europe were, in fact, eager to introduce socialism or socialistic reforms to their countries. It will be noted that these nations, with their peasant farming structure, their prewar decayed aristocracy, their heavily exploitive, miniscule industrial organization were almost classical models of societies poised on the brink of a socialist revolution. Only one of the countries of Eastern Europe, Czechoslovakia, escaped that condition. Czechoslovakia was, despite a preponderance of peasant farming in her eastern provinces, highly industrialized, heavily capitalized, socially fluid, and enjoyed a highly successful tradition of democratic government—not an apt example of a presocialist state.

Whether native socialism would have triumphed in Eastern Europe is something which will never be known. For Stalin was not interested in the success of communism as a native solution to national problems in Eastern Europe. He was interested only in the future security of Russia's western borders. Looking forward to the day when the Red Army would have to return to the Soviet Union, Stalin could not feel sufficiently secure with treaties or alliances in Eastern Europe. Only governments in those nations which were directly, completely, and abjectly subservient to and controlled by Moscow could satisfy the Soviet dictator. The introduction into the governments of Eastern Europe of agrarian liberal leaders and socialists of various hues, far from appeasing Stalin's insatiable craving for security only aggravated it; he viewed postwar moderate socialist leaders in Eastern Europe with the same fearful suspicion he had shown towards all rivals within the Marxist camp since the days of Trotsky.

It may be well to point out here that the Soviet craving for security at any price was not without rational foundations. The Soviet Union had just undergone the most fearful catastrophe in history—a catastrophe brought about partly by the ease with which Germany had dominated Eastern Europe. Furthermore, the dropping of atomic bombs (of which Stalin had not been informed) on Japan in the closing days of the war introduced a terrifying new element of power into the world—and this was a power exclusively in the hands of the United States, a country seen in Communist eyes as the arch-stronghold of capitalism and, wartime alliances aside, the inevitable mortal enemy of communist society. This view was in no way assuaged in the immediate postwar world by the belligerent statements of certain harebrained American political and military leaders.

The truth was that Hitler, by destroying the state structures of the nations of Eastern and Middle Europe, had created a vacuum of political, economic, and social power. The question which emerged was: What forces would move into this vacuum? At first it had appeared that a cooperative effort among all the Allied powers would recreate the domestic power of the nations of that area. The Declaration of Liberated Europe, signed on February 11, 1945, as a part of the Yalta Conference between Russia, the United States, and Britain, had stated that the liberated states were to have the right to form domestic institutions of their own choice and governments which, while they excluded all former fascist and reactionary elements, would be broadly representative and freely elected. Yet even before the war ended, the Allies found themselves quarreling (especially in the case of Poland) over just what was meant by "reactionary" elements, "broad" representation, and "free" elections. It soon became apparent that for Stalin, these were merely meaningless phrases behind which he was determined to impose regimes of his own choosing upon the nations of Eastern Europe.

Yet for about two postwar years, 1945 and 1946, genuine coalition governments existed in Poland, Hungary, Rumania, and Bulgaria. In these governments the local Communist parties played an important but by no means exclusive role; they included also agrarian, socialist, and moderate democratic groups. Yugoslavia and Albania had already been taken over by native communist regimes; Czechoslovakia remained a liberal capitalist democracy. But by 1947, with the deterioration of relations between the United States and Russia, marked by the establishment of the Truman Doctrine (first propounded as a means of providing support for the tottering conservative governments of Greece and Turkey), Stalin seems to have decided that only outright control in Eastern Europe could serve his purposes. Accordingly, in 1947 Communist parties throughout Eastern Europe launched a ruthless campaign to win absolute power in their respective countries. From positions of influence and power previously gained in trade unions, youth organizations, the army, the police, and the means of mass communications, and with the full support of the Red Army where that force was still present, local Communist parties forced other elements in the Eastern coalition governments to either disband or fuse with them. In Poland, Hungary, Bulgaria and Rumania the Communist parties established dictatorships during 1947; in 1948 they were able to seize power in Czechoslovakia through tactics of terror and violence.

All of which may be viewed as not so much a part of the history of the development of Communism as simply another scene in the age-old European drama of power politics. Yet Stalin was not entirely wrong to be afraid of rivals within the socialist world. Even though the governments established in Eastern Europe in 1947 and 1948 were securely under Soviet domination (which is to say, under Stalin's personal control) over the years even the limited local power exercised by these local Communist parties was to prove sufficient to breed leaders and viewpoints which were to importantly alter Communist theory and practice. The first of these leaders, indeed, emerged as early as 1947 while Soviet-controlled governments were being established in Eastern Europe. His name was Josip Broz, better known to history by his conspiratorial name: Tito.

Born in Croatia (part of present-day Yugoslavia) in 1892, Josip Broz was raised in poverty as a blacksmith's son. Taking part during his youth in nationalist agitation against the Austro-Hungarian Empire (of which most of Yugoslavia was then a part), he soon moved politically left until, after World War I, he joined the Communist party. Long considered one of the most militant sections of the Comintern, the Yugoslav Communist party went into a decline from 1929 to 1934.

When Tito (as he was known by then) assumed leadership of the Party in 1939, he had to rebuild it almost from scratch. So successful were his efforts that by 1941 it was a powerful, if underground, element in Yugoslav political life. But the opportunity for power was provided by Hitler's destruction of the Yugoslav state in April 1941. Immediately Tito and the Communists undertook to wage underground and partisan war against the occupying Nazis. By 1944 so successful were they in this effort that more German Army divisions were being tied down in Yugoslavia than by the vast Allied armies in Italy! During the days of partisan warfare, for geographical reasons, Tito could receive aid only from the British and Americans—a fact which had much to do with his subsequent views on the Western democracies. By the time the Red Army arrived in Yugoslavia in 1945, Tito's partisans were in effective control of most of the country. Thus, while he had reason to be grateful for Russian aid (and, be it noted, the Western Allied aid he received by sea across the Adriatic and by air), Tito had largely won his own war on his own grounds. When elections were held in liberated Yugoslavia in 1945, all other political groups simply abstained; Tito and his Communists won overwhelmingly, the Yugoslav ex-king Peter was informed he needn't bother to return from his exile abroad, and Yugoslavia became the first of the "People's Democracies" of Europe with Tito as premier.

The rift which was soon to disrupt Russian-Yugoslav relations, though it was expressed politically, had its roots in the postwar economic chaos that reigned throughout Europe. All of Europe needed a vast program of reconstruction, a heavy influx of new capital for the building and repair of industry and communications which had been devastated by the war. Russia, more than any other nation, with the possible exception of defeated Germany, required a tremendous reconstruction effort. One of Stalin's major purposes in the political reorganization of Eastern Europe undertaken in 1947 was to turn that area into a colonialized region from which Russia might draw desperately needed economic support. Accordingly, the new Communist governments of Eastern Europe were required to sign trade agreements with the Soviet Union which provided that their goods would be very much underpriced in Russia while Russian goods (which they were forced to purchase) would be very much overpriced in their own countries. Trade between the Eastern European nations was discouraged—each was to become a direct economic colony of the Soviet Union. So successful was this Stalinist policy that it has been conservatively estimated that more than twenty-three billion dollars was gained by Russia through exploitation of its Eastern European colonies between 1945 and 1956.

Tito not only would not permit the colonial exploitation of Yugoslavia, he went so far as to attempt to enlist support among other Eastern European nations, notably Bulgaria, for a Balkan Trade Confederation. Furthermore, the establishment of the American Economic Assistance Program to Europe in 1948 (the Marshall Plan), which was rejected as "economic imperialism" (!) by the Soviet Union and, of course, by the Soviet client states of Eastern Europe, demonstrated that there were other possibilities for economic revival than those offered by embracing Russian imperialism. Growing alarmed at the independence demonstrated by the Yugoslav Communists, Stalin attempted to topple Tito from power in 1948. His instruments for this purpose were certain members of the Yugoslav Communist party, Soviet technicians in Yugoslavia, and the Communist Information Bureau (Cominform), which had been established in 1947 (a pale imitation of the old Comintern) with headquarters in Belgrade, Yugoslavia. But Tito was not, nor had he ever been, a puppet Communist imposed on his nation by Moscow. His power and popularity in his own country were entirely too strong to be shaken without an outright Soviet invasion. Unwilling to risk war, Stalin severed relations with Tito and had the Yugoslav Communist party expelled from the Cominform, which moved its headquarters to Bucharest, Rumania. More importantly, he cut off trade between Russia and Yugoslavia.

By 1950 it was apparent to Tito that unless he opened new trade channels, the Yugoslav economy might founder. He therefore accepted economic grants from the United States—grants which were to total more than three billion dollars in the next few years. In return for this massive aid, American officials hoped to establish Yugoslav neutrality in the Cold War and to use the Yugoslav example of independent national Communism as a wedge to separate Russia from her Eastern European satellites. And these hopes were, to a certain extent, fulfilled. In subsequent years Tito did liberalize the Yugoslav economic and cultural structure. In

place of bureaucratic centralized control of industry, workers' councils were established to decide such matters as
factory production and goods distribution; censorship of the
mass communications media was greatly relaxed; Western
tourism was encouraged and soon reached massive proportions. Although the Yugoslav Communist party retained absolute control over the nation's political life, its methods
and policies were democratized to the point where it certainly enjoyed the support of the large majority of the Yugoslav people. Tito did maintain neutrality in the Cold War—
a neutrality which sometimes proved as irritating to the
United States as to the Soviet Union. Most important of all,
Tito's example of independent Communism, liberalized and
freed from Stalinist tyranny, did have important repercussions throughout Eastern Europe, as Stalin's heirs were to
discover.

But if Tito and affairs in Eastern Europe proved trou-
blesome to Stalin during the postwar epoch, they were not
his chief preoccupations. These were, in descending order
of importance, the reestablishment and retention of his personal absolute power within the Soviet Union; the reconstruction of the Russian economy after the ravages of the war;
and the developing Cold War between Russia and the United
States. All of these problems were interrelated, of course.
Soviet production was spurred (and devoted almost exclusively to heavy industry rather than consumer goods) as
part of a "competition" with the United States. American
policy was painted in direst terms to the Russian people in
order to support a partial "war scare" psychology which
would enable the dictator to justify his continued absolutism.
The deepening of Stalin's paranoia found expression in a
new wave of police terror, including the threat of giant new
purges like those of the 1930's. This too was disguised behind hints of plots to disrupt production, or "imperialist
American" espionage and sabotage conspiracies.

It may be admitted that Stalin was largely successful in
his domestic policies after World War II. Production, beginning with a new Five-Year Plan introduced in 1946 increased remarkably. By 1949 the war-devastated Soviet
economy was producing as much as it had in 1941; successive Five-Year Plans increased Soviet production until Russian industrial capacity grew to be the second largest in the
world—not only second largest, but second most sophisticated as well—as the speedy Russian development of atomic

and hydrogen bombs demonstrated and as the Soviet leap into outer space conclusively proved. As far as the Cold War is concerned, while Stalin registered no sensational gains in attempting to expand the sphere of influence of the Soviet Union, neither did he suffer any losses, with the exception of Yugoslavia. And in his campaign to retain and expand his personal power, the dictator displayed his usual cunning sagacity and ruthlessness. During his lifetime no weakening of the absolutist structure of the Soviet regime took place, no dilution of Stalin's personal authority. Indeed, until the very moment of his death, in March 1953, Stalin's closest collaborators, the men who held the highest posts in the Soviet government and the Russian Communist party lived in personal dread of his increasingly insane suspicions.

Of course the reconstruction of the Russian economy and Russia's emergence as a mighty industrial and technical world power, the conquest of Eastern Europe, the intricacies of Cold War relations between the United States and Russia, the deepening of Stalin's tyranny within Russia itself are not particularly germane to the story of the development of Communism in either theory or political fact. And indeed, one of the most important points to be made regarding Communism, at least as developed in Russia, may be gleaned from the fact that as our story has progressed we have found ourselves discussing Communism less and less, while ever greater space is devoted to Russian history as if it was developing entirely independent of the philosophy of Marx or even Lenin. We may take the occasion of the death of Stalin to reflect that Marxism, a theory of the emergence of capitalist industrialism from feudal society, as modified by Lenin to fit peculiar Russian conditions, and enforced by Stalin, had indeed predicted and helped to generate the creation of a state-capitalist industrialized society in Russia. Once that society was established, Marxism-Leninism had *apparently* little more to offer as a philosophical, political, social, or economic guide. The word "apparently" is emphasized here because, under the Stalin tyranny, the study of Marxism and free speculation growing from that study were as rigidly strait-jacketed as all other intellectual activities. If Marxism may be considered to be susceptible to further development rather than as a closed system of thought, then we may say that a history of communism as anything more than the immediate policy of the government of the Soviet Union, came to an end in its Russian phase during the Stalin era—perhaps even as early as the death of Lenin. New directions in communist thought, new dimensions of Marxist philosophy were not to be sought in Stalin's Russia (they have not appeared to this day), but in those areas of the world where a fresh application of Marxism-Leninism produced new problems which required new solutions.

Chapter Thirteen

DRAGON'S TEETH

> The Red Army, never fearing the challenging Long March,
> Looked lightly on the many peaks and rivers.
> Wu Meng's range rose, lowered, rippled,
> And green-tiered were the rounded steps of Wu Meng.
> Warm-beating the Gold Sand River's waves against the rocks,
> And cold the iron chain spans of Tatu bridge.
> A thousand joyous *li* of freshening snow on Min Shan,
> And then, the last pass vanquished, the Armies smiled.
>
> —*Mao Tse-tung*

On October 1, 1949, a short, heavyset, balding man with a pleasantly round face, a man who looked like everybody's jolly uncle, mounted the steps to the balcony of the ancient Imperial Palace in Peking, China. More than half a million people were packed into the great square below the balcony, and they cheered fervently when he appeared. Then the huge throng hushed as Mao Tse-tung, his voice trembling slightly, began to read from a piece of paper he held in his hands: "In the name of the Consultative Political Committee and of the Chinese people, I proclaim the People's Republic of China." With these words, the second largest nation on earth, with a population estimated (at that time) at five hundred million, joined the Communist world. The repercussions of that simple statement created shortsighted elation in Moscow, and equally shortsighted despair in Washington—and those repercussions have not yet subsided. The shockwave sent out from Peking on that crisp October morning has not yet spent itself; in fact, its greatest impact may well lie in the future. And the shortsightedness of outside response to it has left permanent scars upon the political psychologies of both its friends and its enemies.

At first glance, the historical conditions which gave rise to the Communist triumph in China seemed so similar to those which prevailed in Russia before the Bolshevik revolution that the chain of Marxist successes there seemed predictable, link by link. Here again was a vast nation emerging from semifeudalism into the industrial world of the late nineteenth and twentieth centuries. Here again was an overwhelmingly peasant society in which almost all the land was owned by a small class of exploitive landlords. Here again was a society in which early industrialization was a product of foreign imperialistic investment and construction. Here again was a nation which had developed (proportionately) only a small industrial working class and boasted almost no middle class; a nation basically divided between harshly oppressed peasants and a tiny minority of aristocratic landowners, a nation with a large, decaying and incompetent bureaucracy topped by an autocratic ruler who enjoyed absolute power. Here again was a land in which the vast majority of people remained illiterate, prey to disease and crippling conditions of work, suffered widespread famine regularly, and were treated as somewhat less than human by their masters. Here again was a country with no meaningful tradition of political participation on the part of its people and with a deeply paternalistic tradition of obedience which stretched from a father-dominated family to an emperor-dominated government. And, finally, of great importance, here was once again a nation in which the structure of the previous state had been shattered by a devastating foreign invasion.

But there were important differences between the historical matrices from which Russian and Chinese communism arose—and these differences produced different results. First of all, it must be pointed out that the difference between the degree of outside imperialistic exploitation in pre-Bolshevik Russia and prerevolutionary China was so great as to be a difference in kind. While Western capital owned a large share of Russian industry before World War I, and Western capitalists, trading finished manufactured goods for Russian raw materials were certainly relegating the Russian economy to semicolonial status, the majority of Russian industrial enterprises remained in Russian hands, and the entire development of industrialization in Russia was strictly controlled by the Russian tsarist government. But in China, fully ninety-five percent of all industrial enterprises were owned by foreigners. Furthermore, these industries were operated by foreigners, employing Chinese generally only as raw labor. The Chinese imperial government, from about 1850 on was so weak that far from so much as influencing Chinese industrialization, it could not even successfully defend Chinese territorial integrity against foreign imperialism. British, French, American, Imperial Russian, and Japanese armed forces were stationed in Chinese cities; warships of these powers patrolled Chinese rivers; Chinese port cities contained large foreign "concessions" under the direct rule of various foreign powers; huge sections of the nation had been parceled out between foreign powers as "spheres of influence." China, unlike Russia, was a joint colony of the Western nations plus Russia and Japan in all but name. When the feeble Chinese government attempted, from time to time, to assert its rights in its own territory, it was attacked by the armed forces of one or more of the imperialist powers. When the Chinese people themselves rose against domestic and foreign exploitation, the imperialist powers joined forces with the Chinese government to put down the uprisings. It will be seen, then, that any revolution in China, whatever its ideological basis, would have to develop as a *war of national liberation*, not simply a class war between the oppressed and their domestic oppressors.

A second decisive difference between the prerevolutionary societies of Russia and China was also a difference in degree. It was true that both were, very largely, peasant societies, with but small working classes. But the proportion of industrial workers in tsarist Russia to the rest of the population, small as it may have been (about ten percent) was far greater than the proportion of industrial workers to peasants in prerevolutionary China. The Russian working class, concentrated in the large cities was just able to seize power with the temporary support of the Russian peasantry which had been radicalized by the privations of war; the Chinese working class, also concentrated in the large cities, would not be strong enough to seize power, even temporarily. In

China a successful revolution could only be made by the peasantry with the industrial working class a minor ally. Yet, as has been pointed out earlier, from the time of the French Revolution on, an observable phenomenon of peasant revolutions was the fact that once the peasantry had achieved its great aim, ownership of the land, it invariably ceased being revolutionary and lent itself to the suppression of further revolution which might endanger this hard-won ownership. This had been the reason for Lenin's impatience in 1917—he recognized that the Russian peasantry was still a revolutionary force, but that its potential success would convert it into a counterrevolutionary force; thus the Bolsheviks had to strike at an immediately favorable conjunction of worker-peasant interests which might never return. But since, in China, there could be no realistic talk of any very great working-class contribution to the success of the revolution, the peasantry, if it were not to successfully convert itself into a small middle-class farmer group, must somehow be kept in a condition of revolutionary ferment until such time as real state power had been won by the revolutionary Marxist political leadership. This meant that any Communist revolution in China was bound to be a *prolonged* campaign in which the *education of the peasantry to Marxist ideals* would be as important as military successes. The peasantry, even after a successful revolution, could never be allowed to rest on its gains—new class enemies would have to be descried on the horizon as a means of keeping its revolutionary fervor at sufficient heat to give time for an industrialization program which would produce a more solid social basis for a Communist state. Thus, any Chinese Communist revolution would, to a certain extent be a *continuing revolution* even after apparent victory.

That these important differences between the Russian and Chinese experiences were by no means clear to Chinese revolutionaries themselves will become apparent as the story of the emergence of China into the modern world unfolds.

That story may, with a certain degree of arbitrariness, be said to have begun when the European powers, but especially England, first realized that the Celestial Empire was so weak that trade with it could take the form of direct, military-backed exploitation rather than bargaining. The reduction of China to semicolonial status commenced at the beginning of the nineteenth century and continued unabated and with ever-increasing rapacity for the next hundred years. Although this exploitation was, in certain cases, competitive with the domestic exploitation of China carried out by the then-ruling Ch'ing dynasty, it maintained an uneasy alliance with it. Both groups (the Ch'ing dynasty was Manchu—the Manchus were also foreign to China, having conquered the country at the beginning of the seventeenth century) were primarily interested in maintaining their seats of privilege upon the backs of the unhappy Chinese people. In the 1850's, when the Taiping Rebellion, involving many millions of peasants, threatened to overthrow the Manchus, European forces decisively intervened to help the Manchus put it down. On the other hand, when the Manchu government tried to prevent, as it did from time to time, further outside encroachment on its own preserves, the European (and later the Japanese) powers did not hesitate to wage war against it. The imperial capital at Peking was captured and sacked more than once by British and French troops during the nineteenth century, while Japan waged a short but decisive war against Imperial China in 1893. The American contribution to these continuing events, it may be noted, was the famous "Open Door" policy of Secretary of State John Hay—a policy which, in effect, asked that the European powers not completely dismember the Chinese Empire but maintain an open door into it so that others (Americans) could also partake of the feast of exploitation.

Faced with the combined power of the Manchus and foreigners, revolutionary ferment in China took the ancient (for China) form of the establishment of secret societies. In 1900 one of these, the Fists of Righteous Harmony (known in the West as "Boxers") succeeded in raising again the standard of revolt. They were able to rout local Manchu forces (the Empress Dowager fled to the hinterlands) and to besiege the foreign legations at Peking. Immediately English, French, German, Japanese, and American troops were dispatched and within a year they had not only raised the siege of Peking but effectively smashed the Boxer Rebellion and imposed new, harsh indemnities upon the Manchu government for their intervention.

Born into this atmosphere of oppression and rebellion, in the year 1866 was Sun Yat-sen, the man who, more than any other, was to bring about the collapse of the Manchu regime. The child of middle-class peasants, Sun was educated at an English school in Hawaii and later graduated in medicine from an English college in Hong Kong. Rebuffed in his attempt to practice medicine at the Portuguese colony of Macao, Sun decided to devote himself to the cause of revolution. He joined, and later formed, many a secret society in the tradition of the Boxers. His groups attempted time and again to rise against local governments only to be put down with harsh severity every time. To finance his revolutionary ventures Sun traveled all over the world, especially in the United States, speaking to local Chinese emigrant communities. He was, in fact, in Denver, Colorado, on such a tour, when news of a successful uprising led by his lieutenants in China reached him in October 1911. Sun immediately returned to China, only to find that while his followers held power in the south, a former Imperial general, Yuan Shih-kai had seized power from the hastily departed Manchu dynasty in Peking and the north. Yuan Shih-kai had an army and, more importantly, the backing of the European powers who feared that Sun's revolution might endanger their investments in China. The military dictatorship of Yuan Shih-kai (he suppressed Sun's political party and drove Sun Yat-sen himself into exile) lasted until the general's death in 1916. By that time the collapse of government power in China had led to the establishment of semiindependent warlord regimes in much of the country. The only opposition to the warlords was the newly-created (in 1912) Kuomintang (National People's Party) headed by Sun Yat-sen. Not only did Sun (who returned to China in 1916) and his Kuomintang face the power of the private armies of the warlords (a loose coalition of them controlled Peking and the north), but Japan, allied to Britain and France during World War I had seized the occasion of Europe's involvement in that struggle to grab the former German "concessions" and leaseholds in China. She followed this up in 1915 by presenting to the government of Yuan Shih-kai a list of twenty-one "demands" for further economic and political privileges in China, demands which Yuan Shih-kai was unable to oppose. Japan, therefore, could not be expected to look favorably upon Sun's attempt to unite China under a democratic government—nor, for that matter could the Western European powers.

There was one place, however, from which Sun Yat-sen received support: the newly established Soviet Union. As early as 1910, Vladimir Lenin had observed from Switzerland: "Each point in Sun Yat-sen's program is conceived in a democratic spirit which is both combative and sincere."

Now, in 1919 and 1920, eager to strike a blow against the colonial interests of the Western capitalist powers as a means of postponing their "inevitable" assault upon the Soviet Union itself, Lenin offered to help Sun Yat-sen. As early as July 25, 1919, the new Soviet government had offered to give up all the special treaty rights and concessions which had been imposed on China by former tsarist regimes. Although negotiations dragged out until 1924, the new Soviet-China treaty was far more favorable to China than the still-extant treaties she held with Western European powers. More directly, in 1923, one of the ablest of Comintern agents, Mikhail Borodin, was sent as special advisor to Sun Yat-sen in Canton. In return Sun sent one of his more promising young military officers, Chiang Kai-shek, to study at the Frunze Military Academy outside Moscow. Technical advisors, arms, and money soon began to reach Sun's forces at Canton, beginning early in 1924.

Borodin outlined a new party structure for Sun's Kuomintang, one which would ensure greater discipline within the party and enable it to effect direct agitation among the masses of Chinese peasants and workers. At the First Congress of the Kuomintang party, held in Canton in January 1924, the new constitution of the party (written by Borodin himself) was adopted. The Kuomintang Army was revitalized and the Whampoa Military Academy for the training of Kuomintang officers was established. First commandant of the new academy was Chiang Kai-shek, returning from Russia full of enthusiasm for the new Soviet State.

Soviet help and the changes wrought in the Kuomintang and its armed forces bore fruit in 1924. By supporting one warlord (the Manchurian, Chang Tso-lin) against others in the north, Sun was able to strike a bargain which permitted him and his followers to enter China's ancient capital on Christmas Day, 1924. But Sun's triumph was short-lived; on March 12, 1925, Sun Yat-sen died of cancer. Leadership of the Kuomintang thereafter devolved increasingly upon the shoulders of Chiang Kai-shek.

While Soviet Russia had been helping Sun Yat-sen directly, a Chinese Communist party, under the patronage of the Comintern, had been created. The Party was formally declared into existence by a group of nine delegates representing student and labor groups from all over China at a secret meeting held in an empty girls' school in the French concession of Shanghai at the end of July 1921. One of the junior secretaries of this group was a young student from Peking who had become interested in Communism while studying at the university there—Mao Tse-tung.

The problems facing this fledgling Chinese Communist party resolved themselves basically into one: whether or not to support the Kuomintang and, if so, how? Sun Yat-sen's Kuomintang was essentially a party of middle-class, liberal-democratic aims, repugnant to communist hopes. But it was the only effective instrument in sight through which China might hope to unify itself and free itself from foreign domination. Accordingly, the Chinese Communist party (in accord with the views expressed by Lenin at the Second Congress of the Comintern) decided that for the moment they must support the Kuomintang with the aim of helping it to establish a free, unified, industrialized capitalist China. When these ends had been achieved would be time enough to commence communist agitation for a socialist revolution to establish a dictatorship of the proletariat. All of which, it will be seen, was in accord both with the immediate tactical situation and with classical Marxist theory. Although arguments over this problem would continue among Chinese Communists, Comintern officials and Soviet advisors (intensified when Chiang Kai-shek, whom they viewed with suspicion, rose to leadership of the Kuomintang), the Chinese Communist party, while recruiting members for itself, loyally supported the Kuomintang for the next few years.

Beginning in 1925, Chiang Kai-shek felt strong enough to begin that two-year battling march to power which became known as the Great Northern Expedition. Using his highly trained and Russian-equipped new army, Chiang defeated one warlord after another in his march towards Peking. By 1926 most of Southern China was in Kuomintang hands. But by 1927, with Kuomintang forces poised to strike at Shanghai, the contradictions between Kuomintang and Communist party aims had become painfully apparent.

In his struggle to unite China, Chiang Kai-shek felt it necessary to enlist under Kuomintang banners not only peasants and workers, but also China's small but strategically placed middle class, former government bureaucrats, landlords, and even, on occasion, local warlords. Furthermore, fearful of intervention on the part of Western European powers or Japan, Chiang sought to placate them by emphasizing the capitalist-conservative elements in the Kuomintang program. With ultimate victory in sight, all these elements demanded that Chiang take some steps to rid himself of the radical support of both Chinese Communists and his Soviet advisors. Accordingly, in March 1927, as Kuomintang forces entered Shanghai, they turned upon their Communist associates and massacred them. By July 1927 Borodin and his Soviet staff of advisors were packed off to Russia. In December 1927 a repetition of the anti-Communist massacre in Shanghai was held when Kuomintang forces entered Canton. With conservative elements in the Kuomintang, and nervous foreign observers now satisfied that the Chinese Communists had been liquidated, Chiang's forces swept north, entering Peking in June 1928 and establishing a new capital, of the Republic of China at Nanking, the following month.

Clearly, the Communist party policy in China had proved a tragic failure. Communist party forces were disorganized and bloody; Communist party leaders (those who had not been caught and executed by Chiang Kai-shek) were disheartened and divided. It was at this lowest ebb in the fortunes of the Chinese Communist party that the young student from Peking, Mao Tse-tung, rose to prominence and then leadership.

Mao had been born in 1893, in a small village outside Hankow on the Yangtze River. The son of well-to-do peasants, he was educated in local village schools. In 1911 he briefly joined Sun Yat-sen's armed bands to fight for the overthrow of the imperial autocracy, but when Yuan Shih-kai seized power in 1912, Mao quit the army. In 1913 Mao entered the Hunan Normal School in Changsha where he soon formed a New People's Study Society for the discussion of politics and philosophy. When his studies at Hunan were completed, he went to Peking as a delegate to a Congress of student groups being held in the capital in 1918. While there he got himself a job in the library of Peking University and began to study the Marxist classics. By the summer of 1920 he considered himself a Communist; and the following year, as we have seen, he was present at the founding of the Chinese Communist party in Shanghai.

During the period of Kuomintang-Communist collaboration, Mao Tse-tung generally supported the Communist line, but with a significant divergence. While he agreed that the Communists must support the Kuomintang in its drive to unify and liberate China, Mao also wanted the party to organize massive support among the Chinese peasantry as a sort of insurance against possible Kuomintang betrayal. He argued that the Chinese peasantry was a truly revolutionary force and could be harnessed to Communist aims. But traditionalists on the Chinese Party Central Committee clung to the classical Marxist view that only the big-city proletariat could be relied upon to form the backbone of the Party. Mao's views were disregarded.

In February 1927 Mao undertook a field trip among the peasantry of his native province, Hunan, to study conditions. He wrote up the results for the Party Central Committee as a *Report on an Investigation into the Peasant Movement in Hunan.* In this remarkable document Mao reported that the Chinese peasants were on the verge of revolution and that the Communist party must place itself at the head of this incipient peasant uprising. Again, Mao's views were disregarded as being counter to Marxist orthodoxy. If anything, the Central Committee held that peasant revolts ought to be suppressed because they might alarm the landlords of the Kuomintang with whom the Communists were still allied.

When, in the bloody streets of Shanghai and Canton, the Kuomintang at last gave its answer to Communist hopes for collaboration, Mao, without authority from the Party's Central Committee (which was now driven underground) returned to Hunan. There he organized the peasantry and launched a revolt in August 1927, which was to be known as the Autumn Harvest Uprising. By September the successful peasants were able to create what they were pleased to call the First Division of the First Peasants and Workers Army. Kuomintang reaction was swift. The First Division was surrounded and defeated. Mao himself was captured and narrowly escaped execution. Fleeing through swamps and over mountains, Mao emerged again with a mere remnant of his troops to establish, in November 1927, the first Chinese Soviet—in the little town of Tsalin in Hunan province, a village secure in the almost inaccessible mountain fastness called Chingkangshan, "Mountain of Wells and Ridges." To this area, from their bloody defeat in the cities, came the survivors of the Kuomintang's program to liquidate the Chinese Communist party.

With these reinforcements, Mao began to extend the area of his Soviet. In 1928 he wrote an interpretation of the situation entitled *"How Can China's Red Power Exist?"* In this essay Mao demonstrated that a revolutionary army must have a broad territorial base, giving it room to maneuver. This meant that the inhabitants of such an area must share both the work and the benefits of Communist rule. To win peasant support, land must be given them; to win their adherence to the Red Army, the troops of that army must not only behave with impeccable courtesy and honesty to the peasantry, but must help them in their work, must plant and plough and harvest by their side. An ancient Chinese sage said, "The people are the water and the Imperial Government floats atop the water." Mao Tse-tung said, "The people are the water and we are the fishes who swim in the water." Only a true fusion between Red Army and local peasantry could ensure survival. By 1930 Mao's policies had proved so successful that the Communists controlled fifteen "liberated regions" around Kiangsi province and fielded an army of sixty thousand regular troops who could count on the support of fifty million peasants.

Chiang Kai-shek, his power in the rest of China now consolidated, undertook to wipe out the Communist areas. Between 1930 and 1935 he launched no less than five "Final Extermination Campaigns" against the Red forces. All were unsuccessful (Chiang's regiments had a disconcerting habit of defecting to the enemy) until, with professional German military advice, Chiang decisively defeated Mao's Red Army. On October 16, 1934, Mao Tse-tung and the remnants of the Red Army abandoned their base in Kiangsi province. Carrying what equipment and supplies they could, they embarked on a great strategic retreat which became known as the Long March.

This fabulous march, comparable only to the march of the Ten Thousand Greeks as recorded by Xenophon in the *Anabasis,* covered a route of six thousand miles. Forbidding mountain ranges (the "roof of the world"), vast deserts, raging rivers running through mile-deep gorges, miasmal swamps, and battles not only against Chiang Kai-shek's forces but also against primitive tribesmen in Western China —all these faced the Red Army. But on October 25, 1935, Mao and his men reached their goal, the city of Yenan in Shensi province in the far northwest of China. They had marched three hundred and sixty-eight days, crossed eighteen mountain ranges, forded twenty-four rivers, fought a skirmish somewhere along the line every day and fought fifteen major battles. They had passed through twelve provinces and eluded or defeated Kuomintang forces numbering three hundred thousand men, while breaking through the local forces of ten different warlords. They had marched through aboriginal territories in which no Chinese army had been seen for centuries. Their accomplishment made Hannibal's crossing of the Alps or Napoleon's retreat through Russia seem like summer picnics. And their new base in the northwest placed them within easy reach of the Soviet Siberian frontier, Manchuria, Peking, and the rich Yellow River basin. Chiang Kai-shek would have difficulty sending troops into this fastness. Furthermore, from Shensi province, the Red Armies would be able to fight against a new threat to China's national existence: Japanese aggression.

In 1931 Japan had seized China's northern province of Manchuria; in 1932 Japanese naval and military forces seized Shanghai, and conquered the northern Chinese province of Jehol; on July 7, 1937, Japan opened hostilities against China on a wide front. Although not declaring war (the Japanese preferred to refer to their invasion as the "China Incident") the Japanese effectively made full-scale war upon China; within months most of the port cities and much of the interior was being occupied by Japanese forces.

The Chinese Communist response to Japanese aggression as early as 1931 had been to declare war against Japan. Chiang Kai-shek's response was more cautious, and was limited by the now-apparent nature of the Kuomintang regime. Based on cooperation with landlords, middle-class officialdom, and such foreign powers as Britain, France, and the United States, with a tradition of autocratic control and military domination behind it, the Kuomintang could not make use of China's one real weapon against Japan—the vast masses of Chinese peasants and workers. In fact, the Kuomintang undertook to suppress peasant rebellions and workers' trade unions so as not to alarm its domestic and foreign clients. Its regime grew increasingly corrupt, increasingly inefficient, and increasingly oppressive over the years. It could hardly rouse the masses to a great revolutionary struggle against the Japanese.

These restrictions were unknown in the Communist areas, however. There Red Army units, cooperating with the peasantry, waged a ceaseless partisan war against Japanese forces. In so doing they radicalized the countryside in which they operated. Using the same tactics, both military and political, which they had developed in Kiangsi and during the Long March, Mao's Red Armies were so successful against Japan that by the end of the war, in 1945, they held huge "liberated areas" in which many millions of peasants were administered and protected by the Red Army and into which no Japanese dared venture.

Yet effective national resistance against Japan could only be led by Chiang Kai-shek. It was he who had inherited the mantle of Sun Yat-sen, he who was the formal president of the Republic of China, he whose name was known throughout China as a symbol of the struggle for unity and liberation. More importantly, perhaps, it was only the Nationalist regime of Chiang Kai-shek which could effectively cooperate with those Western nations such as Britain, France, and the United States who were willing to help China against Japan. So, while maintaining their independent base in Yenan, Mao's Communists (with the active backing of Stalin who was also worried about Japanese aggression against Siberia), continually urged a united front between Communists and Nationalists in the struggle against Japan. Chiang, ever suspicious of Communist motives, agreed to accept their cooperation only with the greatest reluctance. All during the war against Japan Chiang Kai-shek fought with an eye to the future—that future when, with Japan defeated, he could once again turn to the liquidation of his Communist allies. It may be observed here that the Communists were no less suspicious, and the lands they liberated from the Japanese were consolidated with a view to enlarging Communist control so as to create an impregnable bastion against postwar Nationalist attack.

The Japanese war against China, while it brought no final or lasting victory to the Japanese, went catastrophically against the Nationalist forces. Only when the China Incident was swallowed up in the flames of World War II, when Japan attacked the United States and Britain, was ultimate Chinese victory foreseeable. That victory was won elsewhere —in the waters of the Pacific, on the Pacific islands, in the air over Japan. But China was not neglected by the Americans. What supplies could be sent by air were dispatched; American advisors such as General Joseph Stilwell were assigned the task of attempting to create an efficient Chinese Army; hundreds of millions of dollars were voted by Congress in financial aid to China. Furthermore, at various international wartime conferences, China was hailed as one of the "Big Four" powers fighting the common enemies. In 1945, with the Soviet Union about to declare war against Japan (at the urging of American officials trying to avoid the one million American casualties predicted for an all-out invasion of Japan), Stalin concluded a formal pact of friendship and alliance with the government of Chiang Kai-shek. By implication he disavowed support for the Chinese Communists.

But this was nothing new. For despite the break between Kuomintang and Communists in China (and a subsequent break in Chinese-Soviet relations during the 1930's), Stalin had continued to support Chiang Kai-shek and to withhold support from Mao Tse-tung. Once again Soviet foreign policy was dominated not by Communist theory but by harsh fact. Chiang Kai-shek could lead China against Japan. Japan was a threat to the Soviet Far East. Supporting Mao Tse-tung's ·Communists could only endanger Russian relations with Western capitalist nations. Russia gave no aid to the Chinese Communists until after the end of World War II—and then that aid was scanty. When Mao's armies rolled to victory in 1948 and 1949, they were to be equipped not with Russian but with American arms, tanks, and trucks—captured from Nationalist forces.

But what was decisive in the Chinese Civil War that opened almost as soon as Japan surrendered, was not foreign intervention—either Russian (in Manchuria, from which the Japanese had been driven by the Russian Army during the last days of the war) or American, with its heavy aid in munitions, arms, and money for Chiang Kai-shek. What was decisive was the difference between Nationalist and Communist programs for the industrialization, organization, and unification of China; in short, for the emergence of China into the modern world.

The Nationalists, increasingly bound over the years to landlord, middle-class, and bureaucratic support, could not, without losing that support, undertake the radical measures needed to liberate the Chinese peasantry from its semifeudal oppression. Under the Nationalist regime peasants were taxed as heavily as ever, were conscripted as ruthlessly as ever into the Nationalist Army, and were offered no program whatsoever looking toward their eventual ownership of the land—the great peasant objective. Likewise, the Nationalist regime could offer but little to the big-city proletariat. The dislocations of a devastating war brought fantastic inflation to the cities, reducing the working class to even more abject poverty. At the same time, corrupt Nationalist officials and businessmen openly indulged in profiteering and black-marketeering; objections against this were met by a Nationalist secret police as ruthless as any to be found in the most totalitarian countries.

Not all of this was the fault of Chiang Kai-shek and his top associates. It must never be forgotten that Nationalist China was, basically, destroyed as a state by the Japanese. Furthermore, Nationalist political theory, such as it was, made corruption and dictatorship all but inescapable. Sun Yat-sen had held that the Nationalist revolution would have to pass through three stages. First there would be the military-dominated campaign to unite and liberate China. Then would come a period of "political tutelage" to be carried out by the Kuomintang. During this time the Kuomintang would rule dictatorially, holding the people's rights in trust while the vast illiterate masses of China were educated for self-rule. Only then would the third stage, complete political democracy, be entered. But the first stage, the desperate military campaigns to establish a Nationalist regime for all of China, dictated the second. The military men who led the Kuomintang to victory in 1928 were not equipped in outlook or background to foster the growth of democracy in China. Faced with foreign aggression, the towering problems of educating China's masses in democracy, and, above all, the impossibility of arousing those masses without undermining the structure of the Kuomintang itself, the third phase of Sun Yat-sen's program was constantly postponed. The Kuomintang developed into a dictatorship and, within it, Chiang Kai-shek, who saw himself and was increasingly seen by his followers, as "indispensable," became an absolute ruler. The oppressions, corruptions, and inefficiency which always characterize absolute autocracies became inescapable.

On the other hand, what did Mao Tse-tung's Communists offer the Chinese people? First, and overwhelmingly important, they were able to offer the peasants ownership of their land. Furthermore, they were able to back this offer with practical demonstrations. In those areas in which Red Army troops operated, peasants were financed to buy their land or, in many cases, the land was seized outright from local landlords. This program was not, of course, in accordance with Marxist aims. The land was intended to be transformed into state-owned collective farms. The creation of a small landowning agricultural bourgeoisie supposedly spelled the doom of any Communist revolution. But Mao Tse-tung, as pragmatic as Lenin before him, was developing new tactical methods and new rationalizations of those methods to fit Chinese conditions. In China only the peasantry was strong enough to form the backbone of a Communist revolution. Therefore the Communists would have to give the peasants what they wanted: the land. Furthermore, once they owned the land, the peasants would have to be kept in a state of revolutionary fervor by the threat that without a total Communist victory, outside forces would take the land away from them again. Chiang Kai-shek's government of landlords and bureaucrats obligingly provided this outside threat, as did, later, the Japanese. So Mao was able to both satisfy peasant aspirations and keep the peasants in the forefront of the revolutionary struggle. The fact that eventually the Communist state in China would once again take the land from the peasants to organize it collectively under state control was not made clear; in fact, it was so successfully obfuscated that many foreign observers thought Mao Tse-tung's followers were not real Communists, but simply "agrarian reformers."

Beyond this the Chinese Communists were able to make a direct, classical appeal to the big-city working class, along regular Marxist lines. When the Communists took over, the foreign-owned factories, as well as those domestically owned would be taken over by the state. But the state would represent the workers and peasants. Wages would increase as profits were eliminated, workers councils would take over direction of industry, etc., etc. Furthermore, the Communists were even able to appeal to certain middle-class elements by simply promising an end to graft, secret-police oppression, and government corruption. The Communist party leadership, the Communist party cadres, and the Red Army itself were always careful to display the most austere and impeccably honest behavior wherever they appeared.

In the light of all this it may seem remarkable to us today that foreigners, be they Americans or Russians, could imagine that they could influence events in China. American postwar missions (especially the mission headed by George C. Marshall in 1946 and 1947) which attempted to bring Nationalists and Communists together in a coalition government were doomed to failure. Both sides were convinced of their ultimate victory; neither could compromise with the other without risking their individual identities and power bases. The only question was which side held the more realistic view of the future. This was answered during 1947 and 1948 by massive Communist victories against Nationalist forces, victories marked by the wholesale desertion of entire Nationalist armies to the Communists. Driving south from Manchuria and Yenan and those areas of North China they had previously liberated from the Japanese, Mao Tse-tung's Red Armies gathered momentum as they went. By October 1949 Mao was able to proclaim the "People's Republic of China." By the beginning of 1950, Chiang Kai-shek and a remnant of his forces were forced to flee to the offshore island of Formosa under the protecting guns of the United States Navy. The Nationalist regime in China had crumbled like a "paper tiger" because it had lost the support of the overwhelming majority of the Chinese people. The idea that any American policy short of a full-scale war in China could have prevented this collapse was totally unrealistic.

What Mao Tse-tung and his followers did with their victory will be examined later. For the moment it would be well to bear in mind the differences between Mao's program for victory and the program adopted by Lenin and his heirs. Those differences, as we have seen, were based on the basic economic, social, and historical distinctions between prerevolutionary Russia and prerevolutionary China. From them grew not only Mao's unique recipe for success, but also much of the unorthodox subsequent course of communism in China. It was Mao's ability to adapt Marxist theory to new conditions, his willingness, while paying lip service to Communist dogma, to experiment pragmatically, which brought him, as it had brought Lenin before him, victory in the struggle.

Part Four

REALITY IN SEARCH OF SOME IDEAS

Chapter Fourteen

THE SOVIET STATE

> The contradiction between the State and the individual is a phenomenon which has occurred in history when society has been divided into rival classes. . . . History has already solved that problem in my country. The State and the individual are in harmony with each other; their interests coincide.
>
> *—Andrei Vyshinski*
>
> One hears talk about some sort of absolute freedom of the individual. I do not know what it means. . . .
>
> *—Nikita Khrushchev*

Karl Marx and Friedrich Engels never addressed themselves in any serious way to an examination or projection of what a socialist society would be. They foresaw that immediately following a successful Communist revolution there would have to be a period of dictatorship of the proletariat, a period during which the industrial workers would enforce their will upon the rest of society. This would be for the purpose of wiping out the remnants of the capitalist bourgeoisie, the defense of the revolution against internal or external enemies, the restructuring of society so that the means of production could be taken over communally. Beyond that there would be the necessity of reeducating all members of the revolutionary society, eliminating the psychological hangovers of insecurity, competition, and that individual aggressiveness which had been fostered by capitalist society. When the new "socialist man" had fully come into being, the prophets of Communism had foreseen a time when the state would "wither away." At some time in the far-distant future the state and all its coercive apparatus would no longer be required for the ordering of a society, and conflict, either between classes or individuals, would no longer exist.

Lenin and Stalin, explicitly, and Stalin's heirs implicitly, saw in these predictions a clear, three-phase development. First would be the dictatorship of the proletariat, second the era of "building socialism," finally, the era of full, stateless Communism.

It will be immediately apparent that all of this begs vital questions. The most important of which is: By what means, or through what organs, does the proletariat exercise its dictatorship? By what means or through what institutions does society "communally own" the means of production? By what means does the dictatorship of the proletariat undertake to produce a new, "socialist man"? What standards of behavior and belief are expected of this "socialist man," and who judges them? The answers to these questions have varied but slightly in the Soviet Union since the time of the early Stalin era. After Stalin's death in 1953, a change in the rigorous structure of socialist society in Russia was widely hailed—but this change was by no means basic to Soviet institutions or Communist outlook. The State that Lenin and Stalin built remains fundamentally unaltered in its structure to this day. And despite the fact that the ordering of Soviet Russian society was not and is not an inevitable outgrowth of Marxist thought, as (with the exception now of China) it remains the only spontaneous, domestic Communist society in the world, it will be worth our while to examine it in some detail.

There are two lines of state power in the Soviet Union. One of them consists of the governmental organization, the other of the Communist party organization. Of the two, the Communist party organization is by far the most important. Control of the Party apparatus has brought power to every Soviet leader since the time of Lenin; to Stalin, Malenkov, Khrushchev, and, latterly to Brezhnev and Kosygin. While all top government officials are also top members of the Party hierarchy, decisions reached within Party, not government councils form the basis of state policy.

The formal government and basic laws of the Soviet Union remain built on the Constitution of the USSR handed down by Stalin in 1936. They have been modified several times since that year, but not deeply altered. Supreme state power is vested in the Supreme Soviet, an elected body composed of two chambers: the Soviet of the Union (all-national) and the Soviet of Nationalities (representatives of the various "autonomous" Soviet Republics). In a sense this corresponds to the structure of the American federal government. The Soviet of the Union would compare to the American House of Representatives since its members are elected on the basis of population, while the Soviet of Nationalities would compare to the United States Senate since its members are elected on a regional basis to represent the interests of those regions. Between them, the Soviet of the Union and the Soviet of Nationalities elect a small number of their members to serve on a Presidium of the Supreme Soviet—the actual top governing body of Russia.

The Supreme Soviet and its Presidium also appoint a Council of Ministers to head up the various all-national state executive departments, and beneath them, a descending order of Councils of Ministers and Executive Committees actually charged with the daily administration of the Soviet government on down to the village level. Under the authority too of the Supreme Soviet and its Presidium are the various Supreme Soviets (and their Presidiums) of the individual Soviet Republics. These Republic Supreme Soviets in turn have authority over Regional, District, and Village Soviets within their respective Republics.

Paralleling this government structure is the structure of the Russian Communist party. Its top organ is the All-Union Communist Party Congress which draws delegates on an all-national basis. This Party Congress chooses a small Central Committee from which, in turn, is derived a Presidium. Beneath the All-Union Congress are to be found individual Republic Party Congresses, Regional Party Congresses, Bureaus, District Party Conferences, and Primary Party organizations—each with their Presidiums or Party Central Committees exercising executive power. For clarification the reader is invited to examine the chart on page 235. Such is the formal organization of the government power in Soviet Russia.

All offices in the various scale of Soviets are elective. Deputies to the Supreme Soviet are elected on a nationwide basis; deputies to lower organs are elected on a regional or district or village basis. All citizens of the USSR over the age of eighteen, except for criminals or the insane, are entitled to vote. They also have the right of "recall," that is, anytime a sufficient percentage of the electorate becomes dissatisfied with a deputy they may petition for his recall and for a new election to fill his seat within two weeks. All of which sounds most democratic. Unfortunately, citizens of the Soviet Union, on every and all elective levels are able to vote for *one slate of candidates only*. There are no opposition candidates for elective office in the USSR or any of its member Republics. The voter is thus able either to record a vote in favor of a candidate or a list of candidates, or a vote against, but he is not able to vote for any alternative candidates. Although the ballot is secret, in election after election, beginning in 1936 and continuing to the present day, the voters of Russia have never failed to support the official lists of candidates with majorities of less than 99%! Generally the winning majorities of candidates are announced as hovering (depending on areas and years) between 99.4% and 99.7% of all votes cast. Stalin was never returned to office with less than a full 100% of the votes! Furthermore, those entitled to vote in the Soviet Union do so with an altogether amazing fidelity and perseverance; it is a rare election that does not call forth at least 99.6% of all registered voters!

These state-trumpeted figures are, of course, a dead giveaway. Even without opposition candidates to vote for, it surpasses human credibility that more than 99% (or any figure even remotely approximating that) of voters representing more than 230,000,000 people, sixty language groups, dozens of nationalities, hundreds of occupations, etc., etc., can achieve such near-unanimity. And since the ballot *is* secret, it must be supposed that government electoral commissions entrusted with counting the votes simply announce figures to suit themselves (no doubt subtracting a tiny percentage from 100% unanimity to make things look slightly more realistic).

But if deputies to the various Soviets of Russia are elected by meaningless votes, their duties remain largely meaningless, too. Despite the fact that the affairs of the world's second-most powerful nation must be complex in the extreme (especially considering that the government of Russia is also the employer of most of the Russian people, administering a gigantic national industry), the Supreme Soviet and the Republic and Regional Soviets meet, on an average, for only two weeks every year! During those two weeks they make speeches praising the government and vote, almost

THE THEORETICAL AND ACTUAL POWER STRUCTURE
OF THE SOVIET UNION

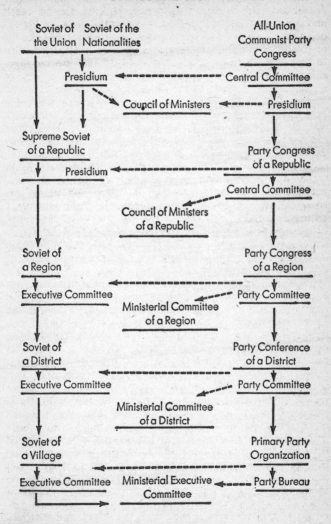

Solid lines indicate theoretical flow of authority; broken lines indicate actual flow of political authority.

always unanimously, to support government policies and programs then in effect or projected. They also vote, again, almost always unanimously, to continue in office the Presidiums they have appointed, or to change their composition. There is no debate in any real sense (occasionally minor criticism of the efficiency on a technical level of various government ministries may be allowed) and no political maneuvering.

If there is but one slate of candidates for which a voter may cast his ballot, from where do these candidates come? On each level they are put forward by either the Party apparatus or Party-supporting groups. The only political group which offers candidates for election in Russia calls itself the Communist Party and Non-Party Bloc. By which is meant that the list will include some candidates who are not necessarily members of the Communist party of Russia, but who are being supported by the Party. No candidates without Party membership or support have ever appeared on any electoral list anywhere in the Soviet Union. Furthermore, on every level of government, from that of the village to that of the Presidium of the Supreme Soviet and the all-national Council of Ministers, *most of the same men* hold dual offices in the respective Presidiums and local governments and the corresponding Central Committees, Congresses, and Executive Committees of the Russian Communist party. The government of the Soviet Union may thus be likened to a body, the skeleton of which is the Russian Communist party. Keeping in mind that this Party counts only about 11,000,000 members and candidates for membership out of a population of hundreds of millions, it will be seen that political democracy does not exist in the Soviet Union, and the government of the USSR on all its levels remains a dictatorship of the Communist party over the people and, on the higher levels a dictatorship of the Party leadership over both Party and government. Yet the era of the dictatorship of the proletariat in Russia was supposed to have passed by 1936—since that time, Soviet leaders and theoreticians have held that Russia was in the second phase of building socialism, looking towards the establishment of full Communism with its withering away of the state.

But it may be objected, on the lower levels, where Communist party candidates are selected to run on the unique electoral list for public office, there must be democratic debate over the qualifications of individuals. This is not true.

Candidates are formally put forward by such Primary Organizations as factory or trade-union committees, neighborhood blocks, collective farms, etc. But what actually happens is that a candidate's name is presented to these organizations by the corresponding level of Communist party leadership and these candidates are then approved with the same record of infallible unanimity by members of Primary Organizations, as they are later elected to office. All candidates must be approved by the Executive Committees through which the Council of Ministers exercises governmental control and administration—and since these Executive Committees are under the real control of the corresponding Party organization, there is no escape from Party approval or disapproval for any particular candidate. Any debate over a prospective candidate's qualifications is confined to the Party organization involved. And since this organization is a minority group of a minority party, there can be no talk of political democracy on any level of government in the Soviet Union.

If citizens of the Soviet Union do not enjoy political democracy, what civil, social, and legal rights are granted them? The Soviet Constitution grants every conceivable right; it is certainly a model of democratic verbiage. But in actuality Soviet citizens may exercise only those rights which the Soviet government at any point in time sees fit to grant them. Citizens are, for instance, guaranteed in the Soviet Constitution the right of free expression through mass media communications, meetings, political activities, street demonstrations, etc. But all means of mass communication, from press to radio and television, to book publishing are both state owned and state controlled. They are censored not only directly, but also indirectly by the fact that as government organs they would, even without direct censorship, express only the government viewpoint. Writers or artists who attempt to publish or display works which do not meet with the approval of the government authorities simply cannot find any means of publication outside the state-owned and operated single publishing entity. Soviet citizens, according to their Constitution, are guaranteed freedom of movement. But Soviet citizens who seek to travel abroad must obtain the consent of the Soviet government—and this consent is only rarely and grudgingly given. Furthermore, Soviet citizens must carry with them domestic passports if they live in any of the large cities or within border areas of the Soviet

Union. These passports must be registered with the police
at every turn and, in the majority of cases, must be renewed
every five years. Since peasants or collective farm workers
are not issued passports, they cannot live in any large city for
more than a few weeks, move beyond their provincial borders, or, in effect, leave their localities. Like serfs of old they
are tied to their land.

But the rigidity of the social order in Russia is not limited
only to agricultural workers. Industrial workers are bound
to their jobs by a complicated system of rewards and punishments. Theoretically they may leave their place of employment after giving two weeks' notice of their intentions.
But they must seek the approval of their factory management (which is, of course, staffed and dominated by local
Party organizations) and, if this is not forthcoming, they
risk the loss of wages, seniority benefits, and social security
rights. Since there is only one employer—the state—in all
of Soviet Russia, there is no escape for a worker from the
permanent approval or disapproval with which he is regarded by his employer.

The criminal code of the Soviet Union is, in some ways
more severe, in others more lenient, than those of Western
democracies. The death penalty is reserved as punishment
for many more crimes in Russia than in the West, but is
rarely invoked for strictly criminal offenses. Crimes such as
robbery, rape, murder, etc., which are personally motivated
—that is to say, are not inspired by a desire to weaken or
attack the state—are generally dealt with by terms of imprisonment ranging from three to fifteen years. Soviet citizens
accused of crimes are neither presumed innocent nor presumed guilty until they are convicted or acquitted; but the
the burden of proving their guilt is laid upon the prosecution. They may be arrested and held without being informed
of the nature of the accusations against them for up to ten
days. After that time they may be held under arrest for
three months before being brought to trial. This initial three-
month period may be extended by higher authority to a
total of ten months. After this time a preliminary trial-
examination takes place before a court. The court (somewhat like an American magistrate's court) decides whether
the evidence warrants trial. If it decides that a defendant
must stand trial then, and only then, is he permitted to engage a defense attorney. Trials are held before courts composed of one judge and two lay persons and their verdicts

are reached by majority vote. These verdicts may be appealed to higher courts (composed only of judges) all the way up to the Supreme Court of the Soviet Union, beyond which there is no appeal. Trial by a jury of one's peers, the right of *habeas corpus,* the right to remain silent until legal advice has been granted, the right to be presumed innocent until proven guilty—in fact, almost all the basic tenets of Western jurisprudence are unknown in the Soviet Union.

But beyond a strictly criminal code (which deals with offenses considered to be crimes in all countries) the Soviet citizen is bound by a legal system which recognizes as "crimes," actions which are not so recognized elsewhere and which establishes means of trial and punishment unique to the Soviet Union. Since, for example, the state both owns and manages all industrial and agricultural enterprises within the nation, actions on the part of industrial or farm workers which would be dealt with on a personal economic level in other countries, may be considered crimes in the Soviet Union. Absenteeism from work, tardiness at work, failure to produce up to the established norm, etc.—all of these may be considered crimes against the state and punished as such. Trial of delinquent workers may be held within the juridical system or before Communist Party Courts composed solely of Party members, and punishments range from reductions in pay to imprisonment or exile. Even away from work, the Soviet citizen must mind his manners and his opinions. For if he is judged guilty of any sort of "antisocial" behavior (a term purposely left vague) he may be called to account before Comradely Courts composed of his fellow-workers or his neighbors. These courts, established and operated by a simple majority of those concerned, may take a citizen to task not only for industrial "crime" but also for making too much noise in his dwelling, for using "foul and abusive language," for not having any visible means of support, for dressing or acting in ways not acceptable to his neighbors. These Comradely Courts may not inflict terms of imprisonment or exile (though they can recommend that cases be turned over to the juridical system) but they can impose public censure and fines.

The Soviet Union offers not only a system of legal and extra-legal jurisprudence unknown in the West, it also offers punishments unknown in the West. Those judged guilty of crimes may be imprisoned in regular jails; they may be executed. But they may also suffer exile or deportation, or "corrective labor." Instead of being sent to jail, a Soviet citizen may be incarcerated for specified numbers of years in a labor camp, of which there are many in Soviet Russia. Or he may be exiled for specified lengths of time to remote areas of the Union. Or he may simply be forbidden, for certain periods of time, to enter other areas of the Union— a sort of domestic deportation. Exile is inevitably to the frozen wastes of Northern Siberia, just as it was in tsarist times. The labor camps, although much more leniently operated today than they were during Stalin's time (when they bore similarity to Nazi concentration camps and millions of people perished in them) are almost always located in forbidding "frontier" areas and the work discipline is harsh indeed, amounting to a system of slave labor not unlike the "chain gang" system formerly employed in parts of the United States.

The severity and structure of the Soviet legal system is, of course, an admission that Soviet society has not yet produced the new "Soviet man," that remarkable individual who will discipline himself to be good, work hard, and avoid all secular temptations simply for the good of society. But not only is there no sign as yet of this Soviet man in Soviet society, there is not even a sign of social and/or economic equality. Soviet Russia, far from being a "classless" society, has witnessed an increasingly rigid social stratification. It is true that certain old classes have disappeared, especially the basic bourgeois class, the ex-owners of the means of production. It is also true that theoretically other old classes can no longer be defined as such; a proletariat which does not toil for a bourgeoisie may not be classified, in Marxist terms, as a proletariat at all; a peasantry which does not toil on privately owned land, likewise may not be defined as a peasantry. But this is mere playing with words. In truth, the Soviet society is made up, basically, of three distinct and apparent classes: the industrial proletariat, the agricultural peasantry, and the "intelligentia" or governing bureaucracy of officials, managers, and technicians. A closer look at each class will support this contention.

The obligation of every able-bodied Soviet citizen to work is inscribed in Article Twelve of the Soviet Constitution, which states: "Work in the USSR is a duty and a matter of honor for every able-bodied citizen, in accordance with the principle: He who does not work, neither shall he eat." This obligation begins at the age of sixteen in cities and towns, at the age of twelve on rural collective farms. The length of the work day varies, but generally, Soviet citizens work a forty-five hour week. As in capitalist lands, they are paid extra for overtime (which, however, they may not refuse without risk) and there are rewards and bonuses for those who either produce more or devise ways of increasing factory efficiency. A surprisingly large percentage of Soviet workers are paid on the old (in capitalist lands) piece-work basis; that is they are paid in accordance with *how much* they produce, not on the basis of the number of hours they work. This provides a built-in incentive system and reestablishes one of those means of worker exploitation so bitterly assailed by Marx and Engels one hundred years ago. Discipline in Soviet factories is rigid; infractions, as we have seen, are punishable as crimes. The management of a factory or industry, under the principle of "one-man command" is granted absolute control of factory procedures, the establishment of production norms, the enforcement of discipline, etc. Management may fire a worker for any number of reasons which generally correspond with reasons for discharge in capitalist countries. But unlike management in most Western democracies, industrial management in the Soviet Union is not handicapped by having to deal with meaningful trade unions.

Trade unions exist in Russia—they exist for every conceivable skill or industry. Furthermore, they are organized to be all-inclusive and have a hierarchical structure which culminates in an All-Union Central Council of Trade Unions. These trade unions are primary Communist party organizations and are administered also as part of both the Party and the government bureaucracy. Their purpose, however, is not to fight against management but to cooperate with management. Since private ownership of the means of production is, in Russia, replaced by "social" ownership because the Soviet is a workers' state, the old functions of trade unions become contradictory. To strike against a factory or industry would mean striking against their own interests. According to Communist dogma, trade unions as we know them, are merely capitalist weapons of class warfare. When class warfare ceases, as it has in Soviet Russia, then such organizations lose their combative function. In fact, in Soviet society, trade unions are simply another means of organizing and controlling the population; the trade unions are instruments of the state, not of the workers. As such, and since the state owns and manages all means of production, they may be likened to the old American "company unions," with the exception that they possess much greater powers over their membership—powers backed up by the juridical arm of the state itself.

Labor fluidity in the Soviet Union is both directly and indirectly controlled by the state. Youngsters graduating from secondary or technical schools are assigned by the state to their first jobs. They are issued labor books in which management inscribes a complete record of their employment, of infractions of rules, etc. These labor books, without which no Soviet citizen may work in industry, are held by management (as, in certain cases, are workers' domestic passports without which they cannot move). Theoretically, since de-Stalinization, workers are free to quit their jobs on two weeks' notice and, with their passports, are free to move anywhere they wish within the Soviet Union. But very often this is accompanied by financial penalties (loss of bonuses, paid-up vacation time, seniority, etc.) as it might be in capitalist countries, and with a loss of housing, since a large percentage of state-owned housing in the USSR is controlled by local factories or industries. If it is important to the state (i.e. the factory management) that a worker *not* quit his employment, the state has many means, both legal and extra-legal, to prevent it. Aside from this, the Soviet State, just like capitalist employers, seeks to hold workers in certain jobs simply by paying them higher wages. Workers in heavy industry earn twenty-five percent more than workers in light industries, for example—a notable commentary on the old Marxist adage: "each according to his needs . . . "

The social benefits enjoyed by workers in Soviet Russia include some unknown in capitalist lands. Since the state is the owner of most housing, as well as the payer of all wages, rents are extremely low, amounting to highly subsidized housing. Likewise all medical costs of every kind are borne by the state. Two-week vacations, retirement plans, institutions for disabled or overage workers, cultural programs that range from factory libraries and clubs to visiting performances of theater, ballet, and even grand opera, accident or sickness benefits—all of these are financed directly by the state. Some, it will be seen, correspond to programs already enjoyed by workers in Western capitalist democracies, the difference being that in the West, workers themselves finance and control these programs through their trade unions or through their governments, paying dues and social-security taxes to do so. In the Soviet Union where the state pays all wages to begin with and directly controls all unions, the payment of special dues or taxes would be clearly redundant: the state finances all these programs by simply paying lower wages. The average wage in Soviet industry is, incidentally, about one hundred dollars per month. But the living standards of Soviet workers cannot be judged by this since, as has been pointed out, rents are much lower and a wide range of services are free. Furthermore, the prices of certain consumer products (of the most necessary, not "luxury" items) are kept, by government policy, within the reach of everyone. The average living standard in the Soviet Union is about one quarter that in the United States. It remains significantly lower, too, than the living standard in such countries as France, England, West Germany, and Italy.

If the conditions of workers in the Workers' State remain somewhat less than satisfactory, what about conditions among the rural population? The overwhelming majority of agricultural workers in the Soviet Union are organized to work on either collective or state farms. While there remain far more collective farms than state farms, the number of the latter is increasing rapidly as virgin lands are brought under cultivation and collective farms are taken over by the state. State farms are those which are owned and directly managed by the state. State farmers are actually agricultural laborers and are organized into unions like industrial trade unions; they are, furthermore, state employees with all the benefits and obligations of government workers. Collective farms, on the other hand, are "voluntary" associations of former private farmers who pool all their material resources plus their labor into the collective in return for an annual share of the collective farm's income. The quotes around the word "voluntary" are in remembrance of Stalin's harsh collectivization campaign of the late twenties and thirties when millions of peasants were "persuaded" to join collective farms by starvation, deportation, and armed force. Collective farms are chartered in the USSR and each farm's charter (its "constitution" as it were) must correspond to the model charter established by government decree in 1935.

The average collective farm tills about 1,000 acres of land and is comprised of about four hundred families. The collective farm does not own land, nor does it own subsoil mineral rights; all this is state property. The Soviet government owns all the land in the Soviet Union and leases some of it to the collective farms in perpetuity. The state determines the amount of produce which must be sown, the harvesting norms to be aimed at, the amount of foodstuffs to be contributed to the state in payment for various state services, and the prices at which the state (the sole consumer) will buy the collective farm's output. All collective farm policy is strictly controlled through the pertinent government ministries.

Soviet collective farmers are not guaranteed either a set annual wage or a set share in the annual sales of their farm. Instead they are paid in accumulated "labor days"—units of work which are entered in their labor books. At the end of the year, a worker on a collective farm will receive a share of its sales (which fluctuate according to government price-setting) on the basis of his accumulated labor days. Furthermore, collective farmers are divided into nine categories according to skill or usefulness of work, and each category is paid a correspondingly higher number of labor days than the category beneath it. The average annual income for a Soviet collective farmer is somewhat less than three hundred dollars. Furthermore, the Soviet government does not undertake to provide many of the social security benefits enjoyed by industrial workers. Old age, sickness or disability benefits, annual vacations, etc., are financed by the collective farm itself which imposes a joint two percent dues upon total farm production during the year. Those collective farms (and they are many) which are located in regions with substandard soil or climatic conditions, or those which suffer natural disasters such as drought in any given year, will obviously lack funds to make their social-security schemes effective.

The collectivization of Soviet agriculture was originally designed to achieve three basic ends. First of all, it offered a means of control over the activities and lives of many millions of Soviet citizens. Secondly, it promised increased agricultural production due to rationalization of methods only possible on large-scale farming units. Thirdly, it was seen as a necessary intervening step between the revolutionary seizure of the land by the peasantry and its eventual outright management as an agricultural factory system by the state.

The first and last of these aims have been and are being achieved. Control of Soviet citizens employed in agriculture is as complete as control of those employed in industry; and, as has been noted, state-run farms on which the workers are actually organized as they are in industry have increased until they account for nearly fifty percent of all Soviet farming. But the desired increase in agricultural efficiency has been only relative. This is not due entirely to government policy or mismanagement. The Soviet Union, though three times the size of the United States, has only about the same amount of arable land. Furthermore, Russian climatic conditions are both violently extreme and unpredictable. Agricultural production in the Soviet Union, producing to feed a population significantly larger than that of the United States, must contend with these natural disadvantages. Agricultural crises are a recurrent feature of Russian life; the Soviet Union has, in recent years, been forced to import significant quantities of grain from Canada and other countries.

But if Soviet agriculture labors under certain natural disadvantages, it cannot be said that government farm policy has not added to these. By wiping out individual ownership, or at least management, of the land, Soviet policy also wiped out a large part of the farmer's incentive to produce. In the early days of collectivization this lack of incentive expressed itself angrily in sabotage of the new collective farms; today it expresses itself largely in apathy. The same severity of legal sanctions against idleness and inefficiency, the same obstacles to free movement or a change of occupations, are placed upon the agricultural as upon the industrial proletariat—bespeaking the same necessity to replace incentive by coercion.

As a concession (and one which successive Soviet regimes have warned is only temporary) to both the necessities and the psychology of agricultural life, the Soviet government permits collective farmers to use very small plots of land adjoining their homes for personal production. These kitchen gardens (they average about one acre in size) may also house one or two cows or horses or pigs. The farmers do not own this land (that ownership is, of course, vested in the state), but they are allowed the private use of it so long as they remain members of the collective farm and fulfill their minimum norm of labor days. Produce grown on this land may be consumed directly by the farmer's family or may be sold in nearby towns. It is estimated that these very small kitchen gardens account for one fifth of the annual income of Soviet collective farmers. Eventually they are to be wiped out, as direct state-managed farms succeed the "independent" collectives.

In describing some of the conditions of existence of Soviet workers and farmers, we have had frequent occasion to use the phrase "working class" and the word "peasants." Theoretically, when applied to these groups in the Soviet Union, these words are incorrect. How can there be a "working class" as differentiated from any other group when there exists no other class? How can there be a true peasantry when all agricultural workers are either directly employed by the state or by vast cooperative collective farms? Yet in the sense that both of these groups have been classically defined as exploited segments of society—the workers exploited by the owners of the means of production, the peasants exploited by the owners of the land—they certainly exist in Soviet Russia. The distinction to be observed is that the ownership of both the means of production and the land is now vested not in private individuals but in the state. If the state did not represent a distinct class as opposed to workers and/or peasants, and if the state was democratically controlled by the majority of Soviet citizens, then one might have to revise one's definitions. But neither of these conditions pertain.

Does the Soviet state, the government of the USSR represent a separate class in Soviet society? Marxist theory has always held that the governments of capitalist lands were but the organized will and power of the ruling, capitalist classes over the toiling masses. A capitalist class is defined as the class which owns the means of production. In Russia the state owns the means of production, but can the "state" be considered a class? For all practical purposes, in Soviet society it can. The government bureaucracy, the members of the Communist party, the managers of Russian industry and agriculture, the technicians, scientists, intellectuals, artists, and the top military officials of the Soviet Union constitute a self-conscious, privileged and distinct class. Their incomes, living standards, and opportunities are significantly greater than those of workers or agricultural laborers, their educations are notably superior, and their interests have shown an increasing divergence from the interests of Russia's masses.

The average youngster in either a working-class or peasant family in Russia may not expect more than a secondary education at best. Generally this consists of trade-school vocational training. Only in the past few years has the government instituted a program of scholarships which would make the centers of higher education available to all Soviet children rather than only to the scions of the managerial class. For the present and the immediate future, the educational gap between the masses of the Russian people and the minority of those enabled to attend institutions of higher education will remain a very real distinction. An even greater distinction is that advancement into the managerial-bureaucratic class depends, very largely, upon either Communist party membership or approval. And since the Party remains a minority with an elitist outlook upon its own organization, such advancement is closed to most Russians. Intellectuals, artists, technicians, and scientists (all of whom, it should be remembered, have had the benefit of higher education) are co-opted by the managerial bureaucracy, in some cases (especially among technicians and scientists) pampered by it and thus, for all practical purposes, drawn into it. Nor can it be said that this represents a ruling class based on merit rather than inheritance; while merit plays a very large part in the attainment of ruling-class rank among Soviet citizens, the children of the ruling classes, due to their parents' greater income, higher educational, and cultural standards, wider opportunities, etc., have a striking advantage over the children of workers or peasants in the competition to rise within Soviet society.

The picture which emerges from this very brief description of the structure of the Soviet state is that of a bureaucratic dictatorship managing a rigid class-society in which the individual, if he is not a member of the top ruling echelons, has almost no control over his own destiny, nor for that matter any choice of destinies. But the Soviet state does not deem it sufficient that its subject citizens display outward uniformity. They must also *believe* in their minds and hearts, not only the Marxist dogmas in their most recent government interpretations, but also a barrage of chauvinistic Russian-patriotic claptrap at which any Marxist worth his salt would presumably scoff disgustedly. The entire weight of the mass communications media, the teaching of the young, official Party and government pronouncements, speeches made by leaders on all levels of the bureaucracy—all are devoted to incessantly dinning into the ears of Soviet citizens a view of the world, the Soviet Union, Communism, and past history which will rationalize and justify the continuance of the status quo.

Russians are told that they live in a classless society; that they enjoy the most complete political democracy known to man; that their standards of living are far and away superior to anything to be found anywhere else in the world; that Russian science not only leads the world in every field but was also responsible in the past for most of the world's great discoveries and inventions; that Russian art, writing, and music are the only healthy art, writing, and music to be found anywhere; that the Soviet Union, as the motherland of Socialism, is beloved by the working classes and downtrodden of all countries.

Russians are told that such absolutist tyrants of the past as Tsars Peter I (the Great) and Ivan IV (the Terrible) were actually "progressive" forces in their times; that the wars of national conquest which the tsars imposed on the peoples of Central and Southern Asia were also "progressive" and "good" for the people thus conquered and colonialized; that they should "piously revere" the memories of such viciously reactionary tsarist generals as Suvorov and Kutuzov (who would have hung any Communists or even liberals who fell into their hands); that Leon Trotsky, aside from being a "fiend," saboteur, and "wrecker of Soviet society," was of no importance during the Russian Revolutions of 1905 or 1917; that Russia, almost alone and without any significant help from the Western democracies, defeated the Axis in World War II; that Russia's last-minute intervention in the war against Japan brought that nation to surrender; that the Russian interventions against the Polish, Hungarian, and Czechoslovakian anti-Communist rebellions saved those nations, to the undying gratitude of their peoples, from semi-fascist reactionary conspiracies to enslave them.

Russians are told that although the peoples of the Western democracies may want peace, their leaders, especially the leaders of the United States, are warmongers against whom Soviet Russia must maintain huge armed forces to preserve the peace of the world; that the vast masses of people in the Western democracies have suffered, since the war, an endless depression; that they live in hunger, joblessness, and misery and look forward only to the day when a socialist uprising will liberate them from their capitalist masters; that the foreign policies of the Western democracies are controlled by the United States and that the foreign policy of the United States is dominated by a greedy, cunning, ruthless conspiracy of the nation's top capitalists, generalized as "Wall Street."

All this and much more is the daily propaganda fare of Soviet citizens. Do they believe it all? Foreign observers living in Russia report that they do not believe it all. But they must at least pretend to believe it. The secret police of the Soviet Union, which, under its various initials (Cheka, OGPU, NKVD, MGB) grew so powerful during Stalin's time as to almost constitute a state within a state, has been somewhat stripped of its privileges and influence by Stalin's successors. But it is still there, hovering in the background. Both the existence of the secret police and the harsh judicial code against "political crimes" make short work of Soviet citizens who publicly question Soviet dogma. Under the supposedly "relaxed" rule of the men who inherited Stalin's empire, several of the best-known Soviet writers have been sentenced to long prison terms for publishing works which painted a less-than-rosy picture of life in the USSR. Painters and composers were warned by Premier Nikita Khrushchev himself that music which was not "melodious" and paintings which were not in the slavishly photographic style of "socialist realism" were "dangerous apings of decadent Western styles" and would not be tolerated in the Soviet Union. As for the youth rebellion which is so vital a phenomenon of Western countries, it is denounced as "hooliganism" in Soviet society and heavily penalized as such. When, in 1966, a mere handful of students attempted to pass out leaflets in Moscow's Red Square questioning the infallibility of Soviet policy, they were promptly arrested, tried, and sentenced to long terms at corrective labor camps.

All of which is a dark picture of life in the "socialist homeland." Are there no rays of light to brighten this portrait? There may be—and we shall examine them later. For the moment one may justifiably wonder at the great distance Soviet society has moved from the vision of individual freedom, personal dignity, and security which inspired the early Communist thinkers. Indeed, if Karl Marx were to observe life in the USSR today, he would undoubtedly set about to rationalize, justify, and construct a theory of the impending "inevitable" socialist revolution there!

Chapter Fifteen

THE TOWER OF BABEL

> Repeat! Tell the United Nations! In the name of
> God, help us; help Hungary!
>
> —*Radio Budapest*
> (Last transmission)
>
> Let them know they are not welcome! Let every
> Russian soldier be told the truth about this invasion!
> —*Radio "Free Czechoslovakia"*
> (Last transmission)
>
> The Moscow revisionists, openly joining the slavering
> pack of imperialistic wolves, have distorted the teach-
> ings of Marxism-Leninism for the purpose of justify-
> ing their unprovoked aggression against the People's
> Republic of China. But the toiling masses of Chinese
> peasants and workers will deal the Russian jackals a
> decisive rebuke!
>
> —*Radio Peking*
> (June 25, 1969)

The "monolithic" house of world Communism, so cherished in both Communist and anti-Communist imaginations,
constructed in Eastern Europe by Stalin and in Eastern
Asia by Mao Tse-tung began to fall to pieces after Stalin's
death. In fact, as we have seen, in Europe it had already
suffered the important breach of the Titoist defection; in
Asia the solidarity of Russian and Chinese Communism had
been but a recent phenomenon; independent Communist
parties in the nations of Western Europe, faced with the revival of national economies brought about through American assistance, found fewer and fewer opportunities to gain

recruits or to influence national policies. Only the under-developed nations of the world, in Africa, Latin America, and Southeast Asia provided a potentially fertile field for Communist expansion.

Stalin died in March 1953. He was succeeded in supreme power by a triumvirate composed of Georgi Malenkov, Deputy Premier of the Soviet Union, Nikolai Bulganin, Vice Premier of the Soviet Union and Nikita Khrushchev, Secretary of the Central Committee of the Communist party. The triumvirate did not last long. Once again it was demonstrated that control of the Party apparatus rather than high government rank was the true source of power in the Soviet state. By 1956 Nikita Khrushchev had made himself master of the situation; soon thereafter his former associates in top governmental positions were on their way to retirement or humiliatingly lesser posts. In Stalin's day they would have been executed, but the death of the old dictator brought a certain relaxation of tensions to the Russian governing bureaucracy. Although Lavrenti Beria, former head of the Soviet secret police, and a few of his associates were shot, the sternest punishments were generally held in reserve.

The heirs of Stalin were, in a sense, trapped. They had inherited an absolute tyranny which extended not only over the Russian domains, but also over much of Eastern Europe. Yet none of Stalin's successors were, by nature, endowed with the ferocity to make successful tyrants. Nor were they endowed with an inheritance which, in a fast-changing world, could indefinitely continue to be administered as an absolutist dictatorship relying upon terror as its primary prop. But to do away with the totalitarian structure of their society would, as they thought, be to open the floodgates to rebellion at home and abroad and, of great significance, to weaken the Communist world in its struggle against the American-led Western democracies. None of which is to say that Stalin's heirs were not Communists. They were, and had risen in the Communist bureaucratic hierarchy not only through their administrative and political skills, but also through their devotion to and ability to manipulate Communist theory and dogma. That the Communist system would eventually triumph over decaying capitalism was an unshaken article of faith ("We will bury you!" crowed Khrushchev to an American visitor in 1956.) with Soviet leaders. But that the survival of Russian foreign power and the furtherance of Soviet domestic industrial progress depended upon a modification of Stalinism, if not of Leninism, was becoming increasingly apparent.

For domestic industrial-technical progress (upon which, in the final analysis, Soviet foreign power depended) in a dawning age of computer technology, automation, and nuclear energy, required the existence of a large, extremely well-educated class of technician-managers and scientists both practical and speculative. The intellectual realms inhabited by such specialists were so remote from Marxist philosophy (despite ludicrous attempts by Party journals to demonstrate, for example, the dependency of biophysics upon "scientific" Marxism) as to be not only beyond the control but also beyond the comprehension of the politicians and bureaucrats of the Kremlin. On the higher scientific intellectual levels freedom of inquiry and freedom from dogma were essential for progress. But a retreat from ideology in the relations between the state and one segment of society would inevitably lead to a weakening of faith and the growth of heresy among lower levels of society. This in turn would perhaps weaken the rationalizations and justifications imposed by Russian leaders on their fellow foreign Communists for complete Russian control of client nations. A weakening of Soviet control in the nations of Eastern Europe, to complete the circle, would surely lead to a weakening of state control in Russia itself.

Despite the all too apparent risks, the Soviet leadership set out on this slippery path of relaxation of dogma in 1956. In February of that year, Nikita Khrushchev, having now eliminated his rivals for supreme power in Russia, made a secret speech to the Twentieth Congress of the Russian Communist party. In it he denounced Stalin as a near-crazed tyrant who had subverted Marxism-Leninism to build a personal, autocratic empire. He revealed that hundreds of thousands of Soviet citizens, including top Soviet leaders had been sent unjustly to their deaths during the great purges of the 1930's and after the Second World War. He pointed out that Stalin had fostered the growth of a secret police power in Russia which had become an instrument of pure terror and tyranny. He declared that the Soviet government was now determined to stamp out all traces of the former "cult of personality" which had been cultivated by the dead dictator; indeed, the secret police had already been cut down to size. In foreign as well as domestic policy the Soviet Union would henceforth follow a "new path." Though Khrushchev did not even raise, much less answer, such interesting questions as to what he and his associates, all of whom had risen under Stalin's tutelage, were doing during the years of tyranny, or how such a personal tyranny could grow in a supposedly socialist, democratic society, this speech had an explosive effect both at home and abroad.

The first repercussions were felt in Russia itself—in Russian Georgia, Stalin's birthplace. There students and industrial workers protested the degradation of their regional hero. (Stalin's pictures, statues, and commemorative plaques were being hastily removed from public view; street and place-names honoring the dictator were changed; Stalingrad becoming Volgograd, etc. The old dictator's corpse was removed from the mausoleum where it rested next to Lenin's outside the Kremlin's walls and reburied in an obscure plot of ground.) But Khrushchev easily reimposed his authority and a program of very moderate reforms continued.

The next repercussions of Khrushchev's speech appeared in Poland. There, in the city of Poznan in June, students and workers rioted outside Party and police headquarters. Only after three or four days was order restored by regular army troops, and the nervous Polish Communist government acted with marked clemency. The truth was that Communist leaders throughout Eastern Europe were uncertain as to what line to follow in the wake of Khrushchev's speech. De-Stalinization might mean only a small amount of reform in a Russia used to decades of Communist dictatorship; but de-Stalinization might well spark full-fledged revolutions in countries in which Communism had been imposed only by foreign force. The Polish leaders, headed by Wladyslaw Gomulka (an old anti-Stalinist) knew that they could maintain themselves in power only by making large concessions to liberal and nationalist feelings. On the other hand, that might still provoke direct Russian intervention. Things came to crisis-point in October 1956. Khrushchev and a gaggle of Soviet marshals descended on Warsaw to chastise the Gomulka government. But they ran into determined opposition. Not only were most Polish Communist leaders determined to liberalize and thereby preserve their regimes, but in the streets of Warsaw thousands of Poles were demonstrating against Russian interference—some with weap-

ons in their hands. Khrushchev, faced with the necessity of
waging all-out war, decided to retreat. As abruptly as he came,
he left for Moscow. Polish jubilation was widespread, but
it was tempered by the realization on the part of government and people that although they might liberalize to a
certain degree (restrictions were placed on the police; inter-
course with the West was reestablished; Cardinal Wyszyn-
ski was released from prison and the Catholic Church allowed
greater liberty), they could risk neither outright rejection
of Communist rule nor any attempt to wriggle out of their
economic, political, and military alliances with the Soviet
Union. Any moves in this direction, directly threatening
Russian power, would surely be met with instant Russian
intervention.

Events in Warsaw during October 1956 sent tremors
throughout the Russian empire. During the first three weeks
of that month the Communist rulers of Hungary had indulged in certain symbolic concessions to their people not
dissimilar to those offered in Poland. But on October 23, a
full-fledged revolution broke out in Hungary—the first revolution ever to take place in a Communist state; an event
unthinkable in Marxist theory, unimaginable in Leninist
dogma. A demonstration against the regime by university
students in Budapest attracted the support of thousands of
citizens. The following day police units, industrial workers,
and certain army forces joined the rebellion. The uprising
had spread from Budapest to the Hungarian countryside;
the entire nation was in flames. The Communist government
called upon Russian forces for aid, but these moved with
obvious uncertainty and reluctance. Concessions offered by
the frantic Hungarian government trailed far behind popular demands. Bloody fighting between the people and a secret
police force fighting for its life ended with the police
dead or in hiding. Leadership of the Hungarian government
was now assumed by the popular Imre Nagy—a Communist
but also a liberal and a man who stood for Hungarian
independence. Nagy was supported by the Russians (who
saw in him their only hope of retaining some sort of control
over events in Hungary), and Russian tanks began to with-
draw not only from Budapest but from the entire country.
Nagy announced extraordinary reforms which went far
beyond any so far offered in any Communist state. Political
democracy with a multi-party system was to be introduced;

all censorship was to be removed; political prisoners were to be freed and the secret police themselves put on trial; the country was to open itself to the West; and Hungary was to become neutral in the Cold War. On October 30 a long communique was issued in Moscow which announced the withdrawal of Russian forces from Hungary and indicated a complete reappraisal of Russian relations with all the countries of Eastern Europe.

On October 31 a secret meeting of the Presidium's Executive Committee met in Moscow. What transpired at that meeting remains unknown. But certainly it was then that the decision was taken to intervene directly in Hungary despite the fact that this meant outright war upon the Hungarian people. What changed Kremlin minds? Partly the fact that Soviet intervention in Hungary ran little risk of opposition from the Western democracies, especially the United States. This was true because, by a tragic coincidence, just at the moment of the Hungarian Revolution's success, Britain and France launched an invasion of Egypt to regain control of the Suez Canal from Nasser's revolutionary Egyptian government. Western eyes were riveted, not upon Budapest, but upon Suez. Furthermore, the Western alliance was in disarray as the Americans, who had had no foreknowledge of the Franco-British attempt, angrily demanded the instant withdrawal of Allied forces. But perhaps of greatest importance in Soviet counsels was the fact that Imre Nagy could not be expected to control Hungarian passions for complete freedom domestically and had already indicated his intention of withdrawing Hungary from her military and economic alliance with Russia. This was a direct threat to Russian power in Europe such as events in Poland had not been. As always, when faced with a choice between Russian security and Communist theory or even the prestige of Communism as a world movement, Russia's leaders chose security. On November 4 Russian tanks and troops reversed themselves and began fighting their way back into Budapest; within a week, after serious amounts of blood had been spilled and 200,000 Hungarians had fled to neighboring Austria and West Germany, the Hungarian revolution was put down. Imre Nagy and other leaders were subsequently arrested, tried in Moscow, and shot. The silence of a graveyard settled over Hungary.

But the tragic events in Hungary, while they shocked not

only Western liberals, but also thinking Communists throughout the world, spurred Khrushchev's search for some new
formula for relations between Russia and her Communist
satellite nations in Eastern Europe. In 1957 he brought forth
what the Russian leadership was pleased to call the "Grand
Design" for such revised relations. Basically it called for a
greater economic independence for the satellite nations and
their economic organization in a Council of Mutual Economic Aid (a Council originated but never much imple-
mented by Stalin years before). Under the COMECON the
states of Eastern Europe would introduce the principle of a
"socialist division of labor." That is, each would contribute
what it was best qualified to contribute to a common market which would include Russia. A supranational planning
board would coordinate and direct these activities. The plan
failed full-scale adoption because the Communist leaders of
certain nations, especially Rumania, objected that it would
freeze economic development; underindustrialized states
would be taken advantage of by those with heavier industrialization. Rumania refused her participation outright;
other states in Eastern Europe showed themselves but luke-
warm to the proposal and eventually COMECON came into
being mainly on a symbolic level.

The only area in the world from which Khrushchev's
Eastern European policies were criticized as *not being harsh
enough* was Red China. But this was only part of a split
between the views of Moscow and Peking that had been a
long time incubating. To understand the split more fully,
it will be necessary to examine events in China since the
Communist triumph in 1949 and 1950.

At first, Mao Tse-tung's Chinese People's Democracy
was governed by a coalition of parties (twenty-three to be
exact) with the Communists predominating. This was a reflection not only of Party policy but also of objective conditions. China had been terribly ravaged, it will be recalled,
by more than fifty years of intermittent civil war and almost
fifteen years of Japanese invasion. The quickest way to re-
vive the Chinese economy, according to Mao Tse-tung, was
to follow a policy not dissimilar to Lenin's New Economic
Policy (introduced after the Russian Civil War for many
of the same reasons). Accordingly, although heavy industry
was taken over by the state, as were central financial institutions (the industrialists and bankers having mostly fled

in any case), smaller capitalists were not molested. Furthermore, smaller landlords (who were not accused of collaboration with the Japanese or mistreatment of local peasants) were allowed (with very much reduced rents) to continue in ownership of their land. But Mao's had been a peasant revolution—and the landlord class would obviously be the first target of his program of socialization.

Accordingly, in 1950, a new Agrarian Reform Law was adopted. Under it Chinese landlords as a class were declared "enemies of the people." Their land was confiscated and turned over to Village Cooperative Societies. These societies, dominated by the poorest peasants and Party agents, proceeded to distribute the seized land to the landless peasantry in their districts. To enforce this policy, "People's Courts" were established in the villages; and these courts dealt ruthlessly with ex-landlords. But fulfilling the Communist promise to give land to the peasantry only raised further problems. First of all, it would not be possible to increase agricultural efficiency and productivity on the basis of millions of tiny farms; only large-scale, mechanized methods could do that. Secondly, by giving the peasants land, China's Communist party was risking that old Communist bugbear, the creation of a lower-middle-class anti-revolutionary majority. At the same time, despite Russian assistance (Russian technicians, factories, and financial aid began to pour into China in 1950), Chinese industrialization, upon which the permanence of a Chinese Communist state would have to rest, could only take place with a heavy investment of capital—and the only capital China had to invest was the labor power of her teeming millions and a hoped-for surplus of agricultural production. Clearly, collectivization of agriculture could not be long postponed.

But Mao, perhaps having learned from the Russian experience, proceeded cautiously with collectivization. Unlike Stalin in the 1920's and 30's, he did not attempt to force China's peasants, at whatever cost, to fit a preconceived pattern of rural life. Instead he proceeded by stages. Thus in 1953 the Chinese government inaugurated a drive to establish agricultural producers' cooperatives throughout China. The land would still belong to its peasant owners, but for purposes of production it would be pooled with other individual holdings into a large-scale cooperative farm on which all the peasants of the vicinity would work and from which all would share in the profits, after government taxes. By 1956 it was reported that ninety percent of China's peasant households (110,000,000 households) were members of farming cooperatives. Outright collectivization of the land (that is, state ownership and state management on the Russian model) was started only in 1957. Its progress has been slow and not unmarked by peasant reluctance and rebellions. But the very cautiousness of the program has, evidently, avoided the near civil-war conditions that Stalin's rushed collectivization brought to Russia decades ago.

The first Chinese Five-Year Plan began in 1953. It was to be succeeded by Five-Year, Seven-Year and even Twelve-Year Plans in bewildering profusion. Since few foreign observers were admitted to China (and these restricted in their movements) it was not possible to accurately gauge the progress of Chinese industrialization. There were to be "Great Leaps Forward" and "Twenty Years' Progress in a Single Day" campaigns without end, but how much actual progress these government slogans represented could not be truly estimated. Most observers are agreed that China's industrial growth rate is the highest of all the underdeveloped countries of Asia. Furthermore, that China has increased in sophistication as well as power was demonstrated by the Chinese explosion of an atomic bomb in 1964 and a hydrogen bomb in 1967.

But, as has been pointed out, the Chinese Communist revolution proceeded from different bases than had the Russian. It was a peasant civil-war revolution taking place also as a war of national liberation. The position of the Chinese peasants remained decisive in Chinese Communist society. Thus, when by 1959 the collectivization drive appeared headed for serious trouble, based on peasant resistance, it was slowed down and, in certain areas, actually reversed. The maintenance of a revolutionary mentality among the peasants, even during the days when they had acquired land, and before collectivization as well as afterwards, was combined with a continuance of the war of national liberation psychology by both subjective and objective factors. The United States, protecting Chiang Kai-shek's Nationalists on the nearby island of Formosa was elevated into a national "hate object," by incessant propaganda. That American actions and policies may have contributed to this cannot be denied. But the extent and ferocity of the hate campaign leveled against the United States suggests that it was, and remains, of greater domestic than international use to the Chinese Communists. Actual war against American forces was undertaken by Red China when it intervened in Korea in 1950. Although Chinese leaders may well have been disturbed by the approach of American forces to the Chinese-Korean border in that year, again, the scale and intensity of the Chinese effort during their undeclared war against United States and United Nations troops indicates that it was designed to meet domestic as much as international needs.

While evidence is not yet available on which to base a concrete analysis of all the reasons for Mao Tse-tung's maneuvers and policies, some things seem self-evident. First of all, it must be repeated, he has had to maintain a revolutionary spirit among the Chinese masses—that is to say, the peasantry. This has meant a continual campaign of education in Communist theory, a heavy reliance on induced fear, and a massive propaganda campaign iterating basic Communist dogma. The disavowal of Stalinism on the part of the Russian Communist leadership, by cracking the dogmatism of Communist belief, represented an unacceptable danger to these efforts. Unlike Russia, China was not yet ready to question any part of the divine gospel of Marxism-Leninism-Stalinism. Khrushchev's revisionism (which it certainly was) could only introduce confusions and uncertainties which might completely undermine the Communist structure in China.

Secondly, China's never-ending war of national liberation, so necessary to keep the population's energies mobilized, could only be channeled after Korea into attempts to help other Asian (and later African) lands in their own struggles to emerge from colonial domination. This meant confrontation with the Western democracies, and especially the United States. But by eroding the position of American power in the underdeveloped countries, China threatened to upset the very delicate world balance of power between Soviet Russia and the United States. This in turn might lead to full-scale atomic war between the two super-powers. And against this, Russia was adamantly opposed. When Chinese propagandists mocked Russian leaders for not pressing the worldwide Communist revolution because they were afraid of war with the United States, Khrushchev stated: "Some comrades abroad claim that Khrushchev is making a mess of things, and is afraid of war. Let me say once again that I should like to see the kind of bloody fool who is genuinely not afraid of war. Only a small child is afraid of nothing, because he doesn't understand; and only bloody fools."

When to these immediate reasons for a split between the interests of the Russian and Chinese Communists is added the historical fact that Russia herself had been included in the pre-World War I group of imperialist powers which all but dismembered China and that Soviet Russian policy even since the Bolshevik Revolution had led to Communist defeat in China in 1930 and had failed to support Mao's independent struggle for power until after the Second World War, the dramatic split between Soviet Russia and Communist China which began in 1956 and grew in proportions steadily until it verged on outright war in 1969 becomes much more understandable. Communism in China had to maintain itself through orthodoxy; the Russian lapse from Marxist orthodoxy had to be combated. At the same time, Russia made almost as convenient a hate symbol for long-memoried Chinese as did the United States. And the war of national liberation might take on physical as well as psychological dimensions along China's thousands of miles of border with the Soviet Union. By 1960 Russian aid to China had ceased and Russian technicians had left the country; by 1963 anti-Soviet demonstrations had come to be commonplace in Peking and even in Moscow on the part of Chinese or Chinese client state students; by 1968 border clashes between armed Chinese and Russian forces had taken place; by 1969 the two nations had approached so close to the brink of war that other powers, including the United States, had grown alarmed.

So unthinkable, in Marxist theory, was a conflict between two socialist societies, that Marxist theoreticians in Moscow and Peking (and all over the world) could account for the Russo-Chinese clash only on the grounds that one or another of their governments were not, in fact, adhering to Marxist principles. In a sense, however, both governments were adhering to Marxism. But Marx, while he had theoretically established the impossibility of conflict between socialist states due to their community of class and interests, had never written on the subject of conflict between nations organized as *state-capitalist* societies. And both Russia and

China were so organized—Russia completely, China incompletely. It was the *discrepancy between the level of organization of state capitalism in each country* which underlay their conflict. If anything, Marx, in his analysis of the growth of contradictions in capitalist society which would inevitably set them to quarreling over economic spoils, and Lenin in his internationalization of that view in *Imperialism,* had shown grounds for expecting the most severe conflicts precisely between those nations in which capitalism had grown into highly concentrated structures, of which state-capitalist societies such as Russia and China must be prime examples. The only thing to note in addition here is that the *density* or *strength* of industrialization, provided always that it is above a certain level, need not be a measure of the *concentration* of economic power in state hands. It is concentration of power, not necessarily the measure of power which is important in provoking conflict—and this for very good reasons summed up outside the Marxist philosophy in the phrase: "All power corrupts; absolute power corrupts absolutely."

The contradictions between Marxist-Leninist theory and actualities both at home and abroad, contradictions which were growing more painful and more apparent with the passing years, were not lost upon the leaders of the Soviet Union or upon their captive Marxist theoreticians. After much preparation, in 1961, at the Twenty-second Congress of the Russian Communist party held in Moscow, a new Party program was adopted. This was a matter of great importance; it was only the third program in the history of the Party, the first having been adopted in 1903, a program for achieving power, the second having been adopted in 1919, a program for preserving power and "building socialism."

Since 1919, according to Soviet theoreticians, the Party had been building a society in Russia based on social ownership of the means of production and distribution according to the criterion: "From each according to his ability, to each according to his *work.*" Now the time had come when the socialist society was approaching the era of Communism in which the new criterion would be: "From each according to his ability, to each according to his *needs.*"

In the coming Communist era, the program predicts: "The demands of the people in all their great variety will correspond to the healthy, reasonable needs of a fully developed man." This statement is so loaded with assumptions that it deserves dissection. What, for example, are the needs of a "healthy" or "fully developed man"? Who will decide what those needs are? Who, in fact, will decide what is healthy and what is the nature of a fully developed man? It is presumed, too, that these healthy, fully developed men will never demand more than their "reasonable needs." It also assumes that these "reasonable needs" despite their "great variety" will be filled—in other words, can be predicted. They can be predicted because the nature of man in the Communist era can be predicted and defined. The nature of man in the Communist era can be predicted and defined because that nature is both malleable and statistically reducible to measurement. In other words, we are back again with "Ideal Man." Never mind what kind of Man is meant by "Ideal." One thing is certain: those men who do not fit into the Ideal pattern will, by definition be something less than men; hence disposable. A power will have to exist to make and enforce all these loaded definitions, and that power will be the state. But, in the Communist era, was not the state supposed to "wither away"? Now we see that this can only take place on the assumption that each and every member of the Communist society fills the Communist version of the Ideal Man exactly and agrees on all matters of ideology, definition, and faith with his fellow Ideal Men. But no two human brains function exactly alike; no two human life-experiences are exactly the same. Hence there must always be disagreement among men, and these disagreements must be resolved. There must be some sort of social machinery to resolve them and, *ipso facto* we are back with the state, no matter how it may be disguised.

The New Party Program outlines, aside from its loaded definitions of the nature of man, something with which the world has recently become familiar—an "affluent society." In brief, it promises abundance of material goods to be produced with less and less labor. The advance of Soviet economy to affluence is predicted to take place in two stages, from 1961 to 1970 and from 1971 to 1980. By that time, to be specific, Soviet citizens are promised that their economy will overtake and surpass that of the United States in the production of consumer and luxury goods and services. "The complete building of a Communist Society," the Program promises, "will be concluded in the subsequent period."

Can the Party keep its promises? It leaves itself an escape hatch in its New Program by stating, "Complications in the international situation and the increased defense expenditure thereby required may impede the realization of plans for increasing the people's prosperity." Thus, any failure of the New Party Program's march to the affluent society can conveniently be blamed on foreign powers. Nontheless, the Soviet Union has achieved its earlier goal of creating a very powerful and sophisticated industrial base. There is no reason, therefore, why it may not, within a very near future, create an affluent society—it has already made significant progress towards that end. Given Soviet economic riches (based, like the American, upon the exploitation of a continental land mass) and the strength of basic Russian industry, only mismanagement or foreign war could seriously threaten the real growth of prosperity in the Soviet Union.

It was because his policies threatened both mismanagement and foreign war that Nikita Khrushchev was removed from leadership of the Soviet Union in 1964—his place to be taken by two bureaucrats: Alexei Kosygin, who became Premier of the Soviet Union, and Leonid Brezhnev who was Secretary of the Central Committee of the Communist party. If the past is any guide to the future, its is Brezhnev who holds basic power, through his control of the vital Party apparatus.

The failures (in Soviet eyes) of Khrushchev were several. First of all, his policy of decentralization of industrial and agricultural control and management, while motivated by a sincere desire to increase efficiency (badly hampered by distant, centralized control from Moscow) did not bring the desired results. It was too abrupt and far-reaching a change to suddenly introduce into an economic structure which had been built and based for decades upon the principle of remote-control management by a centralized bureaucracy. Agricultural crises ensued and to avoid famine the Soviet Union was forced into the humiliating posture of buying grain from such capitalist countries as Canada. There are, as we have seen, very real and continuing reasons for low productivity in agriculture in the Soviet Union; but Khrushchev's decentralization schemes had to bear current blame.

Secondly, Khrushchev was accused of "adventurism" in foreign affairs. Not only had he presided over and been unable to heal the growing and deeply menacing rift between Russia and Red China, his Cuban policies (which will be examined in the following chapter) had brought the Soviet Union to the very brink of atomic war with the United States —and had caused the subsequent humiliation of retreating from this wholly unnecessary confrontation. His inflation of European problems into the Berlin Crisis of 1961 had proved profitless, resulting again in a Soviet retreat and the erection of a symbolic admission of Soviet incapacity, the Berlin Wall. His "rocket rattling" and testing of gigantic hydrogen bombs had failed to shake the defensive posture of the Western democracies, had, if anything, increased Western determination, and had earned Russia the opprobrium of many neutral powers. As for his economic and military fishing in the troubled waters of the Near East, his introduction of Soviet influence into the Arab world, Kremlin leaders found, as had leaders in London, Paris, and Washington before them, that the rewards of such intervention were far outweighed by its headaches.

Finally, despite his denunciation of the "cult of personality" which had been built up around Stalin, Khrushchev himself fostered the creation of such a cult. Soviet histories had been rewritten to emphasize Khrushchev's contributions in the past; his former associates in Soviet leadership had been publicly humiliated and removed from their posts; he undertook diplomatic missions entirely on his own and reached agreements (as with Eisenhower—the "Spirit of Camp David") based not on collaborative assessments of objective factors, but based on his personal judgments of men and affairs. Nor was his very vital, but somewhat (in Marxist eyes) crude behavior (the shoe-pounding at the United Nations; the comradely banquets across America with top capitalists; the impetuous threats and boasts to foreign newsmen) the image that other Soviet leaders wished to project.

That image, in accordance with both domestic and foreign needs, was one of quiet, peacefully inclined, powerful but not militaristic, organization. And this was precisely the image projected by the two, rather faceless, "organization men" who replaced Khrushchev. All signs and indications of the new Soviet leadership are that it is, in fact, collaborative—that no important decisions are taken without the assent of a majority in the Soviet Presidium and the Central Committee of the Communist party. In their attempt to produce an affluent society in Russia, in accordance with the New Party Program, the new Soviet leadership has avoided adventurism in inter-

national affairs. Negotiations looking toward a peaceful settlement of the Russian-Chinese dispute have been undertaken;
a thawing of the icy relations between Russia and the United
States has been sought; temptations to profit from troubles in
the Near East and other areas have been generally resisted;
rocket-rattling and militaristic boasting have been very much
muted.

But the new Soviet leadership has not escaped two very
basic problems. The first of these is how to handle the Russian
empire it has inherited in a period of change both at home and
abroad. The states of Eastern Europe, watching developments
in the Soviet Union towards a more liberalized society and
faced with impatient demands for greater freedom on all
levels from their own populations, have edged towards greater
independence since 1966. The brutal suppression of the Hungarian Revolution was attributed to Khrushchev; such an
intervention seemed unthinkable by the new leadership. Accordingly, in Czechoslovakia, the nation in which, it will be
recalled, there had existed almost no necessity or basis for a
Communist regime other than the force of terror and Soviet
arms, Communist party leaders, under pressures from very
wide segments of their people, instituted a campaign of
liberalization and democratization. So popular and rapid was
this program that Czechoslovakia, like Hungary before it,
threatened not only to return to an open, mixed (socialist and
capitalist) society at home, with a multi-party democratic
system of government, it threatened also to spin completely
out of the Soviet empire, perhaps into neutrality, perhaps
into alliance with the West.

Once again it was demonstrated that no matter what the
current theoretical attitude of Moscow towards political and
economic control might be at home or abroad, no trifling
with Russia's power base in Europe would be tolerated. During
the tragic "Prague Spring" of 1968, a full-scale invasion of
recalcitrant Czechoslovakia was undertaken by Soviet forces
with the aid of units from various of its client Eastern European states. There was less bloodshed than there had been
in Hungary only because Czech resistance took the form of
more or less peaceful mass demonstrations rather than shoot-
ing. But there was no doubt that the Soviet forces were quite
willing to shed as much blood as necessary to bring the Czechs
back into the happy family of socialist nations. The unhappy
Czech leaders who had presided over their nation's attempt

to leave the family were demoted, humiliated, and renounced by the more obediently filial leaders imposed by Moscow. A strict reimposition of Communist party dictatorship over all aspects of the nation's life followed.

Moscow's attempts to justify this brutal intervention in the affairs of a supposedly "sister" socialist republic were pitifully inept. The old bogey of a "reactionary capitalist conspiracy to plunge the Czech people back into the toils of the imperialist powers" was dutifully trotted out, but was so patiently false that even Russian soldiers in Prague and Russian citizens at home found it hard to swallow. Thereupon Leonid Brezhnev came up with a new doctrine. This so-called "Brezhnev Doctrine" was perhaps suggested to the Soviet leadership by the old and long discarded Monroe Doctrine of the United States. It held that the Soviet Union, as the motherland of socialism, had the inalienable right to intervene, by force if necessary, in the affairs of other socialist states in order to preserve their socialist nature and their independence of capitalist domination. This served notice on other nations of Eastern Europe that while they might follow in the footsteps of Russian efforts to liberalize Communism they by no means should anticipate those efforts and, in any event, liberalized or not, they were to remain firmly within the Russian "sphere of influence."

Communism, from Lenin's day and even before, had claimed for itself, as did the Christian Apostles of old, the "gift of tongues." It had been used as a means of extending Soviet Russian power abroad since the earliest days of the Union. The chances of war had enabled it to create a structure of power in Eastern Europe. But despite the "gift of tongues," the international language of Marxism, by 1969 the Soviet power structure in Eastern Europe, and the Marxist group of nations throughout the world resembled a Tower of Babel —with each national Party, in response to national needs tending to go its own way. Despite the Czechoslovakia tragedy, it is hard to imagine that this process will not continue. And the Brezhnev Doctrine is entirely too dangerous an instrument to be employed frequently. The dissolution of both the Soviet empire and the Church of Marxist-Leninist Orthodoxy is a continuing problem for Soviet leadership and Communist theoreticians. It will prove more insoluble as time goes on.

The second basic problem which confronts and will continue to confront the Kremlin leadership is symptomized by the first. Basically it may be stated as the fact that the affluent society imposes its own requirements irrespective of dogma or Communist theory. Even assuming that all economic problems are solved, that Russia does produce abundantly, and even assuming that social problems are solved and this abundance is truly equally distributed within Soviet society, the problems of continued *control* over that society will only be aggravated, not lessened. For very well-educated people, able to maintain and manipulate the terrible complex functions of an affluent society, and satisfied in their economic wants and needs, continue to confront the problems of individual liberty, political democracy, and personal and group freedom. For example, one of the important facets of an affluent society is the ability of its members to enjoy travel all over the world. But Soviet citizens freely traveling abroad will certainly see that very much of the picture painted of the outside world by Soviet propagandists is simply false. In fact, not a few such Soviet travelers have already defected to the West, and foreign travel remains a privilege but sparingly granted by Soviet authorities to their own citizens. Likewise, the sophistication inherently supposed of an affluent society cannot be fed, in its new leisure, with a continued diet of artistic pap. Greater subtlety, greater color and variety, above all, greater freedom to experiment both in the creation and consumption of art in all its forms will be demanded. But this will presuppose the free interchange and espousal of ideas with the West and the tolerance of heretical ideas at home. Yet the fact that Soviet leaders do not feel confident in the ultimate victory of Communist ideas in open competition with other ideas remains amply demonstrated in the stridency of Soviet propaganda, the severity of the Soviet legal code, and the stringent control exercised by both Party and state over any kind of artistic effort or intellectual speculation. Many more contradictions between Communist control of society and the nature of an affluent society might be elucidated. These contradictions seem to be beyond the capabilities of either Soviet leaders or Communist theoreticians to solve. Yet the Soviet Union and its Communist party are committed to the creation of an affluent society—and as that commitment is turned into reality, the brittleness of the Communist political-theoretical control structure will grow. It is only to be hoped that, faced with its inevitable crack-up, Soviet leadership is not tempted to submerge its domestic political problems in foreign adventures.

Yet there are possibilities of evolutionary change for Soviet society. These possibilities are, however, being demonstrated beyond the borders of the Soviet Union, and, oddly enough, they depend to a very great degree upon the responses, actions, and understanding of the Soviet Union's self-proclaimed arch-rival and foe in the contemporary world: the United States of America.

Chapter Sixteen

AMERICAN CONFRONTATION

> Do I believe in Marxism? I believe absolutely in Marxism! ... I am a Marxist-Leninist until the last day of my life!
>
> —*Fidel Castro*
> (Radio Address, 1961)
>
> We had so many silly ideas! Man, I had so many silly ideas, my head—there was so much crap in it!
>
> —*Fidel Castro*
> (Private Interview, 1961)
>
> Last night White America declared war on Black America.
>
> —*Stokeley Carmichael*
> (After the murder of Martin Luther King)
>
> This is a dangerous and uncertain world. ... No one expects our lives to be easy, not in this decade, not in this century.
>
> —*John Fitzgerald Kennedy*

It might not have surprised the pragmatic Lenin to know that four decades after his death, the theory and practice of Communism in the Soviet Union were being vitally affected by events and responses not only in other Communist lands but also in that arch-capitalist United States. Nor would he have been surprised by the fact (indeed, as a Marxist he would have expected it) that social and political developments in the United States were being influenced by events and responses in the Communist world. But he might well have been amazed to know that new directions in the very nature of Marxist philosophy were beginning to arise, not out of the Russian, but out of the American experience in the last half of the twentieth century. Yet such was the case. The Soviet Communist party might proclaim its New Party Program, which amounted to nothing more than a conservative plan to create an affluent society in Russia; the Chinese Communist party, or at least Mao Tse-tung's part of it, might launch a Cultural Revolution, which amounted to nothing more than an attempt to keep alive revolutionary inspiration in the breasts of a peasantry showing signs of developing into a small bourgeoisie; but it was left to American thinkers and rebels, none of whom were to be found within the conservative folds of the Communist party in the United States, to begin a tentative reexamination of Marxist thought to see what in it might be applicable or useful as they strove to comprehend and dominate events in an affluent society increasingly torn by strife—a society which some of them were even calling "prerevolutionary."

As had always been the case in American history, the confrontation of the United States government and of the people of the nation with Communism took place on two levels: the foreign and the domestic. But by 1970, so heavily had these levels influenced each other that they were beginning to merge, dangerously to some, hopefully to others.

The postwar American reaction to world Communism was dominated by three major factors. First, and most important of these, was the Stalinist expansion into Eastern Europe and the slide of China into the hands of Mao Tse-tung. As usual, Americans had gone to war in 1941 inspired by a hodgepodge of ideals—the Atlantic Charter, the "Four Freedoms," the principles of the United Nations, the widespread conviction that once Nazism, fascism, and Japanese militarism were exterminated the world would naturally bloom into political democracy, social justice, and peace. They were encouraged in these dreams by American leaders and the broad streak of transcendental utopianism which had always been part of the American social and intellectual heritage. While very many Americans understood something of the nature of Stalin's domestic tyranny, others—perhaps most—vaguely expected that somehow or other the experience of war and of associating with the Western democracies in a common cause would bring basic changes of outlook and policy to the Soviet Union. In this they were encouraged by Soviet diplomacy and propaganda during the war years. The comedown was harsh. When from 1946 to 1948 it became clear that Stalin placed Russian security above all other considerations, and that this security was to be based not on ideals but on the extinction of independence and freedom in the nations of Eastern Europe, Americans felt both frightened and, more importantly, betrayed. Had they more realistically appraised the causes and course of World War II they might still have felt frightened by Soviet postwar power expansion; but they would not, perhaps, have felt betrayed.

Frightening as was Russian behavior in Eastern Europe, it was as nothing compared to the fear caused by the Communist conquest of China. Here again, most Americans had been badly misinformed for years. Chiang Kai-shek, in the interests of wartime unity, had been painted as a repository of virtues to which he had never pretended; his shaky Nationalist regime had been painted in the most glowing terms. It was hard for many Americans to believe that the Communist victory in China was not, somehow, due to a plot or, at least, due to covert but massive Soviet intervention. The fact that it was a true civil war which had been going on for decades, and in which Mao's forces had won overwhelming support among the masses of the Chinese people was not apparent. A concomitant phase of American reaction to the Communist triumph in China leads us to the second major factor in postwar American reactions to Communism: the power fallacy.

The United States had risen from the depths of the Great Depression through the Second World War to a pinnacle of worldwide military and economic power of which no American could have dreamed before 1945. All wars tend to militarize the societies which participate in them; and the United States after VJ Day had its full quota of jingoists and energetic expansionists eager to flex the newly found national muscles. Some claimed that an "American Century" had dawned. American monopoly of atomic weapons only underscored a basic national chauvinism which, perhaps inevitably, displayed itself after victory. The limits of American power being, by self-proclamation, global, it followed that such a disastrous reversal in American strategic fortunes as the adherence of China's 600,000,000 people to Communism must be due to failings of policy on the part of the United States government or even high treason on the part of American officials at home and abroad. It is a measure of the simplemindedness of American postwar nationalism that so many believed that anything the United States did or did not do could basically affect the outcome of a struggle which had been going on for years, involving hundreds of millions of people many thousands of miles away and inhabiting a country and participating in a culture utterly alien to the American experience.

The third factor in American attitudes towards Communism after World War II was a complex hysteria growing out of the war itself. Unlike what may be termed the "simple" hysteria which briefly followed World War I, the emotional climate of the United States after the Second World War was not exclusively a carry-over of officially inspired xenophobia and hate for the enemy. Among American military men (and very many civilian officials) the unexpected, unprepared-for disaster at Pearl Harbor in 1941 had created an all-but-neurotic craving for absolute security. Never again must the United States be caught unprepared, taken by surprise by any enemy. This "security complex" was dramatically heightened by the existence of atomic weapons; any future Pearl Harbor might well mean national extinction. There was also a very definite element of guilt mixed ·in with this fear. The United States had, without warning and perhaps unnecessarily, employed the atomic bomb; therefore a future potential enemy would no doubt do the same. A new power of unimaginable force and unforeseeable consequences had been unleashed into the world by Americans, and they were the first to suffer from the feelings of doom and insecurity which this force would shortly bring to all mankind.

All of these factors—so many of them subjective—combined to produce a postwar Red Scare in the United States of much deeper and longer-lasting virulence than that which followed the First World War. Accusations of treason and Communist conspiracy were hurled recklessly between private citizens and even high government officials. Especially selected for criticism was the State Department which, being in charge of American foreign policy, was presumably to blame for the fact that the postwar world did not fulfill American expectations. So massive was the anti-Communist hate campaign, which found its leadership in Senator Joseph R. McCarthy of Wisconsin, that the State Department suffered wounds from which it is only now recovering. Although McCarthy and his followers never succeeded in ferreting out a single proven traitor or Communist conspirator in the State Department, many of the Department's ablest men were hounded from office; many others resigned. This, in turn, had a crippling effect upon American ability to assess international issues. Liberals, democrats, moderate leftists in all walks of life were smeared with accusations, almost all of which were unfounded; many fell silent to protect themselves, and their voices were not heard on vital domestic as well as international subjects.

The Communist Party of the United States which, following the Soviet Cold War policies had regained its militancy, was subjected to massive legal prosecution. In 1949 the top leadership of the CPUSA was brought to trial accused of "teaching and advocating the necessity of overthrowing the Government of the United States by force and violence." Note that they were not accused of attempting such an overthrow, nor even of conspiring to produce one, but of teaching its desirability and inevitability. The Party defended itself in a predictably bumbling and bureaucratically legalistic way. Party leaders denied the charges and sought to demonstrate that Party policy and goals, not to say Marxism-Leninism as a political philosophy called for no such violent overthrow(!). The world's great revolutionaries, from Babeuf to Trotsky to Fidel Castro, when brought to trial by the courts of the societies they sought to overthrow, proudly accepted the accusations against them as badges of merit and denounced the courts as agencies of their enemies from whom they neither expected nor begged justice. But the leaders of the CPUSA were not cut from heroic cloth. Their haggling, hairsplitting defense did not, of course, save them from conviction; in the climate of the times no defense could have accomplished that, but neither did it earn them the respect of their fellow citizens of whatever political persuasion. In the end they went to jail and the CPUSA was effectively driven underground. Only years later did the United States Supreme Court rule that various sections of the law under which they had been convicted were, in fact unconstitutional. But members of the CPUSA, though then at liberty to profess their convictions, had to register, under the Smith Act, as "agents" of a foreign power. And so long as the CPUSA faithfully abased itself to the demands of Soviet Russian policy, most Americans would consider that not so much a restriction as a simple statement of fact.

The kind of American response to world Communism which grew out of a decade of fear, confusion, and repression was bitterly illustrated by events in Cuba. The fact that the coming of Communism to that island is to be recounted in this chapter rather than the last, is due to the conviction that Cuban Communism owes its existence primarily to American, not Soviet actions. And it must be seen within the context of a common, global problem faced by both Superpowers.

This problem, which emerged rapidly in the postwar decades was the growth of nationalism among newly free ex-colonial nations of the underdeveloped world. In Asia, Africa, and Latin America the throwing off of former imperialist chains (whether they had been formal or economic) was sparked by an upsurge of intensely nationalistic feelings, and the political parties which reflected such feelings. Both the United States and Soviet Russia attempted to win support for their international positions from these new nations. Both attempted to influence the direction of native nationalism towards their respective economic and political philosophies. In this competition each had certain advantages. Any nationalist revolution or "war of national liberation" could be welcomed and directly supported by Moscow as a blow against the interests of the former imperialist, capitalist nations such as Britain, France, or Holland. In that respect the victory of native nationalism anywhere could only strengthen the Soviet position *vis-à-vis* the West. On the other hand, the United States, with much greater disposable wealth, could offer much greater economic assistance to newly established nations than could the Soviet Union, in an attempt to win them to America's side in the Cold War. But the fact that the Cold War remained "cold" and not "hot" depended on a very delicate balance of terror between the Soviet Union and the United States. Anything that tended to shift that balance of terror, however minutely, was viewed in both Washington and Moscow as a threat to peace. At the same time, shifts in allegiance among newly established nations must, for historical reasons, have worked overall to America's disadvantage. It was the United States and her allies of Western Europe who had formerly enjoyed imperialistic power in the underdeveloped lands, not Soviet Russia. Any change in their former allegiance, whether towards the Soviet bloc or even towards neutrality must in some sense weaken American power. Therefore it appeared in Moscow's interest to encourage, *but cautiously,* the new nationalisms of Africa, Asia, and Latin America, while it appeared to Washington's interest to suppress them.

But competition for support among the new nations depended on another prime factor besides political intervention. Most of the ex-colonial lands were excellent examples of societies ripe for Communist revolutions. Most suffered from the same conditions as had prevailed in prerevolutionary Russia or China. They were often rigidly class-bound societies with a very small layer of rich capitalists (inheritors of ex-colonial business interests) confronting a vast mass of extremely poor peasants and workers; they suffered generally from lack of education among most of their inhabitants; an exploitive attitude towards the national wealth on the part of the ruling classes; a lack of any traditions or development of political democracy; and tremendous underindustrialization. Furthermore, when such nations won their freedom from former foreign exploiters, they were often faced with the realization that unless they industrialized rapidly, their political independence would only be a mask for continued economic slavery; they would be converted into semicolonial sources of raw materials for the industrialized nations and dumping grounds for foreign manufactured goods.

The domestic stability of new governments as well as the actual independence of the new nations depended upon how speedily they could industrialize, educate their populations, and raise living standards. To accomplish these goals they could look for inspiration and direction (and hence, aid) to one or the other of the competing systems. But the American system of capitalist free enterprise combined with personal liberty and political democracy was not usually a relevant example to the new nations. American wealth was based on the exploitation of a virgin and untouched continental landmass; American liberties were derived from the thousand-year-old development of the British and American common law; American political democracy was the result of centuries of experience in England and the United States of participatory self-government and high levels of mass education. Almost none of the newly emerging countries could duplicate any of these conditions. On the other hand, Russia, and now China, were examples of societies very similar to their own which had risen to industrial prowess very rapidly. That this rise had been accompanied by the suppression of personal liberties and the stifling of political democracy were not weighty considerations to nations which had never known either. Capitalism was tainted with traditions of exploitation, Communism was not. Capitalism's success in certain nations was not usually a relevant example; Communism's success in Russia and China was. Therefore, even among those new nations which, like India, enjoyed sufficient sophistication of

political outlook to recognize the threat of tyranny implicit
in Communist development, the Communist system, on inspection, offered greater attractions as a guide than did the
capitalist. To correct this imbalance of appeal, the United
States could offer only massive aid programs (always suspected
of having strings attached), or direct intervention. Thus
American economic and military aid was perhaps sufficient
to keep India from sliding irrevocably into the Communist
camp; direct American intervention (in the form of CIA
agents, money, and arms) was employed to keep Guatemala
in the capitalist camp by overthrowing a socialist regime there.

It was against this background of international struggle
that Fidel Castro's 26th of July Movement waged its successful campaign to win power in Cuba. That island suffered
from classical symptoms of repression. For centuries it had
been a heavily exploited colony of Spain. Its liberation from
Spain during the Spanish-American War in 1898 only transformed it into a political and economic dependent of the
United States. Direct American intervention in Cuban affairs,
from 1898 to 1959 had been frequent and frequently armed.
More than a few Cuban governments during that period
owed their existence, against the will of the Cuban people, to
American support. The Cuban economy was dominated by
American business interests; local public utilities such as
electric, telephone, and gas companies were American owned;
the all-important sugar industry, from cane lands to refineries,
was largely an American monopoly. And the Cuban economy
was exploited for the interests of American shareholders.
Cuba, like China, was an all-but-colonial land. Cuban society
was stratified between a thin layer of the very rich and a vast
mass of the very poor—these latter being split again between
urban workers and a huge rural peasantry. Illiteracy, disease,
hunger, and all the other ills common to prerevolutionary
societies were widespread.

Fidel Castro, who like Lenin, Trotsky, Mao Tse-tung, and
other revolutionary leaders, was the son of middle-class, not
working-class parents, first raised the banner of revolt in
Cuba on July 26th, 1953 in his famous, abortive raid on the
Muntaña Barracks. At that time his objectives were the
toppling of the dictatorial regime of strong-man Fulgencio
Batista, and the establishment of Constitutional, democratic
government in the island. Insofar as this could only be done
by winning a greater degree of freedom from American control, he was anti-American, but not rabidly so. His economic

and social program, expressed in his "History will absolve me" speech made to the Batista court which tried him for leading the unsuccessful uprising in 1953, could be described as very moderately socialist and "progressive." He had obviously done some reading in the Marxist classics, but was obviously not a prisoner of Marxist dogma.

Even Castro's subsequent imprisonment on the Isle of Pines, his months of preparations in Mexico, his bloody campaign to establish himself in Cuba's Sierra Maestre mountains, and the long guerrilla war he waged against Batista forces which brought final victory on January 1, 1959— all of this did not convert Castro to Communism. His experience did modify his program. He called for distribution of land to the peasants, a democratic constitution, freedom from Yankee domination and, in certain economic sectors (but not all) social *control,* not ownership, of the means of production. Furthermore, Castro's victory was entirely his own, won with the support of the vast majority of the Cuban people, and without any foreign aid whatsoever.

The American response to Castro's victory was cautious. Even the CIA admitted that the new Cuban *líder máximo* was definitely not a Communist. If the United States were to retain Cuban friendship, it seemed apparent that it would have to support the Cuban revolutionary government and Fidel Castro. This, at first it did—though suspiciously and somewhat grudgingly (no offer was made to help Cuba economically).

But Castro's program for reforming the Cuban economy ran head-on into American interests and certain classical revolutionary problems. Thus it became evident that if land was to be distributed to the peasants it could come only from rich Cubans and American landowning corporations. These in turn could not be compensated for government seizure of their lands without bankrupting the Cuban economy. Likewise it was found that government control of public utilities and industry did not ensure that these would now serve the public interest—only direct government management of them could ensure that—and such management really meant government ownership, to the detriment again of both wealthy Cuban and American business interests. But without such reforms in the Cuban economy no reforms in the Cuban social structure were possible; and unless these were carried through, Castro's government would not long remain in power. Facing a choice between American opposition and the carrying forward of his revolutionary program, Castro made the only possible decision.

It was only then, after the institution of Cuba's Agrarian Reform Law and the nationalization of certain basic industries and public utilities, that American business interests and politicians began to brand Castro as a Communist and a secret adherent of Moscow's "world conspiracy." This simpleminded view of Cuban reality was an outgrowth, however, not only of the injured interests of American corporations and individuals; it was an outgrowth of the stifling of realistic appraisal of foreign developments which was one of the fruits of two decades of American anti-Communist hysteria. It was also, and perhaps most importantly, a product of the fear of American leaders that any shift in the status quo meant a shift in the balance of power between the United States and Russia and was, ipso facto, a threat to world peace.

The American determination to unseat Castro grew in proportion to the advance of his program to free the Cuban economy from American dependency and his progress toward a position of international independence for his nation. American economic blows (such as the cutting of United States purchases of Cuban sugar, the imposition of a "quarantine" against Cuba's purchase of arms abroad, etc.) only forced Cuba into increasing dependence upon trade and aid from the Soviet bloc of nations. The American anti-Castro program reached its climax when the United States secretly trained and equipped a band of Cuban exiles to invade their country and "topple" Castro from power. But the tragically ill-conceived Bay of Pigs invasion of April 17, 1961—a campaign based on a total lack of comprehension of the nature of guerrilla warfare, political realities, and the essence of revolutionary societies—only demonstrated the fact that Castro was overwhelmingly popular with the great majority of his fellow citizens and very firmly in control of their destinies. But it also revealed, to the Cuban leadership, that the United States would stop at nothing to overthrow them.

All during Castro's years of struggle, and also during his years of power up to 1961, his movement had been at odds with the weak and directionless Cuban Communist party. That Party had sabotaged certain of his efforts against Batista and derided his program of economic and social reform. In turn, when Castro came to power his 26th of July Movement drove Communists from Cuba's labor unions and excluded them from public office. Time and again Castro had publicly denounced Communism as a rigidly bureaucratic and anti-democratic means of organizing society; furthermore, he had declared that he would never substitute Soviet colonialism for the recently ended American variety. By 1961 all this was to be changed.

First of all, the campaign to reform Cuban society, as we have seen, was soon forced to proceed beyond moderately socialistic measures to the emergence of state capitalism—outright government ownership of the means of production. It was becoming apparent too, that land reform would not necessarily accomplish the desperately needed increase in agricultural output and diversification of crops; again, only direct government management which would permit agricultural mechanization seemed to promise that. It was also apparent that Cuban counterrevolutionaries, based in Florida but with some supporters in Cuba posed a well-financed and armed threat to the political stability of the Cuban regime; hence the political democracy promised through the establishment of constitutional government seemed too dangerous an experiment. In other words, objective conditions inside Cuba were apparently, of themselves, fulfilling Communist predictions, following a Marxist road even though such a route had not been officially planned or imposed. What Cuba's foreign relations with her powerful neighbor to the north were we have already seen. To protect himself against American intervention Castro could, realistically, turn only to the Communist world for economic and military support. In the foreign field too, it seemed that Communist propaganda, which painted the United States as a militaristic, imperialist, aggressive nation eager to gobble up its world neighbors, had only been the simple truth. It was all of these factors and more which caused Castro and his government to proclaim themselves Communist *after* the Bay of Pigs affair. If ever a Communist regime was seeded, fostered, and created by American policy, that of Cuba was.

Yet the repercussions of Cuba's adherence to the Communist world were felt not only in Washington. It may be pointed out that their effects in Moscow were not, in the long run, very welcome. For the Cuban situation led Khrushchev to his adventure of placing missiles there in 1962; this in turn led to the famous "missile crisis" of October 1962 during which the interposition of American armed power forced Khrushchev to beat a hasty retreat; this in turn weakened Russian prestige throughout the world and was no small factor in Khrushchev's downfall. Furthermore, the unilateral Russian retreat from Cuba (the Castro government was not even consulted by its Russian ally during the crisis) effectively soured relations between Cuba and the Soviet Union. Castro turned increasingly to Russia's competitor, Red China, for economic and diplomatic support. Beyond that he evidently began to question certain Communist dogmas, at least those apparent in Soviet Russian society and conduct.

All of which has led to an interesting phenomenon: the emergence of yet another deviant example of a Communist society. In recent years Castro has instituted several programs which would be anathematic in Russia. First and foremost is a very real campaign against bureaucracy; the Cuban government seems determined to prevent the establishment and entrenchment of such a conservative governmental bureaucracy as has impeded and burdened Russian development over the years. Secondly, perhaps borrowing a leaf from Tito's book, direct worker participation in the management of the Cuban economy has been emphasized and encouraged by the establishment of workers' councils in factories and productive enterprises. These councils have very real power—and that power may or may not be in opposition to the governing management. Likewise government control of agriculture has proceeded at a very cautious pace (as in China), with the peasants being lured rather than forced into cooperatives and the agricultural cooperatives encouraged to produce and to govern themselves as independently as possible. Thirdly, Cuba has taken increasingly an independent position on international questions. Distrust and hatred of the United States remain, of course; but Cuba by no means slavishly supports the foreign policies of either Russia or China. Finally, it remains to be said, that political democracy, personal liberty, and such cherished Anglo-American rights as freedom of the press are not established in Cuba. The country remains a dictatorship of Castro and his party. But that this dictatorship enjoys the support of the great majority of Cubans is incontestable. Furthermore, the social democracy implicit in Castro's evolution of Communism in Cuba, seems to offer the very real promise of increasing political democracy in the future. Such has been the case in Yugoslavia. While it must be emphasized that neither Cuba nor Yugoslavia are nations which enjoy what Americans would recognize as personal liberty or democratic government, it would seem that if political democracy and its attendant personal freedoms are eventually to emerge in any Communist societies, Cuba and Yugoslavia offer the most promising possibilities.

Both the success and the unorthodoxy of Fidel Castro's movement in Cuba had important effects on the gathering forces pressing for change in American society itself. Castro's youth, his "style"—even his appearance—made a great appeal to young Americans who found themselves caught up in the various struggles of midcentury America to establish social and economic justice at home. Castro offered an example of what a mere handful of dedicated men, unimpeded by theoretical orthodoxy of any kind, could accomplish. In that sense his victory was an important inspiration to the so-called "youth revolution" which was soon to sweep through the Western world. Like Castro, they might borrow certain concepts from Marxism; but these would be rethought, pragmatically applied, and developed to fit real, not theoretical needs, and would be totally independent from official Communist sources.

The central problems with which Americans grappled after 1950 were three: the struggle of black America to liberate itself from economic exploitation, social submergence, and political repression; the continued existence of very large areas of abject poverty in the affluent society; and, finally, the apparent growth of rigidity in American political and social institutions—a rigidity which seemed to oppose all progress. It is not our purpose here to trace the details of the continuing struggle to resolve these problems but rather to assess the real or potential interrelationship between that struggle and Marxist thought.

First of all it is necessary to point out that the Communist Party of the United States, while permitted to take part in the struggle, offers nothing of interest for its theoretical or practical development. The CPUSA's "solutions" to the problems faced by contemporary American society remain drearily dogmatic and utterly impractical. To solve the problems facing black America the Party advocates the creation of a separate black nation somewhere in the South; to solve the problem of continued poverty in large areas of society the Party offers the nationalization of the means of production; to crack the rigidity of certain American political and social institutions the Party offers the even more rigid "dictatorship of the proletariat" and subsequent massive bureaucratic centralization; to curb the expansionist tendencies of the American military-industrial complex, the Party suggests surrender to the Russian military-industrial complex.

What then can be said of Marxist contributions to the solution of America's domestic and foreign troubles in the last half of the twentieth century? First, and most importantly of all, Marxism has provided the sharp tool of economic dissection of social problems. Thus, for example, the realization has finally dawned that social and political progress for black America depends primarily on economic progress for black America. It is finally realized that racial prejudice in the United States has been cultivated as a means of exploiting an entire class for the economic benefit of other groups, and that the racial attitudes of both blacks and whites, whether exploitive or not, are rooted, partly at least, in their economic circumstances. This in turn has led to the realization that the so-called Negro Revolution in America will, in important ways, have to be a total national revolution against an economic structure that imprisons important segments of *both* the black and white communities. Marxism, especially as developed in Lenin's *Imperialism* has also proved itself a valuable tool in helping to bare some of the roots of American foreign policy, insofar as that policy is both fostered by and in turn advances, the interests of the American industrial-military complex or establishment. It is realized that decisions such as those involved in the determination of successive American governments to wage war in Vietnam are derived, to an important extent at least, from concepts created and advanced by domestic economic interests. The Marxist conception of political institutions and political parties in capitalist countries as agencies for the furtherance of ruling-class power and interests, suggests an analytic means of identifying the basis for growing rigidity in such institutions in the United States.

At the same time, the outcome of Marxist theory elsewhere serves as a much-needed warning against the repetition of certain mistakes. Thus it is now realized that the "dictatorship of the proletariat" even though it be the majority group in any nation, must inevitably lead to the dictatorship of the Party and, eventually to the dictatorship of individuals. It is realized that government ownership of the means of production does not guarantee either economic advance or social justice. It is realized that the "remaking" of human nature in order to eliminate such motives as greed, fear, and competitiveness cannot, except at the price of the destruction of all liberty and freedom, be attempted by government manipulation, but will only take place through ages of evolution.

All this and much more could be said about the influence of Marxist thought upon contemporary American society. But these examples must serve to illustrate the point that Marxism today, insofar as it has anything positive to offer, remains an intellectual tool, not a finished dogma; it is a means of thought, not an end product of a closed system of speculation. That tool has grown rusty in the hands of its orthodox Communist manipulators. If it is to be sharpened into current relevancy, that will be accomplished by non-Communists, even anti-Communists in pragmatic day-to-day confrontation with current problems. Ironically, the society most openly facing those problems today, the society from which new directions in the development of Marxist thought may be expected, is the United States of America.

Epilogue

THE AGE OF PESSIMISM

> Everything I see scatters the seeds of a revolution
> which will definitely come. . . . The young people are
> lucky: they will see some great things.
>
> —*Voltaire*

During the golden morning of the Enlightenment, thinking
men assumed that the newly liberated intelligence of mankind
had only to be applied to the problems of this world to
eventually solve them. The future of man's life on earth
was in his own hands, and those hands could be limitlessly
instructed. In every field, from astronomy to zoology, not
omitting politics and economics, a vast and potentially bene-
ficient horizon beckoned. Old evils such as superstition,
bigotry, tyranny, injustice, poverty—these would be overcome
as mankind marched confidently forward into the new day
in which his own will would determine his own fate. Truly,
the Enlightenment was an Age of Optimism.

We have seen how eighteenth- and early nineteenth-century
thinkers assumed the existence of one or another type of ideal
man. These ideal men, whether they were noble savages,
Christian brothers, cooperative sharers, or members of the
working class, were the men hidden within all men; they had
only to be liberated to assume their full stature. Even Karl
Marx, with his supposedly "scientific" view of man in history,
actually supposed the existence of an ideal man, the Communist man who would emerge in the future.

And these ideal men would wield unimaginable power.
For the advances of science and technology summed up in
the magically liberating word "industrialization," would pro-

duce wealth beyond the dreams of former ages—and this with less and less effort on the part of men. It remained only to effect a proper and just distribution of this wealth to free men from their age-old enemies: disease, despair, famine, and poverty. Once freed from these evils, man would have the time and the occasion to devote himself to higher pursuits, such as philosophy and art. If political masters or political systems stood in the way of this vision, they would surely be overthrown. Men might dispute the proper paths into the Golden Age, but they would inevitably arrive there sooner or later.

Two hundred years have now passed since the brightest moments of the Enlightenment; more than one hundred and fifty years have passed since masses of men decided to take their fate into their own hands, to apply their intelligences directly to the solution of political, social and economic problems in the American and French Revolutions. Yet future historians might very well label the twentieth century the Age of Pessimism.

We have lived, and are living in times during which it has seemed that man's intelligence is more to be feared than fostered. The great advances in science foreseen by our predecessors have come, and far from having solved mankind's problems, they have multiplied them. Despite the plenty enjoyed now by a tiny fraction of the world's population in a handful of countries, the great majority of mankind remain gripped by the ancient evils based on poverty. Indeed in certain areas of the world poverty is increasing. Industrialization has liberated some men, but it has enslaved others and befouled the natural environment at the same time. And even those who have benefited from industrialization express a vague feeling of discontent that the abundance of their material rewards in this life cannot seem to satisfy. A more just and equal distribution of the benefits of industrial production, although not a terribly difficult problem to solve, has not been effected.

Furthermore, the social and political obstacles which were brushed aside during the Age of Revolutions, from the dawn of the nineteenth century to the first quarter of the twentieth, have been replaced by tyrannies and tyrants even more fearsome, even more heavily entrenched than those which were overthrown. And these tyrannies have indulged, in our own times, in barbarities the likes of which one can only find in the pages of ancient history. Genocide, massacre, conquest, slave labor, and wars—the most destructive and savage wars in human history—these have been the fruits of "civilization" with which we have lived.

So staggering has been the blow to idealism of any kind delivered by the blood-stained experience of the twentieth century, that many have questioned the very nature of man himself. Here we do not speak of ideal man—ideal man of any kind was long since discarded as a useful conception. We speak of the basic nature of real man. This nature we may believe is intensely savage, murderous, suicidal. Nor is it effectively modified or suppressed by the human intelligence; on the contrary, human intelligence is pressed into service on behalf of man's self-destructive instincts. And since these instincts remain in control of an intelligence which has finally produced the ultimate weapon for man's extinction on earth, it is only a question of time before that sad experiment in natural evolution, man, joins such other failed experiments as the dinosaurs. The dinosaurs at least left a habitable world behind them. Man will not.

Faced with the apparent impasse that man's intelligence has not brought him into a Golden Age, but rather to the brink of race suicide, there are many, especially among the thinking young, who feel that man's only hope for survival lies in a retreat from intelligence, in an attempt to grapple with the more nearly instinctual aspects of human behavior on a more instinctual level. Like the Christians of old they would abandon the decaying empires to their inevitable destruction and seek new evolutionary directions within themselves rather than within further manipulation of their environment. Their attitude is perfectly understandable, even in some respects commendable.

But their assumptions (for they, too, are making assumptions) may be wrong.

They may be wrong because of a failure of perspective and a failure of definition.

It is not necessary to view the history of the past two centuries in the lights provided by either the optimists of the Enlightenment or the pessimists of today. It is not necessary to reach a definition of man's nature on the basis of events during recent decades or on the basis of idealistic hopes. A totally "other" perspective may be postulated. It would run something like this:

The human race, in the light of eternity, is in its infancy. Last year man discovered the uses of fire; last month he invented the wheel; yesterday he began to industrialize his society; one second ago he liberated the energy locked within the atom. Just as one would at least hesitate to pronounce judgment on the nature of a five-year-old child, one must hesitate to pronounce judgment on the nature of man. Just as one would hesitate to describe the personality, character, and mental capabilities of a mature man on the basis of observing him for a few minutes as an infant, so one must be wary of postulating the future development of the human race. In this sense there is no need to make a choice between an optimistic or a pessimistic view of man's essential nature. It would be well, however, to recall that man is born with a brain, that his intelligence is as much a "natural" part of him as his circulatory system. He can no more suppress this essential part of his being than he can suppress his digestive tract—if he attempts to do so he can only mutilate himself.

But does this mean that we must overlook man's behavior during the past two centuries? If we are seeking definitive proof of man's essential nature, yes—the evidence is too scanty. But if we scan the history of the recent past not in search of "proof" or dogma, but rather in search of clues towards man's development in the near future, and clues towards the solutions of the problems he faces in the present, then the evidence may be most useful. But it would be well to maintain a certain perspective upon it and not to lose that perspective in unproductive wrangling over details.

At about the beginning of the nineteenth century, man's accumulated knowledge of his physical environment began to be sufficient for his efficient manipulation of that environment. This efficient manipulation we may call industrialization. The Industrial Revolution which began in England and soon spread to the other nations of Europe, then to America and, in our own day to all areas of the world, was a continuing revolution which fed upon itself; the progress of scientific knowledge and technical mastery was geometric; hence, in terms of the millions of years of prehistory of the human race, incredibly rapid.

But industrialization brought with it social and economic problems, such as the problem of equalizing the benefits of industrialization, the problem of controlling it for the social good, the problem of coping with its impact upon older human institutions such as the family, the state, and man's environment, both urban and rural. Various schemes, plans and suggestions were made as to how the problems of industrialization could be solved. One of these plans was developed into the philosophy of Marxism. Through Marxism several groups of men have attempted to solve the problems of industrialization which have faced and continue to face all men. They have not, up to this time, succeeded any better than anyone else. Other schemes for solving the social problems attendant upon industrialization have been advanced. These schemes, under the name of fascism or Nazism have not only failed to solve the problems of industrialization, they have been in actual rebellion against the human intelligence which made industrialization possible. Where industrialization coincided with (both fostering and being fostered by) political, social, and intellectual revolutions against the rigid society which the nineteenth century inherited from the eighteenth— as in England, France and the United States—the problems of industrialization were generally left to solve themselves in a haphazard system which has developed into free-enterprise capitalism. In these cases certain political problems such as individual liberty and the establishment of democratic government were solved *before* industrialization. In other countries political problems were not solved before industrialization and remained to plague late-industrializing states such as Russia, Germany, and China.

Marxism, which sought to provide a blueprint for heavily industrialized societies, actually provided a justification and suggested a means of industrializing nonindustrial societies. In nations where political revolution had not taken place, had not liberated national energies for capitalist industrialization, and in nations where lack of wealth prevented the necessary accumulation of private capital to fuel industrialization, Marxism offered a vision to inspire and a plan to follow. This plan, substituting the social ownership of the means of production for their private ownership really meant, to under-industrialized nations, the substitution of social development of the means of production rather than private development. But the only available political form that social development or control or ownership of the means of production could take was the state itself. And since, as we have seen, Marxist development only took place in those states which had not enjoyed an early democratic revolution, state control or ownership of the means of production meant state tyranny over the means of production, there being no tradition of, or means for, the people to control their states. Hence Marxism led the way not to socialism but to state capitalism. As such it may be seen as a theory of capitalism, not Communism. But however it is viewed, Marxism's vision of men ultimately freed from toil, from bondage to human failings, from the state itself, is definitely an Enlightenment view and as such may be said to be optimistic.

The failure of Marxism, capitalism in its various degrees and forms, the several anti-intellectual ideologies called fascist, and every other plan or scheme advanced to solve the social, political, and economic problems growing from industrialization have contributed to the feelings of pessimism so widespread today. But is this a valid response?

First of all it must be remembered that as fast as industrial-technical progress has been, industrialization has actually taken place in only a fraction of the world. And in those areas where it has occurred, even in the most advanced nations, industrialization is still in its primitive, paleolithic stage. What the social effects of industrialization will be when automation and computerized production become commonplace, when men are divorced from their machines, is something to be but warily predicted. Secondly, the failure of such systems of thought as Marxism to provide answers to past and current problems posed by industrialization does not prove that answers cannot eventually be found. It does not even prove that Marxist thought may not, in the future, indicate directions towards those answers. It may, on the other hand, be aid to demonstrate once again that total systems, total answers to social and human problems must always fail since humanity cannot be dealt with on a total basis but only on an individual basis. Finally, the apparent failure of the application of human reason to the human environment to usher in the Golden Age within a couple of centuries, does not, of course mean that such application is futile. On the contrary, a very good case may be made, especially in the light of recent events, that the application of human intelligence has not been *sufficient*, that greater efforts must be made.

In sum, if the Age of Optimism failed to allow for age-old human frailty, the Age of Pessimism fails to allow for age-old human ability. If the history of Marxism may teach us anything it is that optimistic or pessimistic views of humanity or human society are not useful—only *realistic* views are relevant. In the present low stage of human knowledge about human society and human self-knowledge, realistic views can only be arrived at on a pragmatic and tentative basis. This, of course, presupposes political, economic, and social freedom to inquire and experiment; it presupposes a very real effort to rid ourselves of presuppositions. Individuals, institutions, or nations which attempt to block this free application of human reason to the human condition must inevitably fail. For if contemporary events may teach us anything, it is that the revolution so gladly foreseen by Voltaire is still going on. It hasn't ended yet.

BIBLIOGRAPHY

A Suggested Reading List will be found at the end of the Bibliography.

PRIMARY SOURCES:

Engels, Fredrich.

The Peasant War in Germany (1850)
Germany: Revolution and Counter Revolution (1852)
The Housing Question (1872)
Anti-Duhring (1878)
The Origin of the Family, Private Property, and The State (1884)
Ludwig Feuerbach and the Outcome of Classical German Philosophy (1886)
Dialects of Nature (posthumous—1927)

Mao Tse-tung.

On Practice
On Contradiction
On Dialectical Materialism.
On Protracted War
On New Democracy
On the Correct Handling of Contradictions

Marx, Karl.

Das Kapital (Capital) 3 vols. (1867-1894)
The Civil War in France (1872)
The Poverty of Philosophy (1847)
The Eighteenth Brumaire of Louis Bonaparte (1852)
Critique of Political Economy (1859)
Value, Price, and Profit (1865)
Critique of the Gotha Programme (1875)
Selected Correspondence of Karl Marx and Friedrich Engels (1952)

Marx, Karl, and Engels, Friedrich.
> *The Communist Manifesto* (1847)

Lenin, Vladimir I.
> *What Is to be Done?* (1902)
> *One Step Forward, Two Steps Back* (1904)
> *Two Tactics of Social Democracy in the Democratic Revolution* (1905)
> *Materialism and Empiric-Criticism* (1909)
> *Imperialism: The Highest Stage of Capitalism* (1916)
> *A Letter to American Workers* (1918)
> *"Left-Wing" Communism, an Infantile Disorder* (1920)

Stalin, Joseph V.
> *Foundations of Leninism* (1924)
> *Problems of Leninism* (1926)
> *Dialectical and Historical Materialism* (1938)
> *The History of the Communist Party of the Soviet Union* (1938)
> *Marxism and Linguistics* (1950)

Trotsky, Leon.
> *The History of the Russian Revolution* (trans. Max Eastman) (1932)

SELECTED BIBLIOGRAPHY:

Armstrong, John A. *The Politics of Totalitarianism.* New York: 1962

Barnett, A. Doak. *Communist Economic Strategy.* Washington, D.C.: 1959

Bates, Marston. *The Prevalence of People.* New York: 1963

Bauer, Raymond A. *How the Soviet System Works.* Cambridge: 1956

————. *The New Man in Soviet Psychology.* Cambridge: 1952

Beck, F. and Godin, W. *Russian Purge and the Extraction of Confessions.* New York: 1951

Bell, Oliver: *The Two Chinas.* New York: 1962

Berdyzev, Nicholas. *The Russian Revolution.* Ann Arbor: 1961

Berlin, Isaiah. *Karl Marx, His Life and Environment.* New York: 1959

Berliner, J. S. *Factory and Manager in the USSR.* Cambridge: 1957

Berman, Harold J. *Justice in Russia.* Cambridge: 1950

Borkenau, Franz. *European Communism.* New York: 1953

Brinton, Crane. *The Anatomy of Revolution.* New York: 1952

Burnette, O. L. and Haygood, W. C. *A Soviet View of the American Past.* New York: 1960

Brzezinski, Z. K. *The Permanent Purge.* Cambridge: 1956

Campbell, John C. *Soviet Economic Power.* Cambridge: 1960

Carew, Hunt, R. N. *The Theory and Practice of Communism.* New York: 1958

Carr, E. H. *Studies in Revolution.* London: 1950

Chandra-Sekhar, Sriptai. *Red China; An Asian View.* New York: 1961

Cohen, Arthur A. *The Communism of Mao Tse-tung.* Chicago: 1964

Conquest, Robert. *Power and Policy in the USSR.* New York: 1961

Counts, George S. *The Challenge of Soviet Education.* New York: 1957

Cressey, George B. *Soviet Potentials: A Geographical Appraisal.* Syracuse: 1962

Crankshaw, Edward. *Khrushchev's Russia.* New York: 1959

Crossman, Richard. (ed.) *The God That Failed.* New York: 1952

Curtiss, John S. *The Russian Church and the Soviet State.* Boston: 1953

Dallin, Alexander. *The Soviet Union and the United Nations.* New York: 1962

Dallin, David J. *Facts on Communism.* Washington: 1961

Deutscher, Isaac. *Prophet Armed: Trotsky, 1879-1921.* Oxford: 1954

———. *The Prophet Unarmed: Trotsky, 1921-1929.* London: 1959

———. *Stalin, A Political Biography.* New York: 1949

Djilas, Milovan. *The New Class.* New York: 1957

Dobb, Maurice H. *Soviet Economic Development.* New York: 1948

Draper, Theodore. *American Communism and Soviet Russia.* New York: 1960

———. *Castroism: Theory and Practice.* New York: 1965

———. *The Roots of American Communism.* New York: 1957

Ebon, Martin. *Malenkov—Stalin's Successor.* New York: 1953

Fainsod, Merle. *How Russia Is Ruled.* Cambridge: 1963

Feis, Herbert. *Between War and Peace: The Potsdam Conference.* Princeton: 1960

———. *The China Tangle.* Princeton: 1953

Fischer, George. *Soviet Opposition to Stalin.* Cambridge: 1952

Fischer, Louis. *Russia Revisited.* New York: 1957.

Florinsky, Michael T. *Russia: A History and an Interpretation.* New York: 1953

Foster, William Z. *History of the Communist Party of the U.S.* New York: 1952

Freedman, Robert. (ed.) *Marx on Economics.* New York: 1961

Galbraith, Kenneth. *The Affluent Society.* Boston: 1958

Garthoff, Raymond L. *Soviet Strategy in the Nuclear Age*. New York: 1962

Glazer, Nathan. *The Social Basis of American Communism*. New York: 1961

Granick, D. *The Red Executive*. New York: 1960

Grant, Nigel. *Soviet Education*. Baltimore: 1964

Gsovski, Vladimir. *Soviet Civil Law*. (2 vols.) Ann Arbor: 1948

Guernay, Bernard G. (ed.) *An Anthology of Russian Literature in the Soviet Period*. New York: 1960

Hazard, John N. *The Soviet System of Government*. Chicago: 1964

Hicks, Granville. *Where We Came Out*. New York: 1954

Hindus, Maurice. *House Without a Roof*. New York: 1961

Hoetzsch, Otto. *The Evolution of Russia*. New York: 1967

Hook, Sidney. *Marx and The Marxists*. Princeton: 1955

Hu, T. C. (ed.) *Chinese Education Under Communism*. New York: 1964

Inkeles, Alex, and Bauer, Raymond A. *The Soviet Citizen*. Cambridge: 1959

Inkeles, Alex. *Public Opinion in Soviet Russia*. Cambridge: 1958

Isenberg, Irwin. *Eastern Europe*. New York: 1965

Jacobs, Don N. (ed.) *The New Communist Manifesto*. New York: 1962

Jasny, Naum. *The Socialized Agriculture of the USSR*. Stanford: 1949

Keep, John, and Brisby, Liliana. *Contemporary History in the Soviet Mirror*. New York: 1964

Kennan, George F. *On Dealing with the Communist World*. New York: 1964

———. *Soviet Foreign Policy, 1917-1941*. Princeton: 1960

———. *Russia and the West, Under Lenin and Stalin*. Boston: 1960

Kulski, W. W. *The Soviet Regime: Communism in Practice*. Syracuse: 1963

Labedz, Leopold, and Johnson, Priscilla. *Khrushchev and the Arts*. Cambridge: 1964

——— and Laqueur, Walter. *Polycentrism*. New York: 1962

Lewis, John W. *Leadership in Communist China*. Ithaca: 1963

Li, Choh-ming, *Economic Development of Communist China*. Berkeley: 1959

Lindsay, Michael. *Is Peaceful Co-existence Possible?* Ann Arbor: 1960

Lukacs, John. *A New History of the Cold War*. New York: 1966

Marcuse, Herbert. *Soviet Marxism: A Critical Analysis*. New York: 1958

Mazour, Anatole G. *Russia, Past and Present*. Princeton: 1963

Mehnert, Klaus. *Stalin Versus Marx*. London: 1952

———. *Soviet Man and His World*. New York: 1962

Meyer, Alfred G. *Leninism*. Cambridge: 1957

Milosz, Czeslaw. *The Captive Mind*. New York: 1953

Murray, Robert K. *Red Scare: A Study in National Hysteria*. Minneapolis: 1955

Moseley, Philip E. *The Kremlin and World Politics*. New York: 1960

Niemeyer, Gerhart. *Communists in Coalition Governments*. Washington: 1963

————. *The Communist Mind*. Philadelphia: 1963

Nove, Alec. *The Soviet Economy*. New York: 1961

O'Brien, Frank. *Crisis in World Communism*. New York: 1965

Pipes, R. *The Formation of the Soviet Union*. Cambridge: 1954

Pitcher, Harvey J. *Understanding the Russians*. London: 1964

Poppino, R. E. *Communist Movements in Latin America*. New York: 1964

Possony, Stefan T. A. *A Century of Conflict*. Chicago: 1953

Rauch, George von. *A History of Soviet Russia*. New York: 1957

Reed, John. *Ten Days That Shook the World*. New York: 1925

Rossiter, Clinton. *Marxism: The View From America*. New York: 1960

Rostow, W. W. *The Dynamics of Soviet Society*. New York: 1953

Salisbury, Harrison E. *The Soviet Union*. New York: 1968

Schapiro, Leonard. *The Communist Party of the Soviet Union*. New York: 1959

————.(ed.) *The USSR and the Future*. New York: 1963

Schwartz, Harry. *Russia's Soviet Economy*. New York: 1954

Seton-Watson, Hugh. *From Lenin to Malenkov*. New York: 1953

Shabad, Theodore. *Geography of the USSR*. New York: 1951

Simmons, Ernest J. *Through the Looking Glass of Soviet Literature*. New York: 1953

Spinka, Mathew. *The Church in Soviet Russia*. New York: 1956

Tang, Peter S. H. *Communist China Today*. Washington: 1961

Timasheff, Nicholas S. *The Great Retreat*. New York: 1946

Towster, Julian. *Political Power in the USSR*. New York: 1946

Triska, Jan F. (ed.) *Soviet Communism, Programs and Rules*. San Francisco: 1962

Ulam, Adam B. *The New Face of Soviet Totalitarianism*. Cambridge: 1963

Utechin, S. V. *A Concise Encyclopædia of Russia*. New York: 1963

Vernadsky, George. *A History of Russia*. New Haven: 1954

Werth, Alexaander. *Russia at War*. New York: 1964

Wilson, Edmund. *To the Finland Station*. New York: 1941

Wolfe, Bertram D. *Three Who Made a Revolution*. New York: 1964

Wolin, Simon (ed.) *The Soviet Secret Police*. New York: 1957

Yarmolinsky, Avrahm. *Road to Revolution*. New York: 1959

Yuan-li, Wu. *The Economy of Communist China*. New York: 1965

Zenkovskii, Vasilii V. *History of Russian Philosophy*. New York: 1953

SUGGESTED READING:

Berlin, Isaiah. *Karl Marx, His Life and Environment*. New York: 1959

Borkenau, Franz. *European Communism*. New York: 1953

Brinton, Crane. *The Anatomy of Revolution*. New York: 1952

Crankshaw, Edward. *Khrushchev's Russia*. New York: 1959

Crossman, Richard. *The God That Failed*. New York: 1952

Deutscher, Isaac. *Prophet Armed & Prophet Unarmed.* Trotsky, *1879-1929*. London: 1959

———. *Stalin, A Political Biography*. New York: 1949

Djilas, Milovan. *The New Class*. New York: 1957

Draper, Theodore. *The Roots of American Communism*. New York: 1957

Fainsod, Merle. *How Russia Is Ruled*. Cambridge: 1963

Fischer, Louis. *Russia Revisited*. New York: 1957

Freedman, Robert (ed.) *Marx on Economics*. New York: 1961

Kennan, George F. *Russia and the West Under Lenin and Stalin*. Boston: 1960

Kulski, W. W. *The Soviet Regime: Communism in Practice*. Syracuse: 1963

Lukacs, John. *A New History of The Cold War*. New York: 1966

Marcuse, Herbert. *Soviet Marxism: A Critical Analysis*. New York: 1958

Reed, John. *Ten Days That Shook the World*. New York: 1925

Salisbury, Harrison E. *The Soviet Union*. New York: 1968

Werth, Alexander. *Russia at War*. New York: 1964

Wolfe, Bertram D. *Three Who Made a Revolution*. New York: 1964

Wilson, Edmund. *To the Finland Station*. New York: 1941

Fiction:

Koestler, Arthur. *Darkness at Noon*. New York: 1941

Orwell, George. *Animal Farm*. New York: 1946

Solzhenitsyn, I. A. *One Day in the Life of Ivan Denisovich*. New York: 1964

Swearingen, Rodger. *What's So Funny, Comrade?* New York: 1961

INDEX